LABOR IN THE NEW URBAN BATTLEGROUNDS

**Frank W. Pierce Memorial Lectureship
and Conference Series No. 12**

LABOR IN THE NEW URBAN BATTLEGROUNDS

Local Solidarity in a Global Economy

Edited by
Lowell Turner and Daniel B. Cornfield
with a foreword by Peter Evans

ILR PRESS, AN IMPRINT OF CORNELL UNIVERSITY PRESS

ITHACA AND LONDON

First published 2007 by Cornell University Press
First printing, Cornell Paperbacks, 2007

Printed in the United States of America

Library of Congress Cataloging-in-Publication Data

Labor in the new urban battlegrounds : local solidarity in a global economy /
edited by Lowell Turner and Daniel B. Cornfield ; with a foreword by
Peter Evans.
       p. cm. — (Frank W. Pierce memorial lectureship and conference
      series ; no. 12)
  Includes bibliographical references and index.
  ISBN 978-0-8014-4551-4 (cloth : alk. paper) — ISBN 978-0-8014-7360-9
(pbk. : alk. paper)
    1. Labor movement—United States.   2. Labor unions—United States.
3. Community development, Urban—United States. I. Turner, Lowell.
II. Cornfield, Daniel B. III. Title. IV. Series.
  HD6508.L223 2007
  331.880973—dc22

                                   2006036017

Cornell University Press strives to use environmentally responsible suppliers
and materials to the fullest extent possible in the publishing of its books.
Such materials include vegetable-based, low-VOC inks and acid-free papers
that are recycled, totally chlorine-free, or partly composed of nonwood fibers.
For further information, visit our website at www.cornellpress.cornell.edu.

Cloth printing   10 9 8 7 6 5 4 3 2 1
Paperback printing   10 9 8 7 6 5 4 3 2 1

Contents

Foreword

Peter Evans

Labor in the New Urban Battlegrounds is an energizing, optimistic book. By using the contemporary metropolis as a comparative laboratory to see what contexts and strategies contribute best to labor revitalization, Lowell Turner, Daniel Cornfield, and their collaborators generate a fresh sense of positive possibilities for labor and new insights as to how creative actors can best take advantage of those possibilities.

Energizing optimism should not be confused with seeing things through rose-colored glasses. The book fully acknowledges the odds against labor revitalization and the structural obstacles to a more equitable society. Optimism is generated by pairing obstacles with possibilities, often brought to light by another city in which similar obstacles have been overcome with innovative strategies. This book builds on a new tradition of recent analyses of U.S. labor that compellingly contests previous premature obituaries of the labor movement while making a distinctive contribution. Its power is rooted in the "comparative metropolis" analytical theme and the editors' skill in bringing a diverse baker's dozen of substantive studies to bear on it.

The individual chapters are empirically diverse, complementing a gamut of metropolitan areas in the United States with comparative cases from Europe. They employ varied methodological approaches to look at the "social infrastructure" and strategic choices that underlie urban successes and failures. Many chapters are in-depth case studies of individual cities, while others (e.g., Greer, Byrd, and Fleron; Hauptmeier and Turner) are paired comparisons. Still others (Applegate; Luce; Reynolds) draw their evidence from larger numbers of cities. One (Sellers) employs an ingenious analysis of cross-national data to draw inferences about differences in urban strategic possibilities. The result is much more powerful analytically than it would have been had the editors collected thirteen metropolitan case studies and then tried to figure out their comparative implications.

Empirical range and methodological diversity augment the power of the volume, but the overarching focus on comparative metropolitan analysis is what gives the book its distinctive analytical punch. Even though a variety of organizations and social actors populate the stage—campaigns, nongovernmental organizations, individual unions, and ethnic communities—defining the urban area as the stage on which the dramas occur was a critical decision. From this decision flows the book's special contribution to refocusing contemporary labor debates.

"Local solidarity in a global economy" is not just a catchy subtitle—it captures the book's principal analytical message. Success in bargaining with employers and government officials will continue to be central to the future of the labor movement, but the underlying key to labor revitalization is building coalitions among disprivileged but mobilizable groups in civil society. As Turner points out in his introduction, traditional approaches to labor and the labor movement have tended to focus on labor's contests with employers and the state, neglecting the role of civil society alliances in achieving labor's ends and the centrality of the labor movement to a vibrant civil society. There is, of course, a long tradition of studies of urban coalition building that focus primarily on other actors. Now there is a burgeoning literature on social movement unionism (or, to use the broader term favored in this book, "social unionism") that is "bringing civil society back in" to studies of labor. Civil society alliances play a central role in such recent books on the U.S. labor movement as Dan Clawson's *The Next Upsurge* and Rick Fantasia and Kim Voss's *Hard Work*. Nonetheless, this book is unique in the clarity with which it focuses on civil society coalitions while highlighting the central importance both of those coalitions to labor and of labor to those coalitions.

The spotlight on the role of civil society coalitions in the revitalization of the U.S. labor movement is reinforced by comparisons with European cities. As Sellers points out in chapter 2, urban "social infrastructure" in the United States is "civic localist" in character and "local coalition building has special significance for the civic localist setting." This doesn't mean that local coalitions are absent in Europe (as Holgate and Wills show in chapter 12, on London). Nonetheless, if labor revitalization does succeed in the United States, the salience of local coalition building is likely to be considered one of the movement's distinctive contributions relative to the traditions created by the apparently more powerful trade union movements of Europe.

The comparative dimension points toward one of the book's implicit challenges. What if its analytical strategies were applied to the metropolises that will dominate global debates on the future of the labor movement in the twenty-first century—cities such as São Paulo, Mumbai, Mexico City, Johannesburg, or (most challenging of all) Shanghai? Some early work (e.g., Seidman 1994) suggests that coalitions with civil society will be even more crucial in these urban areas than they are in the United States. Reading *Labor in the New Urban Battlegrounds* whets the appetite for a collection of studies that applies the comparative metropolitan lens to the possibility of labor's revitalization in the global South.

There is another, very different, challenge raised by reading this book—that of potentially missing readerships. The same kind of coalitional strategies advocated for labor should apply to the book itself. It should be widely read (and adopted in courses) by those who focus on labor revitalization, but it would be a shame if the book's readership did not extend equally to readers in coalitional arenas: those who see themselves as primarily interested in social movements, community-based organizations, and organizing in ethnic communities.

Readers are in for an intellectual and political treat, but reading should also entail responsibility to follow the volume's lead and explore the usefulness of the analytical frame in new urban venues, including those very different from the ones described here. It is hoped that readers will also use this volume as a vehicle for the coalition building it advocates. Every reader should make sure that this timely book is read by at least one other person who approaches urban coalitions from a starting point different from their own.

Acknowledgments

Most chapters in this book were originally presented at a conference at Cornell University hosted by the School of Industrial and Labor Relations in October of 2004. We are grateful to the ILR School's Pierce Fund for support of that conference. Several authors were also supported in their research efforts by the Ford Foundation, the U.S. Department of Education, and above all, by the Hans-Böckler-Stiftung.

Ideas, concepts, arguments, presentations, and papers were developed in lively discussion among chapter authors, conference participants, and other colleagues in academia and in the labor movements of the United States, United Kingdom, Germany, and at the European Trade Union Confederation. Specific acknowledgments are expressed by the authors at the beginning of each chapter. In addition, we extend special thanks to Peter Evans for reading and commenting on our manuscript and writing a generous foreword for this book, and to Janice Fine and Immanuel Ness, who each made detailed critical comments that helped guide our final revisions.

Other colleagues provided significant suggestions and criticism, including Lee Adler, Mark Anner, Rose Batt, Lourdes Beneria, Kate Bronfenbrenner, Susan Christopherson, Lance Compa, Maria Cook, Robert Hickey, Richard Hurd, Harry Katz, Nathan Lillie, Barbara Lynch, Saskia Sassen, and Sidney Tarrow.

Fran Benson, Nancy Ferguson, and Candace Akins at Cornell University Press (ILR Press imprint) guided the production of this book with great enthusiasm. John Raymond offered superb copyediting while Do Mi Stauber contributed her typically first-rate index. Brigid Beachler wore two hats in her indispensable contributions as a graduate student commentator at the original conference and as an administrative manager from her base in the Department of Collective Bargaining, Labor Law, and Labor History at Cornell University. Finally, the coeditors would like to thank their chapter authors for timely submissions and in some cases heroic efforts to add new material, revise, and synthesize by our strict deadlines, and to push us sometimes forcefully concerning the analysis in our framing introduction and conclusion. Sometimes we even managed to hear what they were saying and did our best to incorporate their wisdom, along with the insights of the colleagues mentioned above, in what we hope is a contribution to a developing body of work that examines and supports the revitalization of contemporary labor movements at home and abroad.

ACORN Association of Community Organizations for Reform Now
AFGE American Federation of Government Employees
AFL American Federation of Labor
AFL-CIO American Federation of Labor-Congress of Industrial Organizations
AFSCME American Federation of State, County and Municipal Employees
AFT American Federation of Teachers
AGENDA Action for Grassroots Empowerment and Neighborhood Development Alternatives
APWU American Postal Workers Union
BCTC Building and Construction Trades Council
BYNC Back of the Yards Neighborhood Council
CAAs community action agencies
CAP Community Action Program
CBA community benefits agreement
CBDOs community-based development organizations
CBI Community Benefits Initiative
CCLW Community Coalition for a Living Wage
CDCs community development corporations
CDU Christian Democratic Union
CEJ Coalition for Economic Justice
CHAOS Create Havoc in Our System
CIO Congress of Industrial Organizations
CLC central labor council
CTW Change to Win
CWA Communications Workers of America
DALF Denver Area Labor Federation
DC Demonstration Cities
DGB Deutscher Gewerkschaftsbund, German Confederation of Trade Unions
EDG Economic Development Group
EZs "enterprise zones" or "empowerment zones"
FAUI Fiscal Austerity and Urban Innovation
FRESC Front Range Economic Strategy Center
GDP gross domestic product
GEW German teachers' union

GLA Greater London Authority

GMB General and Municipal Workers Union

GOTV Get Out the Vote

HERE Hotel Employees and Restaurant Employees

HUD Department of Housing and Urban Development

IAF Industrial Areas Foundation

IAFF International Association of Fire Fighters

IAM International Association of Machinists

IBEW International Brotherhood of Electrical Workers

IBT International Brotherhood of Teamsters

IFPTE International Federation of Professional and Technical Engineers

IG BAU German construction, agriculture, and environment union

IG Metall German metalworkers' union

ILA International Longshoremen's Association

ILR Cornell University School of Industrial and Labor Relations

ILWU International Longshore Workers Union

IWW Industrial Workers of the World (Wobblies)

JfJ Justice for Janitors

JwJ Jobs with Justice

LAANE Los Angeles Alliance for a New Economy

LBK Landesbetrieb Krankenhaeuser

LELO Northwest Labor and Employment Law Office

LIUNA Laborers International Union of North America

NAFTA North American Free Trade Agreement

NALC National Association of Letter Carriers

NEA National Education Association

NHS National Health Service

NLRB National Labor Relations Board

NWOs nonworker organizations

NYPA New York Power Authority

OEO Office of Equal Opportunity

OLAW Organization of Los Angeles Workers

OPEIU Office and Professional Employees International Union

ÖTV Öffentliche Dienst, Transport, und Verkehr (German public sector union now merged into ver.di)

PLA project labor agreement

PWOC Packing Workers Organizing Committee

RISEP Research Institute on Social and Economic Policy

ROC Restaurant Opportunity Center

SBLC South Bay Labor Council

SDS Students for a Democratic Society
SEIU Service Employees International Union
SF JwJ South Florida chapter of Jobs with Justice
SJRA San Jose Redevelopment Agency
SMART Santa Monicans for Responsible Tourism
SNCC Student Nonviolent Coordinating Committee
SPD Social Democratic Party
SPEEA Seattle Professional Engineering Employees' Association
TELCO The East London Communities Organisation
TGWU Transport and General Workers Union
TRANSNET German railway union
TUC Trades Union Congress
TWO The Woodlawn Organization
UAW United Automobile Workers
UFCW United Food and Commercial Workers
UFT United Federation of Teachers
UFW United Farm Workers
UNISON the dominant British public sector union
UNITE Union of Needletrades, Industrial, and Textile Employees
UNITE HERE the merged union of UNITE and HERE
USAS United Students against Sweatshops
USWA United Steelworkers of America (in current usage just USW)
UTD United Teachers of Dade
ver.di Vereinte Dienstleistungsgewerkschaft, or United Services Union
WC Worker Center
WPUSA Working Partnerships USA
WTO World Trade Organization

INTRODUCTION

An Urban Resurgence of Social Unionism

Lowell Turner

Growing inequality is a defining social crisis of our era. In addition to the great gulf that separates the global North and South, domestic economic polarization increasingly characterizes the more prosperous countries of the North. Most obvious in the United States, economic inequality is now widening even in the social democracies of western Europe. It is no coincidence that this growing divide has been accompanied by the declining membership and influence of labor unions, a long-term phenomenon in the United States and United Kingdom, but one that has gained momentum more recently even in countries with stronger labor movements such as Germany.

A revitalization of the labor movement is arguably a necessary precondition for the reversal of this spreading social cancer at the heart of contemporary industrial societies (Weir 2004). Our purpose in this book is not to argue this point but to examine one increasingly significant locus for efforts aimed at union renewal: the urban labor movement. While studies of unions and labor-management conflict have typically concentrated on national, sectoral, and firm-level analysis, regional and local arenas have increasingly become important battlegrounds in union efforts to rebuild economic and political power.

The essays presented here examine the emergence, successes, and failures of contemporary urban-based labor movements, especially in the United States, where such developments are most significant, but also in the United Kingdom and Germany in comparative perspective. Our central question is why such labor movements have emerged prominently and achieved significant successes in some cities but not in others. A comparative analysis points to the central role of two factors: agency, specifically the choices and strategies pursued by union leaders and their organizations; and opportunity structure, located in the presence or absence of particular barriers in the institutional, political, and social context. Although opportunity is important, we also find contrasting outcomes for local labor movement influence given similar opportunities and similar outcomes given contrasting opportunities. Innovative strategies offer potential for strengthening labor's urban-level influence in any circumstances.

URBAN BATTLEGROUNDS IN A CONTESTED GLOBAL ECONOMY

As cities in an increasingly global economy swell with immigrant and ethnic minority workforces, economic and social polarization deepens, laying a new groundwork for social unrest even in the prosperous North (Abu-Lughod 1999, 271–85; Sassen 2001, 251–325). As labor comes under increasing pressure at national, sectoral, and firm levels, local/regional arenas, especially the metropolitan area, provide new possibilities for innovation and resurgence (Gordon 1999; Herod 1998, 1–36). And in some cases urban labor movement revitalization contributes directly to battles at the global level. A dramatic example can be found in the high-profile 1999 demonstrations against the World Trade Organization in Seattle.

The story line and significance of the Seattle events are well known (Hawken 2000; Levi and Olson 2000; Steger 2003, 122–26). The fifty thousand demonstrators from across the United States, Canada, and other countries, brought the global justice movement to the public eye, inspiring a series of subsequent mass demonstrations in Quebec, Washington, D.C., Prague, Genoa, and other places. The Seattle demonstrations are widely seen as a watershed for a variety of overlapping movements aimed at protesting the spread of global liberalization without democratic regulation. What is less widely known is the central role played in this story by the labor movement in Seattle.

In an unprecedented alliance with environmental organizations and other social groups, the AFL-CIO and its member unions brought more than half the demonstrators (about thirty thousand by most estimates) to the streets of Seattle in late November and early December of 1999. They did this because Ron Judd and his colleagues at the King County Labor Council persuaded John Sweeney and other labor leaders to take advantage of this historic opportunity. Judd could speak convincingly as the key leader in a series of successful campaigns and coalitions that brought together an increasingly vibrant and cohesive labor movement in Seattle in the 1990s.[1] Not only did a renewed local labor movement add credibility to Judd's arguments inside the AFL-CIO, the labor council and its member unions provided the organizational foundation on which the "Battle of Seattle" was waged. In short, a reinvigorated local labor movement persuaded national unions to make the critical organizational contribution to a pathbreaking challenge to a prominent global institution.

Seattle and other urban cases show that the revitalization of union strategy and a renewal of union influence are possible even in a broader context of global liberalization and union decline. Recent successes are typically associated with a

---

1. See, for example, chapter 6 by Greer, Byrd, and Fleron.

return of social movement unionism, a shift in orientation and strategy from established insider or business union approaches to the innovations of a mobilization-based social unionism.[2] In examining such processes, we focus on coalition building, arguably both a litmus test and a necessary feature for contemporary labor movement revitalization, whether at international, national, or local levels. More specifically, our purpose is to examine labor-inclusive urban coalitions, their causes and effects, and to compare such coalitions across a range of cities in the United States and Europe.

Thus our focus is on two interrelated processes: the circumstances under which such coalitions emerge, expand, and are (or are not) sustained; and the relative success and specific accomplishments of such campaigns. Explicitly or implicitly, we examine the extent to which such coalitions contribute to the building of a social justice infrastructure, a concept that includes both movement and institution building. Based on active networks of social actors in ongoing relationships and engaged in multiple campaigns, a social justice infrastructure includes both institutions and a transformed local politics in which labor's influence as a progressive social actor expands. In the best cases, labor-inclusive coalition building may contribute to a revitalization of civil society and democratic participation (Johnston 2001; Osterman 2002, 185–88).

OPPORTUNITY AND CHOICE

Labor in the United States and elsewhere finds itself at a historical conjuncture in which new union strategies become necessary and are in many places emerging. The conjuncture, which can be understood as a product of sweeping political and economic forces (neoliberalism, global liberalization), is characterized for union strategy by a new focus on social coalition building and grassroots mobilization at the urban level. New strategies are targeted especially at service industries such as health care, education, hospitality and building services, as well as other urban-tied industries such as transportation and construction—workforces that in many cases include large numbers of immigrant, minority, and female workers. Manufacturing is still central to the economy and to the labor movement, but for a number of reasons, including capital mobility and a continuing decline in manufacturing employment, it is no longer at the center of union organizing efforts. Our purpose is to explain the emergence of a new kind of unionism aimed at rebuilding capacity and power in the new context—we call it social unionism—to

2. In contrast to "social partnership," the social union concept includes both coalition-based social movement and economic development unionism.

explain where and why it does or does not emerge in selected metropolitan areas. Our explanation centers on opportunity located in institutions and society—in particular institutional openings and social context—as well as strategic actor choice. Our perspective builds on but is also critical of the narrow scope or outdated analysis of literatures on institutions, civil society, and industrial relations.

To be more specific about the relevant aspects of opportunity, institutions can be enabling or constraining. In the postwar period in all three of our countries, less so in Germany, more so in the United States, labor institutions have gradually changed in ways that make them less enabling and more constraining. In their efforts to break out of constraints, located largely at national, sectoral, and firm levels, unions have in some places opened up a new battleground—the city—that is in important ways more favorable. Thus the spatial dimension takes on new importance. It is in urban environments where unions are most likely to find new allies to help them build new power. It makes a difference whether institutions at the urban level are more open or more entrenched, but in either case strategic innovation by unions aims to exploit opportunity afforded by institutional openings, fragmentation, rigidity, loss of legitimacy, and conflicts among institutional officeholders and power brokers.

Comparative political economy, sociology's new institutionalism, and conventional industrial relations analysis have viewed institutions as enabling or constraining, or as shaping behavior, or as configurations that change over time (historical institutionalism). In our perspective, institutions are also power structures that can provide elements of an opportunity structure—opportunities that open up when institutions lose cohesiveness or legitimacy—that can be used to challenge institutionally embedded power.

Society is important for the social context in which unions seek new allies in their efforts to build capacity and power. The urban context is especially important because that is where people live and social networks are built. Identity politics come into play as defining characteristics of potential social allies—whether the identities are based on ethnicity, immigrant status, gender, religion, neighborhoods, or other identities.[3] In mobilizing or participating in social coalitions, unions build on bases in society well beyond the workplace to gain public support and build new political power than can also feed back into workplace power.

Thus institutional openings and social context are key elements of the opportunity structure faced by unions seeking to innovate, to build social and political capacity. Although the more opportunity, the better, unions may or may not act on given opportunities, or they may seek to create opportunity with aggressive coalition-based campaigns. Thus the *critical role of agency:* unions may or may

---

3. Dan Cornfield develops the central role of worker identities in his conclusion.

not pursue new strategies such as organizing and coalition building. Whether they do so may depend on leadership change, "bridge builders" (activists with backgrounds and experiences that span different types of social movements), internal organizational reform, or the demands of members or other social groupings. A full explanation of why unions do or do not innovate is beyond the scope of our analysis, although such questions are addressed in the city cases, adding richness to the book even if we can't generalize an argument in this regard. The essential point is that unions have real choices to make as they face the opportunities provided in urban areas by institutional openings and social context.

CASE STUDIES AND CONTRASTING OUTCOMES

The book's collection of original essays is based on primary research by a group of labor scholars whose attention has shifted toward the surprising revitalization of unions in some cities accompanied by its absence or blockage in other cities. We believe this edited collection on urban coalition building breaks new ground as a comparative study of innovative local union strategies aimed at labor movement renewal through expanded alliances outside the workplace.[4] The core chapters present case studies of (1) particular urban issues and institutions around which coalition campaigns are built (living wage, community-based development organizations, local politics, central labor councils); (2) "union towns" (New York, Boston, Buffalo, Seattle); (3) "frontier cities" (Los Angeles, Miami, San Jose, Nashville); and (4) European cities in comparative perspective (London, Frankfurt, Hamburg).

For analytical leverage, cities are divided into established union towns, with entrenched, influential labor movements in the postwar period, and frontier cities, with weak or less established labor movements at least until the 1990s. For both groups, selected cities include those in which labor movements are resurgent and those in which labor has made little progress. While chapter authors take distinctive approaches with particular emphases, the overall analytical task is to explain contrasting outcomes, especially with reference to the extent and relative success of union coalition efforts and their spillover effects in the building of social justice infrastructures and a pro-labor progressive local politics.

City cases are selected for a diversity of outcomes. Thus two of the union towns—Seattle and Buffalo—show innovative coalition building resulting in new areas of union influence, while in two others—New York and Boston—social coalition building has been significantly blocked.

---

4. For earlier efforts that focus on central labor councils see, for example, Ness and Eimer 2001 and Reynolds 2004.

In similar fashion, we look at two frontier cities—Los Angeles and San Jose—where coalition building has taken off, with positive effects for union influence, and two—Miami and Nashville—where such efforts are in much earlier stages. For both union and frontier cities, contrasting outcomes allow us to sort out and suggest key causal forces at work.

Finally, our European cases cast additional light on causal processes. Why, for example, do we find significant local coalition building efforts in London and Hamburg but not in Frankfurt? What additional insight can we gain by comparing the blockages to coalition building in a union town such as Frankfurt with similar processes in New York and Boston; and by comparing coalition-building efforts in London and Hamburg with both similar and contrasting outcomes in Seattle and Buffalo?

With contrasting outcomes in similar cities and similar outcomes in contrasting cities, our case studies point toward the limitations of conventional social science explanations, whether institutional, political, economic, or cultural. Actor choice, strategic or otherwise, that is not predetermined by external or internal factors takes a central place in this analysis as a causal force in its own right, which is explored from a variety of perspectives throughout the book. Combined with opportunity structures, an elaborated strategic choice perspective goes a good way toward explaining a significant shift toward social unionism in some cases but not others. Although we cannot develop a fully consistent causal argument based on the diverse research and analysis of twenty scholars, these two variables, choice and opportunity, are prominent across all the cases.

Opportunity structure is a central concept in the social movement literature of the past three decades (Tarrow 1998, 71–90). An opening in the political opportunity structure—based on weaknesses in state authority through loss of legitimacy, policy failure, and/or divisions among the powers that be—is often cited as an explanatory factor in the emergence of a social movement cycle (McAdam, Tarrow, and Tilly 2001, 14–15). Although limited in most formulations by a focus only on the state, the concept as appropriately expanded here is useful for our purposes. Opportunities for urban labor movements are located most significantly in the social context and in the institutional arrangements in which union activity is embedded.

In Los Angeles, for example, the social context includes a growing Latino workforce concentrated in low-end jobs and ripe for mobilization through extensive social networks.[5] The institutional context confronting labor was in important ways wide open for strategic innovation, given a historically weak labor

---

5. The following city cases, with the exception of Houston, do not include citations since the summaries presented here are based on subsequent chapters in this book.

movement unencumbered by institutional embeddedness. When key unions adopted grassroots mobilization and coalition-building strategies in the 1990s, the labor movement in Los Angeles grew rapidly in organizing, bargaining, and political influence.

That opportunity structure is not enough is made clear in a comparison between Los Angeles and Houston, where similar social contexts and weak institutional incorporation for labor prevailed.[6] While Houston does have the institutional disadvantage of its location in a right-to-work state, it shares both the large Latino population and the rather wide-open institutional context. What stands out are differences in the choices and strategies pursued in each city by local union leaders and central labor councils. The innovative approaches that have led to a mushrooming of coalitions and the growth of a cohesive and politically powerful labor movement in Los Angeles have been present until recently to a lesser extent in Houston—and so has the expansion of labor movement influence and power (Meyerson 2004; Karson 2004).[7]

Other cases present variations on the basic argument. In New York and Boston, the emergence of social coalition building has been stunted by the presence of strong insider union locals cutting their own political deals and bargaining agreements. Here the institutional arrangements in which key local unions are embedded have allowed those unions to choose the status quo over innovation, blocking a broader pattern of mobilization and coalition building. In New York, a small number of powerful locals have often been at odds with one another and have shown only limited interest in central labor council coordination, while in Boston a few strategically placed locals have cut deals with local and state governments that have at times benefited their own unions at the expense of broader labor and social interests.

The Seattle and Buffalo cases demonstrate, however, that entrenched unions incorporated in the local political economy can make different choices. In Seattle, innovative union leadership emerged from the previously conservative building trades to join with other unions in the promotion of an increasingly cohesive social unionism. In Buffalo, traditionally strong manufacturing unions have

---

6. Although Houston is not presented in our case studies, this city is useful for comparison here. In our research we have looked at more cities than can be presented here as detailed case studies, and the larger number of cases has been helpful in working out the comparative analysis (see chapters 2 and 4, for example, for additional urban cases including Houston).

7. Significantly, a major breakthrough in Houston came with a Justice for Janitors campaign that organized five thousand new SEIU members in the fall of 2005. A coalition strategy modeled on victories in other cities such as Los Angeles offered possibilities for spillover into other Houston campaigns and city politics. See Steven Greenhouse, "Janitors Drive in Texas Gives Hope to Unions," *New York Times,* November 28, 2005 (available at http://www.nytimes.com/2005/11/28/national).

banded together in a broad coalition with employers, government, and social actors to promote innovative economic development. Although the Buffalo case does not fit the social movement approach found in most coalition-building efforts in our other city cases, developments there do reflect substantial innovations in union strategies—and also include environmental and social justice dimensions.[8]

As in Los Angeles but in contrast to Miami and Nashville, labor leaders in San Jose, most importantly at the central labor council, have pulled together a cohesive, innovative labor movement that has gained considerable political power, given the opportunities afforded by a significantly open landscape in which labor incorporation was historically weak. In Miami and Nashville, by contrast, where the landscape is similarly open but where labor continues to play a less influential role, union leaders have been slower to build the coalitions necessary to turn things around. The opportunity structure in both cities lacks a relatively homogeneous immigrant/ethnic community as in Los Angeles and to a lesser extent in San Jose. Opportunity matters, shaping the range of choice available to social actors—but opportunity alone is not enough to explain outcomes. More recently in Miami, but not in Nashville, the central labor council together with well-placed activist local unions have consciously promoted selected coalition campaigns aimed at building labor power and a more extensive social justice infrastructure—with some significant successes that demonstrate the potential for continuing advances.

The institutional context is particularly important where states have right-to-work laws. Thus unions in Nashville and Miami have a harder row to hoe, which accounts for some of the difficulties those local movements have had in exploiting their particular opportunities. These cases strengthen the argument for the significance of institutional arrangements and cause us to temper our emphasis on actor choice. But as the case studies make clear, Nashville unions have not done what they could, for example, in reaching out to immigrant groups, while Miami unions are doing this as a central component of a new strategic orientation, with growing success.

Another factor that tempers our analysis is ethnic diversity. In all of our city cases, growing immigrant and ethnic minority workforces occupy a central position in labor's prospects for successful organizing and political clout (e.g., Milkman 2000). Los Angeles has built a labor movement resurgence in part on the mobilization of a large Latino community and its advocacy organizations.

---

8. On the economic development variant of social unionism beyond the Buffalo case, see also the chapters by Ron Applegate (community-based development organizations), David Reynolds (regional power building), Ian Greer (Hamburg and Seattle), and Nari Rhee and Julie Sadler (San Jose).

Greater ethnic and immigrant diversity in Miami and Nashville raises the bar for a coalition-based social unionism, and one could argue that this is a decisive factor that again undermines our emphasis on actor choice. Yet the difference in innovative initiatives remains, with a broad social union fermentation in Miami that is lacking so far in Nashville. And in the San Jose case, a substantial Latino community is balanced by an equally large Asian population (about 25 percent each in the metropolitan area), an ethnic diversity that has not limited the labor council's grassroots efforts, especially in the Latino community.

Given very different institutional contexts, our European city cases are admittedly a bit of a stretch for this comparative analysis. Still we find useful insights and to some extent confirming outcomes as we move across national boundaries. More work needs to be done in this broadened field of comparison, but in the meantime the signposts are promising. Frankfurt, for example, looks very much like New York and Boston in important ways: existing institutional arrangements are not favorable to alternative strategies nor have the dominant unions pursued them. Several unions, including the powerful Metalworkers Union (IG Metall), have their national headquarters in Frankfurt and are focused on sectoral bargaining and nationally coordinated campaigns. There has been little opening for independent local initiatives, especially innovations in strategy such as coalition building to promote a more socially activist urban labor movement. Nor have local unions made much effort in this regard.

In London, unions have also focused on national strategies to the detriment of local initiatives. Yet here firm-level bargaining (as opposed to the sector bargaining that dominates German collective bargaining) has opened the door for local and regional campaigns. Important unions such as the Transport and General Workers Union (TGWU) and UNISON (the dominant public sector union) have in some cases built coalitions with other social actors and community groups in London to campaign for local legislation such as living wages and for targeted multifirm organizing such as sustained campaigns at the Canary Wharf corporate and financial complex in East London. Key local unions, with and without national support, have developed significant place-based strategies. In contrast to Frankfurt, the London case offers more institutional opportunity, although it is limited enough that differences in the strategic choices of local actors appear significant.

Hamburg offers a middle case, in which local innovation is tempered but not overwhelmed as in the Frankfurt case. Here, Germany's two largest unions, IG Metall and ver.di (Vereinte Dienstleistungsgewerkschaft or United Services Union, a vast service workers union that spans the public and private sectors) have each built winning coalition campaigns around particular local issues, but without much spillover into a more cohesive urban labor movement. That German institutions, in spite of a well-anchored national and sectoral focus, do not present insurmountable barriers to ongoing coalition-based social unionism is demonstrated in the case of Stuttgart. Here determined local actors, especially ver.di, have developed coordinated campaigns that have both brought in other social actors and influenced national mobilizations in defense of the welfare state in 2003 and 2004. As in the Seattle case, the Stuttgart labor movement's activism laid a foundation for events of national import.[9]

To summarize case-study findings, we have identified a significant break with traditional business or insider unionism in many urban contexts. The divergent path is characterized by what we call social unionism, in most cases based on social movement approaches such as grassroots mobilization and coalition building. While in some cities such initiatives are limited or suppressed, in others we find an expansion of innovation that broadly overtakes traditional approaches. Our cases demonstrate the decisive significance of two factors in the emergence of urban social unionism, as indicated by the spread of social coalition building as a prominent feature of local labor movement activity. The first is the *range of opportunity* faced by unions in a given urban context. The most significant aspects of the opportunity structures appear to be located in existing institutional arrangements and social context. Institutions and patterns of labor incorporation (or exclusion)—the presence or absence of powerful deal-cutting insider unions, the presence or absence of right-to-work laws—can either open the door for innovation and revitalization or block the way. Cross-national institutional differences are also significant in this regard, as Jefferey Sellers shows. The social context can offer more or less in the way of potential coalition partners and social networks through which mobilization efforts can spread. Immigrant groups are particularly important in contemporary organizing efforts, and in this regard relative homogeneity in immigrant/ethic composition is a significant factor in the opportunity structure.

The second and decisive factor in the emergence of socially activist urban labor movements is the *strategic choices made by local unions.* New or reformed local leaders and bridge-building activists have a range of choices even in the most difficult circumstances. Although institutional and social contexts offer more or less opportunity, local unions have important choices to make. They can take advantage of openings to move toward social mobilization and coalition building, or they can choose to stay with the traditional approaches they know. Strategic innovation is to be sure not an up-or-down choice. Reform-minded leadership is most likely to emerge where real possibilities for reform are apparent. And the

---

9. Although the Stuttgart case is not a subject of study for this book, related research indicates the significance of developments there for a broader comparative analysis.

success of such leaders—as shown in the cases presented by David Reynolds in chapter 4—also depends on the development of appropriate leadership skills.

As Dan Cornfield and Bill Canak argue in chapter 9, the strategies that unions and other social actors pursue depend in large part on how they choose to frame the issues and to mobilize resources. Coalition building is based on a reframing that emphasizes common interests with other social actors, and it is also a potentially effective way of expanding available resources. Thus even when barriers are great it is possible for innovative, aggressive unions to develop strategies aimed at breaking through the constraints, and in such situations—Miami, Boston, Stuttgart, London—significant advances for social unionism cannot be ruled out.

If the range of outcomes runs along a continuum, at one end are cases of considerable opportunity and strategic innovation, such as Los Angeles and Seattle, while the other end is occupied by cases of limited opportunity and strategic traditionalism, such as Nashville and Frankfurt. We are impressed, however, and our analysis is colored, by the fact that in any case unions can use social movement or economic development strategies to push the envelope. It is important for analysts as well as trade unionists to know the constraints, but our findings persuade us that innovative union strategies can make gains in any context.

COUNTERARGUMENTS

We have combed through our case studies to see if alternative arguments make sense. *Economic structure* or restructuring is obviously important for the circumstances labor and other social actors face at any level of engagement. As manufacturing disappears from many urban areas, or shifts from large-scale operations to light manufacturing, or disperses into suburbs and exurbs, union membership takes a beating while opportunities for new organizing are less favorable. A corresponding expansion of service sector employment—in health care, education, building services, domestic services, transportation—requires innovative organizing strategies and confronts unions with new challenges. Changes in economic structure clearly affect the constraints and opportunities faced by labor and its potential allies. Such processes characterize all advanced industrial societies at national, regional, and local levels. Although the pace, extent, and substance of change vary, all of our city cases show broadly similar processes of economic restructuring, with impacts powerful enough to overwhelm the differences for union innovation. We find no explanatory help in the variations that exist from city to city in the specific content of contemporary economic change.

Nor do existing local *political structures or processes* appear decisive. Stephanie

Luce does find that urban governance structure matters in that local governments with city administrators are likely to be resistant to living wage legislation and implementation. Sustained pressure from labor and its social alliances is especially necessary to counter such resistance. But neither this nor other structural differences in local political frameworks appear linked to the rise or relative success of social coalition building. Contrasting national political and economic institutions do matter for the range of choice in each country, as Jefferey Sellers shows in chapter 2. But that range is wide enough that locally specific opportunities and choices can be decisive, and we do find similar as well as contrasting outcomes in countries with very different institutional frameworks.

Closely related to political structure and process is *government policy* toward unions. Friendly governments such as those led by mayors Ken Livingstone in London and Antonio Villaraigosa in Los Angeles can offer significant support to union organizing and coalition campaign efforts. Yet historically labor-friendly governments in cities such as New York and Frankfurt have done little to open the door for innovative coalition-based labor strategies. And in Los Angeles, San Jose, and Seattle, resurgent labor movements have transformed local politics in ways that have weakened opposition and strengthened support for union-backed public policy.

The relative effects of *globalization*, whether the emphasis is on economic integration, intensified competition, or neoliberal governance, also do not help very much in explaining the variations we have found. An expanding immigrant workforce, for example, is important in all our urban cases, including the more recent "interior globalization" represented in this book by the Nashville case. We began this project with the assumption that global cities such as New York, Los Angeles, London, and Frankfurt would display converging workforce characteristics, including a vast influx of low-end immigrant labor and a growing economic and occupational polarization, which might lead to converging strategic innovations by labor and its social allies. What we found, instead, was that all of our cities are characterized by increasing global penetration and expanding immigrant workforces, and that union strategies vary as much across the classic global city cases as between more and less globally integrated urban areas.

Finally—although we cannot claim to have exhausted the list of potential counterarguments—*employer opposition* is widely cited as a powerful explanatory force driving union decline. Across our U.S. cases, however, aggressive employer opposition is almost a given in the present era. Although especially intense and effective in Nashville and Miami, where right-to-work laws prevail, antiunion employer strategies are nonetheless standard practice throughout the U.S. political economy. Battles to organize and negotiate at major hotel chains, for example, require intensive comprehensive campaigns in Los Angeles just as they do in

Boston and Miami—and the same is true for London. Even where institutions of social partnership mute the opposition in countries such as Germany, we nonetheless find quite different union strategies and social coalitions in cities such as Frankfurt, Hamburg, and Stuttgart.

In contrast to the conventional arguments outlined above, our analysis points to the influence of social and institutional contexts in shaping opportunities for innovation, while privileging the independent decision-making capacities of social actors such as labor unions, central labor councils, and the social coalitions in which they participate.

REVITALIZING THE LITERATURE

Because we believe that national and global politics build to a large extent on the local, the growth of social coalitions and networks at the urban level affords an important window into the prospects for progressive reform in an era dominated by neoliberal globalization. This perspective also contributes to a refocusing of labor scholarship somewhere between the traditional and often narrow framework of industrial relations and the broad political and institutional approaches of comparative political economy. What is missing from much previous work in these fields is civil society. Yet labor today operates not just at the workplace, firm, sector, and in the grand arenas of national politics but also as a social actor, one among many, drawing on logics of social movements, urban conflict, and a politics of place.

The diminishing substance of contemporary civil society, like the decline of the labor movement, has been a subject of much analysis and a source of widespread concern (Putnam 2000; Skocpol 2003). In this regard, efforts to revitalize the labor movement can be viewed as an important element in efforts to revitalize civil society. Urban-based coalition building can expand union influence, and vice versa, in the reconstruction of modern social justice infrastructures. Labor movement revitalization, where it does occur, offers a potentially significant contribution to struggles for broader social transformation.[10]

In this context, the studies presented here aim to deepen our understanding of the possibilities for labor's contribution to a broader renewal of progressive politics and institutional reform. The analysis confronts existing theoretical perspectives: the transformation of industrial relations (Kochan, Katz, and McKer-

---

10. The recent and growing literature on labor movement revitalization includes, among other work, Bronfenbrenner et al. 1998; Turner, Katz, and Hurd 2001; Nissen 2002; Cornfield and McCammon 2003; Frege and Kelly 2004; Fantasia and Voss 2004; and Milkman 2006.

sie 1986), a prominent school of thought from which we take our grounding in strategic choice but one that is limited by an overemphasis on the firm and work-place, missing the broader social context; varieties of capitalism (Hall and Sos-kice 2001), now prominent in comparative political economy, a perspective limited by an assumption of institutional stability that allows little room either for labor movement revitalization or for a renewal of progressive political and economic participation and policy; a promising recent literature on actor-driven institutional change (Streeck and Thelen 2005) that nonetheless focuses mainly on incremental neoliberal advances in a context of global liberalization; and a so-cial movements literature now broadened into a framework of contentious poli-tics (McAdam, Tarrow, and Tilly 2001), yet still limited by a focus on protest aimed at the state, with a relative neglect of the contemporary potential of labor as a social movement actor targeting the multinational corporations that domi-nate the global economy. Emphasizing actor choice, strategic innovation, and coalition building, our book contributes to an expanded theoretical perspective that brings back labor and civil society with insights from studies of labor revi-talization, social movements, democratic renewal, and institutional reform.

CONCEPTS AND DEFINITIONS

The following concepts should be seen only as clarifications rather than as at-tempts at precise definition. In any case, our creative group of chapter authors could never be pinned down to strictly harmonized usages. These loose defini-tions express an attempt by the editors to generalize our meanings as best we can, without any attempt to jam current or future work into straitjackets of restrictive analysis. Flexibility is after all a watchword of the day.

We use the terms city, local level, local arena, region, and metropolitan area more or less interchangeably. Our intent is not to provoke our colleagues in the field of urban studies (who we very much hope will read this book and join us in a dialogue about the place of labor in urban discussions), but for our purposes here *urban area* refers to the entire metropolitan region. While much of our re-search centers on the core city, since that is where much current labor movement action occurs, organizing efforts in the suburbs and surrounding areas, often as an extension of city campaigns, are significant for the prospects for successful union innovation.

Labor movement revitalization is also a term that gets used in various ways not only in this book but throughout the literature. In some usages, revitalization refers to new vitality and strategic innovation, including coalition building and grassroots mobilization. In other cases, the term refers to the accomplishments and breakthroughs—in organizing, collective bargaining, and local politics—to which innovative unions contribute. My own view is that labor movement revitalization should appear on the former side of the equation, referring to new vitality: innovation, internal organizational reform, newly awakened unions pursuing activist strategies aimed at concrete successes. Revitalized unions may or may not achieve their goals, just as a revitalized army or political party may or may not win the battle.[11]

Social movement unionism is used here to indicate an activist mobilization-based unionism that, in contrast to established insider unionism, pushes for substantial social change (Waterman 1993; Turner and Hurd 2001). The concept is at once condensed and broadened in the term *social unionism* to encompass both social movement approaches and other coalition-based innovations in areas such as economic development. Social unionism should not be confused with social partnership, which is typically an insider form of unionism. Where social partnership is strong and stable—Norway, Sweden, and Finland, for example—a more activist social unionism may not appear on the radar screen. Where social partnership relationships have weakened, as in Germany, there are new stirrings of social unionism. And in nations such as the United Kingdom efforts to build insider social partnership at the firm level are counterposed to alternative grass-roots mobilization efforts.

There is a difference between social movement unionism and social movements (Turner and Hurd 2001, 11–12). The latter are much broader and happen in the fullest form at particular historical moments, such as the 1930s and 1960s.[12] Social movement unionism, by contrast, refers to union strategies that use social movement–type approaches, such as coalition building, grassroots mobilization, aggressive organizing, demonstrations, and civil disobedience, and which typically operate outside established channels. Such approaches are more difficult when social movements are not widespread, and thus the contemporary situation presents major challenges for innovative unions, which must push upstream. There are no broad social movements to sweep unions along in their efforts at power building—which is one reason why so many unions have resisted innovation. Coalition campaigns that spill over into other campaigns and influence local politics, in cities such as Los Angeles, San Jose, and Seattle, may take on the

---

11. This formulation is not common usage in some of the chapters that follow, as well as in this author's previous work. In this new area of inquiry, based on contemporary developments, research and analysis are still in the early stages. Contradictions in usage of the term "labor movement revitalization" in my own case reflect (at best) a trial-and-error process of concept development.

12. The social movement concept used here is contrasted to the narrower "new social movement" characterization that, like the term "labor movement," applies to particular interest advocacy (such as environmental or women's rights) that may or may not function as an active "movement."

characteristics of social movements and are based on social movement–type strategies. But they are not social movements in the full meaning of the term.

Social coalition building refers to alliances of social actors, sometimes with the leadership of or at least participation by labor unions, whose campaigns are typically aimed at firms and governments.[13] As campaigns gain steam, or sometimes at the outset, local officials and candidates sign on to press demands on their own governments or firms doing business in the city, not incidentally to win popular support. And when campaigns focus on economic development, the participation of key employers and local governments is essential for success. Social coalitions seek among other things to contribute to an expanded *social justice infrastructure* that includes both movement and institution building. Based on active networks of social actors in regular relationships, a social justice infrastructure includes both institutions—such as the living wage boards, community-based development organizations, and central labor councils considered in this book—and a transformed local politics.

The social union concept includes, therefore, both social coalition building and the drive to expand a social justice infrastructure. Coalition-based campaigns are typically framed as battles for social justice. Expanded union participation in alliances with social groups acknowledges the multiple identities so important to the politics of contemporary campaigns. Urban labor movements find essential allies in social groups organized around the interests of immigrants, women, minorities, consumers, and communities. In many cases, such alliances become possible only in conjunction with internal union reform efforts, including organizational restructuring and leadership change, that expand internal inclusiveness and in so doing lay the groundwork for externally inclusive coalition campaigns. Identity-based social coalition building is a defining characteristic of the current transformation, elaborated in Dan Cornfield's concluding chapter, from manufacturing-based industrial unionism to the multijurisdictional unionism of an increasingly service-based economy.

In referring to *institutions*, we build on the standard contemporary definition found in Hall and Soskice (2001, 9): "a set of rules, formal or informal, that actors generally follow, whether for normative, cognitive or material reasons, and organizations as durable entities with formally recognized members, whose rules also contribute to the institutions of the political economy." This broad definition reflects common usage, and for our purposes it includes the structures and regularized processes through which labor, business, government, and other social actors pursue their interests and interactions. Unlike much contemporary insti-

---

13. For a sample typology of union coalition building, see, for example, Frege, Heery, and Turner 2004.

tutional literature, we do not take institutions as given but rather as the product of past, present, and future battles in which, for example, social movements can and do reform or transform institutions (Turner 2003).

ISSUES AND CASE STUDIES

To lay the groundwork for the urban case studies, the essays in part 1 present several issues central to the efforts of social coalition building at the local level. Stephanie Luce opens with an analysis of the living wage campaigns that have resulted in new legislation in more than seventy U.S. cities since 1994. Almost always including the participation if not the leadership of unions, living wage campaigns have brought together community, religious, ethnic, and immigrant organizations in coalitions that have won public support and often spilled over into further collaboration. Ron Applegate highlights the institution-building capacity of community coalitions. In the community-based development organizations (CBDOs) he examines, unions, long at odds with such efforts, have begun to enter the local economic development arena in alliances that build community power and at the same time provide bases for further collaboration. As cutting-edge cases demonstrate, a comprehensive approach enables both unions and CBDOs to challenge the political and economic constraints that have blocked their respective efforts to advance agendas of social justice.

In the broad cross-national comparative analysis offered by Jefferey Sellers, national infrastructures matter yet still leave a range of choice for local actors based on urban context, including the strength of community organizations and the nature of the policy-making process. Sellers emphasizes that local alliance building allows unions to expand opportunities present in the social and political context. And in another multicity case study, David Reynolds demonstrates the capacity of local unions to build regional power in the United States. Transformed by a new generation of activist leaders, previously dormant central labor councils have emerged as focal points in coalition campaigns that bring social actors together to expand progressive political influence across a range of urban areas. Such initiatives move beyond traditional efforts to elect pro-labor candidates toward more comprehensive strategies for engagement in regional governance.

The chapters in part 2 present case studies of "union towns" in the United States, where insider unions have long occupied positions of well-established political and economic influence. Heiwon Kwon and Benjamin Day examine the Boston case, where a few political deal-making unions have made gains for their own members at the expense of a broader mobilization to expand organizing efforts and a more cohesive social unionism. Ian Greer, Barbara Byrd, and Lou Jean

Fleron show the critical role of political entrepreneurship in innovative union efforts to build coalitions that have moved traditional unions in Seattle and Buffalo into central positions of influence in the economic development arena. Finally, Marco Hauptmeier and Lowell Turner provide a bridge to the next section in a comparison between the limitations of social unionism in New York and the transformation in Los Angeles of traditionally weak unions into a politically powerful labor movement, building in part on coalitions rooted in a growing Latino community.

Part 3 builds on the Los Angeles case to consider urban areas in which unions did not exert significant political and economic influence prior to the 1990s. For Miami, Bruce Nissen and Monica Russo explain both the blockage of union influence in an area characterized by diverse immigrant groups in a right-to-work state as well as the more recent transformation of the central labor council and the potential for an expansion of strategic social unionism. Daniel Cornfield and William Canak identify a similar blockage in Nashville, illustrating the lack of labor mobilization with an in-depth study of recent immigration patterns and the continuing distance between labor and immigrant support groups. Coming full circle back to a successful case similar in some ways to Los Angeles, Nari Rhee and Julie Sadler show the pathbreaking role played in San Jose by innovative leadership at the central labor council, in building the coalitions and political power necessary to redefine the labor movement as an influential actor in public policy-making processes.

Going solo this time, Ian Greer provides a bridge between U.S. and European cases by opening part 4 with a comparative study of Hamburg and Seattle. Although labor in Seattle coalesced earlier than Hamburg as a cohesive labor movement, unions in both cities have in recent years pulled together impressive coalition campaigns around particular issues. Jane Holgate and Jane Wills present a mixed picture for labor in London, where coalition-based living wage and union organizing campaigns have broken new ground in a labor movement still largely characterized by national, firm-specific, single-union campaigns. Otto Jacobi's Frankfurt story concludes the case studies with a graphic demonstration of the barriers to local labor campaigns in a context marked by strong labor institutions focused at the national, sector, and firm levels.

Finally, Dan Cornfield adds a systematic analysis of patterns of immigration and identity for processes of labor movement revitalization, while at the same time making a heroic effort to summarize our collective insights into the meaning and significance of contemporary union coalition-building efforts.

And now, please join us where the rubber meets the urban road. . . .

Part I

URBAN ISSUES AND CAMPAIGNS

1

THE U.S. LIVING WAGE MOVEMENT

Building Coalitions from the Local Level in a Global Economy

Stephanie Luce

In the last decade, U.S. unions have sought out opportunities to build coalitions with potential allies. In part, this is a defensive measure: faced with declining density and power, unions must search for partners to help them rebuild and be "good community citizens" in order to strengthen their reputation among potential members. It is also a proactive measure: numerous union leaders today come out of the new social movements of the 1960s and 1970s and realize the need to incorporate broad demands into labor's agenda. Finally, some unionists pursue the strategy because they simply believe "it's the right thing to do."

In this chapter I examine one possible avenue for building labor-community coalitions: the living wage movement. The modern U.S. living wage movement began in 1994 with a campaign in Baltimore to raise wages for city residents making the minimum wage. The result was an ordinance that required employers holding service contracts with the city to pay their workers a wage close to the federal poverty line for a full-time worker with children. Since 1994, activists have engaged in living wage campaigns around the country, typically building coalitions of labor, community, and faith-based groups to pass local ordinances directed at city or county governments. I discuss the types of coalitions built through the movement and examine their successes and failures in terms of their capacity to build city-based networks and to revitalize union organizing.

AN OVERVIEW OF THE LIVING WAGE MOVEMENT

The United States established a federal minimum wage as part of the Fair Labor Standards Act of 1938, which sets a minimum hourly rate of pay for covered employers. The minimum wage is not indexed to inflation, so it must be raised by Congress on a regular basis to keep up with the cost of living. Congress failed to do this in the 1970s and 1980s, and by the early 1990s the real value of the minimum wage had fallen far below its historic levels—and well below the amount necessary for a worker with a family to meet the federal poverty line.

In addition, public sector workers, who had fought and won the right to unionize in many places, also saw an attack on their wages in the form of privatization, or contracting out. Local governments, faced with reduced federal aid and declining populations and tax bases, looked to balance their budgets by contracting out government services. This effort was spurred in the 1980s by an ideological move toward downsizing government and the expansion of free markets (Sclar 2001). The result was that many unionized public sector jobs were lost, and low-wage positions without benefits developed in their place.

In response to these trends, the incidence of workers living in poverty grew, and community and labor organizations looked for solutions. At the same time, labor and community groups were feeling under attack more generally and looked for avenues for local campaigns that would unite them with allies and offer the opportunity for winnable reforms.

The living wage movement was one solution to these issues. Framed primarily as local campaigns, they allowed unions, community, and faith-based groups to work together in coalition to raise wages for some workers. These coalitions have looked for any form of leverage they could find to raise the wages of workers, most of whom had been unable to raise their own wages through collective or legislative action. Initially, the leverage was found through getting cities and counties to pass ordinances attaching living wage requirements to service contracts. This was later expanded to cover firms receiving economic development assistance from cities, firms operating concessions on city-owned property, and direct city or county employees.

As they waged more and more campaigns, activists became more successful at winning. Scholars such as Nissen (2000), Merrifield (2000), and Tilly (2003) argue that at some point the campaigns came together into a social movement. It appears that they contain the three components that social movements scholar Charles Tilly (2004) argues must be present. First, the living wage movement is an ongoing effort that makes public demands on authorities—primarily city and county legislators, but others as well. Second, the campaigns employ a range of tactics, such as lobbying, rallies, marches, petitions, direct action, and the creation of new coalitions. Finally, the participants present their issue as worthy and their campaigns as a unified demand representing large numbers of committed people. The campaigns rely on existing organizations and networks, but they also pull in new activists.

These activists began working together across cities, coordinating their work directly with one another at times and learning from each other. Activists expanded the movement in several directions. First, campaigns went beyond simply mandating wages. Many ordinances now index the living wage to inflation, provide health benefits, and may include benefits such as paid days off. Some include community hiring halls and language that gives some preference to union employers.

The movement also expanded the types of employers covered by the laws. In addition to service contractors, subsidy recipients, subcontractors, and direct city or county employees, the ordinances now also cover universities, school boards, transportation boards, and ports. In recent years, we have seen campaigns designed to raise the minimum wage for all employees in a particular locality. The New Orleans minimum wage passed in 2002 was overturned by the Louisiana Supreme Court, but subsequent ordinances passed in Santa Fe, San Francisco, and Madison.[1]

Living wage advocates have also been connected to statewide minimum wage campaigns. In states such as Massachusetts, Vermont, California, Oregon, Illinois, and Washington, efforts to increase the state minimum were tied in with living wage language and activists. In November 2004, voters in Florida and Nevada passed statewide minimum wage laws by a large margin. Both set the minimum wage at one dollar above the federal level, and the Florida law also indexes the wage rate to inflation.[2]

The living wage itself varies from city to city. Initially, campaigns set out to win a living wage that was set to the poverty level for a family of four, assuming a full-time worker. Activists recognized that this does not "solve poverty," as many workers do not work full time, and the poverty level itself is still quite low. Still, it is an improvement over the minimum wage. For example, in 2004 the federal minimum wage was $5.15 an hour, and the living wage as defined by the poverty level for a family of four was $9.28. After the movement achieved some success, campaigns tried to win higher wages—such as 110 or 120 percent of the poverty line. In 2004, the average wage won in traditional living wage campaigns was $10.89— or 117 percent of the poverty line.[3]

---

1. Not all cities have the right to pass their own minimum wage laws. Louisiana is a "home rule" state that does allow cities this right. New Orleans living wage activists collected the necessary fifty thousand signatures to put the minimum wage proposal on the city ballot in 1996. However, the hotel and restaurant lobby went to the state and got the legislature to outlaw cities from passing wage laws. The law allowed the state to override home rule in this case because a city wage law would do "undue economic harm to the state." Activists challenged this law, and the courts ruled that the measure had to be allowed on the ballot. The measure passed with strong support, and opponents immediately challenged it. The first ruling was in favor of the living wage, but the Louisiana Supreme Court upheld the state law, nullifying the city ordinance.

2. Other states will have minimum wage referendums on the ballot in coming years.

3. In addition to the minimum wage, the United States also has "prevailing wage" laws. These primarily apply to the construction industry and require the federal government (and some state and

After the first ten years of the movement, more than 120 living wage ordinances were on the books. A handful of these have been overturned or repealed (which will be discussed later), but most still stand. Living wage ordinances can be found throughout the country—in large cities and small; cities with Democratic and Republican leaders; traditional "progressive cities" such as San Francisco and Madison, as well as more conservative or mainstream ones such as Lincoln and Cincinnati. However, Isaac Martin (2004) finds that the cities with ordinances tend to be concentrated outside the South in urban centers, or at least in large metropolitan areas in liberal cities with dense organization levels "including labor unions, congregation-based organizations, and low-income community organizations." Because the ordinances are more likely to be found in large cities, this suggests the cities with ordinances are those with a greater percentage of people of color.

For the most part, the living wage movement has been targeted at the municipal level. First, the constituency groups that are involved in most of the campaigns are rooted there. Most community organizations and churches have a local focus; the municipal level is where the base of these groups exists. These groups are used to mobilizing at the local level and have the infrastructure to do so. This is less true of unions: union locals may be used to mobilizing at the firm level and internationals at the national level. But the growth of the living wage movement coincided to some degree with the rebirth of the central labor councils, making for a natural partnership.

The second reason for the local focus was that the campaigns had a greater chance of winning. State and federal campaigns take a lot of money, which these campaigns did not have. It is also much easier to use people power at the local level—getting members to meet with elected city representatives, for example. Finally, the local focus allowed groups to build the kinds of coalitions they wanted to create.

BUILDING COALITIONS

Living wage campaigns and ordinances differ greatly from city to city, making it difficult to characterize the movement or the impact of the laws. Despite the variation, one thing most campaigns have in common is that they are run by labor-community coalitions. In many cases, these coalitions bring together groups that have never worked together before or that have not developed strong relation-

city governments) to pay the prevailing wage (usually defined as the union wage) for any publicly funded construction work.

ships. The living wage concept is popular with a wide spectrum of organizations—indeed, with the general population—so it makes a natural issue around which to build alliances. The most common coalition partners include labor councils or unions that represent low-wage workers such as the Service Employees International Union (SEIU) and UNITE HERE, which was formed by the merger of UNITE (Union of Needletrades, Industrial and Textile Employees) and HERE (Hotel Employees and Restaurant Employees International Union); national community organizing groups with local chapters, such as the Association of Community Organizations for Reform Now (ACORN); faith-based groups, such as the Industrial Areas Foundation (IAF); and labor-community collaborations, such as Jobs with Justice (JwJ). In any one campaign, a host of other organizations, ranging from environmentalists to civil rights organizations, might sign on. In many cities, new relations have developed between labor, faith-based, community, and student groups. Some coalitions form to pass the ordinance only, but many have gone on to work on other projects together.[4]

Not all the coalitions include labor. Some campaigns are led primarily by community organizations, and some include labor unions only as endorsers rather than as full participants. A few campaigns are run primarily by community organizations such as ACORN. In some cases, the ordinances are pushed through primarily by elected city officials. The Hayward, California, a living wage ordinance was passed primarily by local Democratic Party activists.

However, most campaigns do include labor unions in some capacity, and labor has participated in almost all the successful campaigns (Martin 2004). These involve two basic types. First are the unions or central labor councils that participate in living wage coalitions to build new alliances or strengthen ties with community allies. For these unions, the coalition building is the primary goal of the campaign. The second group consists of unions that become involved in living wage campaigns to advance specific goals, such as organizing workers or winning raises for workers they already represent. This involves cases where unions are in the coalitions from the start, as well as cases where the unions come on board after the laws are passed—when they see opportunities to use enforcement campaigns to their benefit.

Not all campaigns include workers who would be covered by the ordinances. Sometimes the movement is an extension of previous organizing efforts, such as the unsuccessful unionization drives at the hotels in Santa Monica, California, or an outgrowth of low-wage workers self-organizing around their own demands about what constitutes a living wage, as in Providence, Rhode Island. On the other hand, many campaigns have little or no contact with the affected workers and are

---

4. For more on this, see Luce 2004.

run instead by what Harvard economist Richard Freeman refers to as nonworker organizations, or NWOs (Freeman 2005). Freeman notes that the presence of NWOs has grown as the official labor movement has weakened. He argues that these organizations can "fight for other folks' wages" on behalf of vulnerable workers "who cannot improve their situation by themselves" (Freeman 2005, 17). However, NWOs differ from other worker organizations in that they are not controlled by the workers. Instead of workers electing their own leaders, NWOs choose what workers they want to fight on behalf of. Sometimes this gives workers little or no voice in fighting for their own demands. At other times, it can be a successful partnership that creates a space for workers to form their own organizations or creates alliances between NWOs and existing workers' organizations.

Building Labor-Community Alliances

The chance to build new alliances is perhaps the most important reason some labor unions have been involved in living wage campaigns. This has been especially important for central labor councils trying to increase their visibility in their communities. In some cities, central labor councils have initiated the campaigns, such as in San Jose, Tucson, and Madison. In others, they came on board as major participants, such as in Atlanta and Los Angeles.

As Southern Arizona Labor Council president Ian Robertson explained his role in the 1997–1999 living wage campaign in Tucson: "I'm tired of being called a labor boss, and that we're only interested in collecting dues. Here was an opportunity for labor to be a community partner" (Luce 2002). In Cleveland, labor council president John Ryan notes that even if the living wage ordinance didn't result in immediate organizing gains for labor, the campaign was important in itself for its ability to help some families move out of poverty.[5]

Beyond central labor councils, local union members and leaders have also found living wage campaigns a useful way to build alliances. Coalition building is important in its own right, but it also creates the foundation for broader social movements with a workers' rights agenda. A Sonoma County, California, living wage coalition includes unions—SEIU, the International Brotherhood of Electrical Workers (IBEW), and the Carpenters—political groups (the Green Party), and groups such as the Sonoma County Council on Aging, Sonoma County Peace and Justice Center, and Women in Action. According to Marty Bennett, a lead organizer in the effort, labor unions lost a close vote on a project labor agreement (an agreement between the city and stakeholders to build a new development un-

---

5. John Ryan, interview with the author, May 19, 2004.

der certain conditions favorable to workers) in a city council meeting in 2000. That woke them up to the fact that they needed to work in coalition to pass labor's political agenda. Steve Benjamin of the IBEW notes, "Any time you can establish new relationships like this, it's a good thing" (Luce 2002).

In Boston, the main anchors of the 1997 living wage campaign were ACORN and the Greater Boston Central Labor Council. According to Monica Halas, a living wage advocate and lawyer with Greater Boston Legal Services, the campaign brought together ACORN and the labor council in a way that other issues had not. The alliance may not seem a natural one, as ACORN's base is primarily African American residents, while the labor council has stronger ties in the white working class in a historically segregated city. Yet the organizations were able to institutionalize their relationship by requiring the city to establish a Living Wage Advisory Committee, with seats for both, to monitor and enforce the law. According to Halas, the committee "really cemented their relationship, and there have been so many positive spin-offs out of that" (Luce 2004, 204). These spin-offs include the successful effort to raise the state minimum wage in 1998, pass a statewide and Boston earned-income tax credit, and introduce a state corporate accountability law. When Boston Justice for Janitors went on strike in 2002, ACORN president Maude Hurd and labor council leader Tony Romano were arrested together in an act of civil disobedience supporting the janitors.

In Los Angeles, the 1996–97 living wage campaign helped build not only a labor-community coalition but a citywide movement. Living wage advocates as well as opponents and journalists point to the living wage campaign as a catalyst for this movement, which has brought a slew of victories: community benefits agreements for major economic development projects in the city, the election of labor-backed candidates for city governance, winning the largest pay raises in many years for city employees, and growth in union power. City council member Joel Wachs, who had been in office for twenty-seven years, noted in 1998 that "the city employee unions are stronger than I've ever seen them with respect to influence over the City Council. Most council members will not buck the unions. There are more council members today who will vote 100 percent for what the unions want."[6]

Living Wages and New Organizing

The link between union organizing and the living wage is complex. Although some living wage opponents claim that unionization efforts are the main motive

6. Patrick McGreevey, "Unions Gaining Power in L.A." *Daily News,* September 7, 1998, N1.

behind the movement, not all union leaders are convinced that living wage campaigns can lead to new organizing. Some believe the campaigns hurt organizing efforts: If workers can get higher wages through legislation, why would they fight for a union? Anecdotally, union leaders from a variety of unions and regions have made this claim, including those from the American Federation of State, County and Municipal Employees (AFSCME), United Food and Commercial Workers (UFCW), the building trades, UNITE HERE, and others. In general, however, these opponents are in the minority, and most union leaders are supportive of the living wage concept.

According to Ken Jacobs, former head organizer for the San Francisco living wage campaign, living wage campaigns can either help or harm unions. Unions that have been strategic about involvement in campaigns have seen positive results. Where unions are neutral toward or skeptical of the campaigns and stay out of them, living wage ordinances can be a detriment to new organizing (Luce 2004).

There are several ways in which unions can use living wage campaigns or ordinances to assist new organizing. First, the campaigns can simply be a way to meet new workers and let them know about the power of a union. If a union is an active participant in the campaign, they can help workers to see that winning a living wage might be the first step in a longer campaign for more rights. In Burlington, Vermont, the Living Wage Coalition helped pass an ordinance raising wages for direct city employees. The workers got a $2.25 per hour pay increase and went on to successfully seek representation with AFSCME.

Second, unions can build language into the ordinances that give them advantages in organizing. Taft-Hartley prevents cities or states from requiring firms to honor card check and/or neutrality agreements outright (Sahu 2001). Instead, unions have been able to win weaker language in ordinances that gives some advantages to unions, such as "labor peace" provisions that allow cities to deny contracts or subsidies to firms with a poor labor relations history; gives preference in handing out economic development monies to businesses that "engage in responsible labor relations"; and prohibits the use of public money for antiunion activities. This kind of language can be found in about a quarter of the ordinances passed.

Over a third of ordinances passed also contain language that explicitly prohibits employers from disciplining or firing workers who exercise their rights under the living wage law. This can aid union organizing efforts because workers who speak out about their right to join a union will be protected from job loss if they are also speaking about their right to receive a living wage.

In the first ten years of the movement, there have been a handful of cases in which unions have been able to use this direct ordinance language to organize workers. In Santa Cruz, the living wage ordinance requires covered employers to remain neutral in union campaigns. When a known antiunion employer wanted to get a city contract to drive city buses and vans, they granted a card check agreement to the United Transportation Union Local 23. The union then organized and won a contract for the 150 workers. In the same city, SEIU Local 415 won a card check agreement with the city to cover its 550 nonunion temporary workers.

Success has also come in indirect organizing victories, where the campaign has in some way spurred a new drive or assisted an existing one. For example, Tucson passed a living wage law in 1999 that applied to service contractors. The living wage raises put contracted workers' wages higher than some city workers' wages, so city workers began an organizing campaign. Communication Workers of America Local 7026 organizer Rolando Figueroa, who had been active in the living wage campaign, approached the workers and launched an organizing drive. Eventually, fifteen hundred workers won recognition and a first contract with the city. Figueroa asserts that the Communication Workers campaign might never have happened without the living wage campaign because the victory gave workers confidence to take on a union drive. Figueroa notes that "many workers are reluctant to join unions because they are afraid to make the commitment, or think the effort is futile. But seeing a living wage coalition join together to fight for and win a living wage ordinance opens their eyes to the power of collective action, and the potential power of working with other workers in a union" (Luce 2001).

Many university-based living wage campaigns are closely related to efforts to organize workers. In 2001, the University Student Labor Action Coalition at Wesleyan University in Connecticut helped janitors on campus (working for a private contractor) organize with SEIU Local 531, as the initial step toward a living wage campaign.[7] In the spring of 2005, after three years of pressuring the administration, students at Georgetown University went on a hunger strike to win a living wage policy for campus janitors. After nine days, the administration agreed to raise workers' wages to $15 over three years. According to senior and Georgetown Living Wage Coalition member Mike Wilson, winning a living wage was not enough:

> We wanted Georgetown to commit itself and its contractors to a policy of neutrality in union campaigns, because we felt that this was important in our fighting for it with the workers at Georgetown. We wanted the workers themselves to feel empowered so that they could continue this fight after most of those working on the campaign graduate and leave. We wanted the workers to keep the power. (Democracy Now 2005)

---

7. For a fuller account of the Wesleyan effort, see Clawson 2003.

As a result, the university agreed to commit to union neutrality and include this requirement in all its contracts. A few weeks later, students at Washington University—St. Louis held a sit-in on their campus to demand a living wage for university employees. After nineteen days, the administration agreed to $1 million in salary and benefit increases for campus employees and to form a committee to work on ensuring that campus workers have freedom of association.

Other successful efforts to link living wage campaigns to unionization have occurred in cities such as Berkeley and San Jose, California; Alexandria, Virginia; and Miami, Florida. Perhaps the most extensive connection between the living wage and union organizing has occurred in Los Angeles. The campaign was spearheaded by the Los Angeles Alliance for a New Economy (LAANE), a union-based social justice organization founded in the 1990s by HERE. After the ordinance was enacted, LAANE had staff monitor city meeting agendas for upcoming service contracts and economic development projects. This information was shared with unions, which then attempted to work with the bidding employers to obtain card-check/neutrality in exchange for helping the employer get the contract.

At the same time, LAANE worked with the Los Angeles County Federation of Labor and area unions on an independent organizing drive at Los Angeles International Airport, which was covered by the ordinance. Some of the airport contractors hold long leases—some that were adopted right before the ordinance was passed were not due to come up for another ten years. The unions decided to pressure the employers to adopt the ordinance voluntarily. Their efforts paid off: according to Larry Frank and Kent Wong (2004), "When the living wage law was passed 30,000 out of the 50,000 airport worker were not in a union. Since this time, HERE has gone from representing roughly one out of five airport workers in its bargaining to four out of five. SEIU has moved from representing one in ten workers within their jurisdiction to representing more than half."

LAANE and its living wage coalition allies, including the faith-based Clergy and Laity United for Economic Justice, continued to use the momentum from the campaign and the power of the living wage rhetoric in related efforts to win community benefits agreements for economic development. As of 2005, LAANE has won six such agreements, which provide things such as living wages for workers in development projects, such as the new Academy Awards center, as well as union neutrality agreements, which have helped UNITE HERE organize workers.

Unionized Workers Win Better Contracts

Some living wage campaigns have furthered the cause of organized workers in other concrete ways. When Alexandria, Virginia, passed its living wage law in 2000, the ordinance resulted in raises for parking lot attendants at city-owned lots, represented by HERE. The union had only been able to win wages of around $7 per hour, which was higher than the wage paid to other parking lot attendants in the area but still below a living wage. With the ordinance in place, wages jumped to $10.21 an hour. Similarly, in Chicago, living wage advocates made sure that the ordinance covered home-health-care workers represented by SEIU Local 880. The ordinance raised those workers' wages from $5.30 to $7.60 an hour.

The living wage movement has provided support to National Education Association (NEA) organizers around the country who are trying to win higher wages for teaching assistants and other school support staff. In Vermont, the NEA built a contract campaign around the demand for a livable wage of $9 to $10 per hour plus health benefits. In Boston, orderlies, clerks, and technical workers represented by SEIU settled a contract in 2002 with Boston Medical Center using living wage guidelines. Under the agreement, workers would receive raises to bring their pay up to at least $10.55, the Boston living wage at the time.[8] Campus campaigns have also used living wage campaigns to assist in contract campaigns for already organized workers—such as at Harvard, Stanford, and Vanderbilt universities.

REVITALIZING THE LABOR MOVEMENT

These examples suggest that the living wage movement has had some success in helping revitalize labor—by helping build labor-community alliances, organizing new workers, and raising wages for already unionized workers. What can we conclude about the kinds of campaigns and coalitions built and their ability to achieve success?

First, in cases where unions have used living wage campaigns as a way to pursue new organizing or win raises for already organized workers, building a labor-community coalition has led to some victories. Unions have been creative in finding ways to craft ordinances and use them as leverage in organizing and bargaining. Coalition building can assist in these efforts by providing unions with good publicity, making contacts with new workers, and adding moral force to

---

8. Jennifer Heldt Powell, "Boston Medical Center Settles Contract with Workers," *Boston Herald*, October 9, 2002, 34.

unionization drives. But for this to happen the unions must be prepared to use the campaigns for organizing purposes. As Ken Jacobs notes, they must be strategic about how to use the campaigns or ordinances to launch organizing drives or assist contract campaigns. Unions cannot simply sign on to a living wage campaign and assume it will directly help them.

It is difficult to estimate the number of workers who have benefited directly or indirectly from the living wage movement. While the traditional living wage ordinances covered only a few dozen workers at most in some cities, they affected tens of thousands in cities such as New York and San Francisco. However, the statewide minimum wage campaigns that have emerged out of the living wage movement are clearly covering many more workers. For example, economists estimate that the Florida minimum wage law passed in 2004 will directly affect about three hundred thousand workers (Pollin, Brenner, and Wicks-Lim 2004). In addition, many workers have received "ripple effect" wage increases due to the living wage movement. These are workers already earning the living wage or slightly above, who also received a raise with the passage of the new law. In many cases, these indirect raises are larger than the direct raises. For example, 550,000 workers in Florida are expected to benefit from "ripple effect" raises from the 2004 law.

Second, the examples about implementation struggles suggest that living wage advocates cannot assume that passing a living wage ordinance will automatically result in higher wages for the covered workers. Diligence is needed to ensure the city enforces the law. Furthermore, some ordinances are blocked from implementation altogether or even repealed after passage. Perhaps surprisingly, I found that strong implementation is more likely in cases where living wage advocates are involved in the implementation process and where the campaign itself was relatively contentious. Although a contentious campaign doesn't guarantee strong enforcement, it can force living wage advocates to build real and deep coalitions that may be needed later to keep the ordinance on the books. Contentious campaigns can push coalitions to test themselves and learn about their own strengths and weaknesses, as well as build institutions that can be used for implementation down the road.[9]

Third, even when the campaigns have not resulted in new organizing gains or in living wage gains for large numbers of workers, the opportunity to build labor-community coalitions can be considered a victory in itself. In Los Angeles, Episcopal minister Dick Gillet noted that many in the religious community had negative images of unions and that the living wage campaign created an ideal place for dispelling some of these notions: "The living wage victory in Los Ange-

---

9. For more on this point, see Luce 2004.

les raised the possibility that a real awakening and a willingness to rekindle the fires for a new agenda for justice might be at hand in the form of a promising new partnership of religious faiths with the diverse and progressive sectors of the community, and even with some politicians with a conscience."[10] In Milwaukee, the executive director of the job training organization Esperanza Unida remarked that the Campaign for a Sustainable Milwaukee was different from previous coalition attempts: "I've never seen so many people working together to focus on the root cause of our social problems."[11]

Many in the labor movement now acknowledge the necessity of building coalitions with community partners. However, recognizing the need for coalitions and the ability to build them are often far apart. The challenges to building real labor-community coalitions are many. In some cities, unions have a legacy of exclusion and discrimination against African Americans, making it difficult to find enough trust to work together. In many cases, labor unions possess greater resources (including staff, infrastructure, and money) than most of their potential allies, leading to an imbalance of power within the coalitions. Labor unions feel pressure to spend dues money wisely—often on providing services to members or organizing new members, rather than on efforts with vague outcomes.

Living wage campaigns appear to provide a way to get beyond some of these obstacles. The movement has created a way for unions to build coalitions that they had not necessarily been able to create through other means. In Cleveland, former Jobs with Justice staff person Steve Cagan says the living wage campaign "was a real movement" for two years—the coalition was grassroots, diverse, and broad, and people realized that building the movement was as important as winning the ordinance.[12]

Richard Freeman (2005, 16) cautions that living wage campaigns on their own can turn into "cul-de-sacs drawing activist energy from national reforms that could improve the well-being of low-wage workers more widely." However, most living wage activists realize that the campaigns alone will not cover many workers and that the movement must "scale up" to address poverty more fundamentally. To this end, they continue to wage campaigns at the local level, but they have expanded their efforts to statewide minimum wage campaigns and pay ongoing attention to openings at the national level to raise the federal minimum wage. In some cities, the coalitions have passed ordinances and then died off, but in other places the campaigns have built new and lasting coalitions and sparked a host of

---

10. Richard Gillet, interview with the author, January 29, 1998.

11. Jack Norman, "Activists Work on Economic Plan with Jobs in Mind," *Milwaukee Journal,* September 23, 1994, B1, B6.

12. Steve Cagan, interview with the author, May 20, 2004.

successful organizing to build working-class power. For example, in July 2006 members of the Chicago living wage coalition came together to pass a Big Box Ordinance requiring large retailers in the city to pay a living wage of $10 an hour and another $3 an hour in benefits, indexed for inflation.

What explains the appeal of the living wage movement? In part, it rests on the basic popularity of the issue: voters have broadly supported the concept of the federal minimum wage since it was established in 1938. The idea carries a deep moral resonance and is relevant to a wide range of groups. And as expressed by *The Black Commentator* (2002), the movement fulfills a fundamental need: "Living Wage campaigns create legal, economic and political environments in which workers and entire communities can fight the power of money."

2

UNIONS AND THE STRATEGIC CONTEXT OF LOCAL GOVERNANCE

A Comparative Overview

Jefferey M. Sellers

Throughout advanced industrial countries and beyond, local politics has histor- ically provided a crucial focal point of organizing and influence for working-class movements. The comparative case studies in this book highlight how this local focus has again emerged as a major element in the opportunity structure of union politics. In this chapter I employ cross-national statistics to analyze national and local variations in the political opportunities for unions and other groups con- cerned with social justice within communities. Whatever the national context, the analysis shows that urban coalition building with other political and social groups plays an important role in effective union politics. Cross-national local compar- isons also reveal how the opportunities and risks of urban coalition building in the United States differ from those in much of the rest of the developed world.

In the early phases of industrial unionism in nineteenth and early twentieth century Europe, local political regimes and coalitions governing industrial cities were as crucial to working-class politics as unions and parties at the national level (Katznelson and Zolberg 1986; Dogliani 1992). Under conditions of relatively sta- ble capitalist organization, and in alliance with middle-class reformist move- ments as well as working-class parties, unions furnished critical support for "municipal socialist" regimes at the local level (e.g., Steinmetz 2001). These local formations provided housing and educational, recreational, and health services that often grew into components of national welfare states and helped mobilize workers in national politics. In the multiethnic, more fragmented context of working-class organization in the United States, the big-city political machines of Northeastern cities brought unions parallel channels of incorporation (Corn- field 1993; Katznelson and Zolberg 1986).

In the contemporary era, high-tech manufacturing, service capitalism, eco- nomic globalization, and media-driven politics have limited the opportunities for

The author would like to thank Jeffrey Whitten and Yooil Bae for research assistance and Jeb Barnes, Dan Cornfield, Nathan Lillie, Merrill Silverstein, Janelle Wong, and two anonymous reviewers for comments and suggestions.

unions to pursue local coalition building around municipal socialist agendas. Accounts of contemporary capitalism that focus solely on the organization of firms and international markets (e.g., Hall and Soskice 2001), however, neglect the important political opportunities that persist for unions to make gains through urban coalition building. Rights to good jobs, decent wages, local services, and environmental quality remain a common cause between unions and an array of social justice movements within communities. The place-dependent business interests inherent in such services as tourism and retail distribution have opened up new opportunities for community-level politics (Sellers 2002, chap. 5). The rise of environmental and neighborhood movements concerned with the quality of life may furnish a new common ground with working-class politics. And in many cities disenfranchised immigrant workers offer potentially potent new constituencies for movement unionism around social justice.

In this chapter I offer a systematic contemporary snapshot of how the context of local politics varied in the 1980s and 1990s across the developed world and the consequences for union influence at the local level. Statistical comparison will bring out both the effects from legacies of national institution building in politics, the economy, and civil society, and the common dilemmas unions face.

LOCAL INFLUENCE IN NATIONAL AND TRANSNATIONAL POLITICAL ECONOMIES

The strategic context of unions in local politics needs to be understood in light of both the other types of groups and political organizations that are also active in local politics and the relation between different arenas of contestation in advanced industrial society. Much of the politics of local coalition building around social justice plays out in arenas distinct from the firm itself or relations among firms. The institutionally distinct arena of local government, policy, and politics also furnished part of the local opportunities for labor, as does the sphere of civic and social organization known as civil society (see Linz and Stepan 1994, chap. 1). Synergistic relations between these different arenas played a crucial role in the municipal socialist politics of earlier eras. Parallel synergies continue to be critical to contemporary union empowerment through local politics.

The overlapping nature of relations between these arenas can be conceptualized as a set of interrelated arenas (see figure 2.1). Local government, for instance, can regulate such aspects of firm activity as local plant construction and location or local wages. Local political parties can draw on union support, provide benefits for union members, and furnish part of the agenda for union organizing. By the same token, unions that seek to mobilize support within civil society for ef-

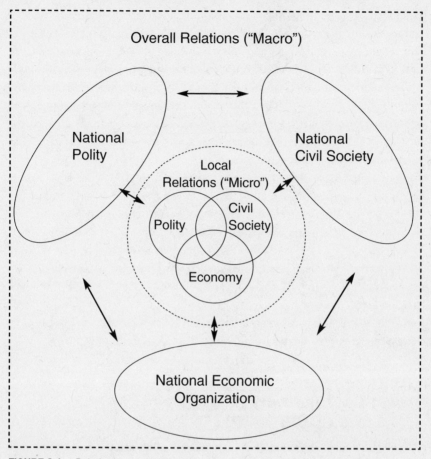

FIGURE 2.1.   Relations among national and local polity, civil society, and economy

forts to improve working conditions or wages may find it useful to advocate broader community agendas that affect the interests of union members even outside the workplace. Alliances with social justice groups in spheres beyond the firm make sense as a means of garnering support and of furthering the interests of common constituencies. Unions can gain allies in the community and can further the pursuit of social justice for union members far beyond the confines of firms.

  Reaching out to the community to build coalitions also holds potential costs for unions. As Claus Offe and Helmut Wiesenthal argued decades ago (1985), political and civic interest formation outside the economic arena often coalesces around agendas that diverge from the interests of workers. A pluralistic political or civic arena leaves unions in the position of being only one among many potential interest groups. Resource mobilization theory (McCarthy and Zald 1977; Tilly 1978) predicts that more mobilized unions will be more successful in setting political agendas. But powerful allies that share agendas for social justice may also be crucial to making cross-sectoral coalitions work in the interest of both unions and the working class. As Peter Evans (2002) notes, the resulting opportunities may be as much a matter of initiatives, responses, and solicitations from officials and established institutions as they are a product of what unions themselves do. Unions themselves can also represent narrower group interests or less disadvantaged groups.

In the following analysis, I use mass survey data from the World Value Surveys and elite data from the Fiscal Austerity and Urban Innovation (FAUI) Project to analyze what makes a difference for union influence in the local political process. As resource mobilization theory suggests, influence is partly a matter of mass mobilization. Where unions and other social justice groups have organized more of the population, they can be expected to have greater influence. Coalitions with each other and with other social, civic, and political associations can also enhance this influence. As cross-national comparison of local variations shows, different histories of working-class organization, civic association, and local institutions have given rise to systematically different patterns of union influence.

MOBILIZATION AND INFLUENCE IN LOCAL GOVERNANCE

A localized view of policy and the opportunities to influence it necessitates multilevel analysis of institutions and politics (Sellers 2002, 2005). This analysis supplements the numerous data sets already available for variables at the national level with the most extensive data set now available at the local level, the cross-national (FAUI) surveys of small samples of mayors between 1985 and 1999 (e.g., Clark 2000). The analysis joins this data set with the systematic evidence on associational membership and participation from the World Values Survey, the largest cross-national survey of individual political behavior and beliefs (see also Inglehart, Basanez, and Moreno 1998). The combination of local elite and individual-level surveys enabled simultaneous comparative national assessment of both the influence of unions and related organizations within local government and the degree to which unions and other organizations mobilized citizens.

Participation and Mobilization in Local Organizations

The World Values Survey offers a clear cross-national overview of overall levels of mass mobilization.[1] In addition to a question about participation in unions, the survey question battery about mass participation in voluntary organizations includes two categories that also measure participation in other organizations that often represent disadvantaged groups. One of these, focused on voluntary organizations engaged in "community action," covers those addressed to "issues like poverty, employment, housing, racial equality" (Inglehart, Basañez, and Moreno 1998, 24). The other, encompassing "social welfare" organizations," includes those providing "social welfare services for elderly, handicapped, or deprived people" (ibid., 19). At the same time, the battery asks about participation in an array of other types of civic associations less targeted toward social justice, from religious to cultural and environmental associations. The survey thus offers an overview of how self-reported participation by individual citizens in associations devoted to social justice compares to wider patterns of civic participation (see table 2.1).

The patterns of participation in unions and social justice organizations, on the one hand, and other civic associations, on the other, fall into four broad types. In both the United States and Canada union participation is low on average, but participation in social justice organizations besides unions remains comparatively high. Most strikingly, strong participation in more general civic associations dominates average rates of participation in all social justice organizations. Since Tocqueville, observers of the United States have pointed to the high levels of civic association (Ladd 1999; Putnam 2000). The relatively low level of participation in social justice organizations in the United States has also long been noted (Verba, Nie, and Kim 1975). U.S. citizens participate in general civic associations on average more than 9 percent more frequently than in social justice organizations.

The two Scandinavian countries, by contrast, have a long history of working-class as well as general civic mobilization, and strong welfare states that have emerged alongside unions and social democratic parties (e.g., Esping-Andersen 1985; Stephens and Stephens 2001). The highest participation here occurs in unions and more generally in social justice organizations. Participation in social

---

1. Subsequent administrations of the World Values Survey, particularly the one in 1995–98, also enable a comparative overview of different levels of activity in an array of organizations. Although the results largely correspond to those reported here, this analysis focuses on the 1990–93 data. These correspond most closely to the period of the FAUI survey for most countries but also employ categories of disadvantaged groups that correspond more closely to those of the FAUI survey. Unfortunately, the differences in question formats between waves of the World Values Survey makes it difficult to compare the results from these surveys over time.

■ Table 2.1 Rates of membership in associations serving disadvantaged groups and in other civic associations, 1990–1993 (in percentage of respondents)

COUNTRY	UNITED STATES	CANADA	BRITAIN	AUSTRALIA	FINLAND	NORWAY	JAPAN	KOREA	FRANCE	ITALY	HUNGARY	SWITZERLAND
Disadvantaged groups (mean)	7.7	8.3	8.3	(22.5)	16.7	18.7	3.0	8.7	5.0	4.0	11.7	6.0
Community action groups	5	5	4		3	3	0	13	3	2	1	3
Social welfare groups	9	8	7	(24)	11	11	2	6	7	4	2	9
Unions	9	12	14	(21)	36	42	7	7	5	6	32	6
Other local civic groups (mean)	16.9	14.3	9.1	(29.5)	11.7	13.1	4.1	12.3	5.6	4.1	3.8	9.4
Religious organizations	49	25	16	(39)	18	11	7	39	6	8	11	11
Educational or cultural associations	20	18	10	(28)	20	14	6	11	9	4	3	7
Women's groups	8	7	5		3	3	3	3	1	0	1	
Environmental groups	9	8	6	(12)	5	4	1	2	2	3	1	11
Professional groups	15	16	11	(24)	15	16	4	13	5	4	6	14
Youth groups	13	10	4		5	6	1	7	3	3	2	4
Sports clubs	20	23	18	(52)	23	33	9	17	16	10	4	
Health groups	8	9	4		7	12	1	15	3	3	4	
Other civic groups	10	13	8	(22)	9	19	5	4	5	2	2	
Disadvantaged versus others	−9.2	−6.0	−0.8	(−7)	5.0	5.6	−1.1	−3.7	−0.6	−0.1	7.9	−3.4

Source: World Values Survey, 1990–1993. (Australian results from 1995–1998 World Values Survey.) Totals exclude those for several organizations with more limited national data or a predominantly nonlocal focus (peace movement, animal rights, third world development).

Note: Australia results reflect different question wordings of 1995–1998 World Values Survey, which substituted "Charities" for social welfare groups (approximately), "Arts" groups for educational and cultural, and did not include other categories. This survey also gave respondents a choice of either active or inactive membership.

welfare organizations remains among the highest of any advanced industrial democracies. More general participation in voluntary associations, although higher than anywhere except in North America, falls below the rates in social justice organizations.

In a third, more diverse, group of countries, mobilization in unions, other social justice organizations, and general civic associations remains comparatively lower than in either of the first two groups. Participation ranges from generally high in the United Kingdom to generally low in Japan. In a final category, Hungary as a post-Communist setting retained high participation in unions despite low participation in all other kinds of organizations and associations (see Howard 2003).

Activity and Influence in Local Politics

Alongside overall citizen participation rates, our attention focuses on organizational mobilization and influence at the local level. It is at this level where smaller civil associations are mainly centered and where the rank and file of many kinds of mass membership organizations is most active. The FAUI survey, carried out among local elites from the mid-1980s to the mid-1990s, provides the most useful comparative indicator of the role of unions and other social justice groups at this level.

The survey data reported here asked mayors or their representatives in national samples of municipalities of more than eight thousand population to rate the activity and influence of a range of different groups in the municipal budgetary process. Usually based on a five-point scale, this data permitted statistical comparison of the influence of each of these groups both in relation to one another and among different cities domestically and abroad.[2]

Two separate questions for each type of local association or other actor were used to elicit this response. First, respondents rated how active the group or actor was in the local budget-making process. Second, they assessed either the extent of the local response to the efforts of this actor in the process or (in a few cases) the general influence of the actor in the process. This data provided a clear snapshot of how much the infrastructure of local state-society relations, including the local organizational landscape as well as the official decision-making

---

2. Numbers of respondents varied between 415 in the United States to 89 in Finland. Variable response rates necessitate some caution in interpreting the FAUI data. Measured in relation to the number of questionnaires, these ranged from 40 percent in the United States to as low as 14 percent in Japan. However, no other current data set provides a similar combination of local demographic and political data.

process, incorporated a given group. Any group that scored high in activity had mobilized enough to come to the attention of local officials. Any one rated high in influence or response had clearly managed to parlay activity into effective power within local decision-making processes. These findings can be considered alongside the individual-level data of the World Values Survey from the same period (1990–93).[3]

FAUI survey responses on union activity and influence provide a gauge, filtered through the perspective of the local mayor, of how active unions are in the local budget process and how much influence they exercise. Each average rating (shown in table 2.2), taken from a five-point (in Finland a four-point) scale, is represented on a standardized, 100-point scale on which 100 is the highest and 0 the lowest reading. Two categories taken directly from the different versions of the national surveys offered somewhat distinct versions of the same question. One of these, posed in Finland, France, Italy, Norway, Switzerland, and Korea, asked about unions in general. The other, used in Australia, Britain, Canada, Finland, Italy, Japan, and the United States, inquired about unions along with public employees or professional local staff in general. Although this formulation excluded a large portion of unions and asked about public employee influence beyond that of union organizations alone, it provided a useful comparative referent to the questions about unions in general.

Broad national differences in union influence stand out despite the limited parallels in the questions. Part of the variation corresponds to what resource mobilization theory might predict as a consequence of national differences in union density. In the two Nordic countries, the ratings of activity for unions in general average among the highest. What stands out in these settings is the unusually high level of responsiveness to unions in local government, some ten points on average above the level in any country except Japan, and higher on the scale than the rating of activity itself. Not only are unions more mobilized but local corporatist practices have institutionalized regular opportunities for them to exert influence (Pierre 1999). Although professional unions in Finland are significantly less active, respondents rate them slightly higher in influence. Clearly unions are a major player in local budget politics here.

The indicators of union influence in the English-speaking countries need to be understood in light of the identification of unions with the public sector. Here, where mass participation in unions is lower but civic participation higher, we find generally less union influence. In Australia and Britain, despite somewhat high levels of union density, unions are the least active and the least influential. In the United States and Canada, the activity of municipal unions and employees ranges

---

3. National sample sizes ranged from 1,002 (France) to 1,839 (United States).

■ Table 2.2 Unions: Mayoral ratings of activity and influence in local politics (100-point scale), with national rates of participation

	UNITED STATES	CANADA	AUSTRALIA[e]	BRITAIN	FINLAND	NORWAY[c]	SWITZERLAND	JAPAN	KOREA	FRANCE[b]	ITALY[d]
Union Activity General Mean (Standard Deviation [SD])	53.01 (26.01)	47.03 (25.86)	31.79 (27.10)		55.11 (24.81)	48.8 (45.97)	33.62 (24.47)		66.77 (25.86)	45.20 (21.40)	39.25 (22.25)
Union Influence/Response[a]	48.29 (27.48)	43.84 (28.8)	33.77 (27.74)	32.42 (28.76)	58.69 (12.33)	75.5 (29.5)	47.78 (20.41)		50.64 (22.78)	44.50 (27.10)	46.75 (23.00)
Aggregated Union Activity and Response[b]	51.48	47.06	33.95		57.51	63.95	40.7		58.71	44.85	43
Public or Municipal Employees and Their Unions					39.56 (23.05)			50.79 (23.48)			39.25 (31.25)
Influence/Response					59.82 (13.56)			56.11 (24.38)			44.75 (30)
Aggregated Public Employee Union Activity and Response					49.77			54.07			41.98
Rate of national participation (%)	9	12	(21)	14	36	42	6	7	7	5	6

Sources: Local activity and influence data from Fiscal Austerity and Urban Innovation Project surveys of local mayors between 1985 and 1995, standardized to 100-point scales; rate of national active participation from International Survey of Human Values, 1990–1993; (for Australia) 1995–1998.

[a]Aggregated Union Activity: (Union Activity + Union Influence or Response)/2

[b]Union Influence/Response: (Union Influence + Union Response)/2

[c]The Norwegian question for activity was whether the group contacted the mayor on the budget. The Norwegian measure of influence was whether the group had increased in influence in the past few years and the response categories were more active, about the same, and less active.

[d]For France and Italy, union influence/response data comes from "influence."

[e]Australian rate of participation reflects generally higher rates in the 1995–1998 World Values Survey.

considerably higher. Yet in both of these countries, responsiveness to unions falls well below the average rating of local union activity. Municipal unions in Finland, although less active than their U.S. and Canadian counterparts, exercise much greater influence in local budget politics.

Among the remainder of countries, where union as well as civic density remained generally low, the ratings of local activity and influence vary widely. Mayors in Japan and Korea rated union activity as high or higher than their Nordic counterparts, and even French and Italian mayors assigned unions significant levels of influence despite low mass participation in union organizations there.

Within local politics, the activity and influence of other groups oriented toward social justice varies in largely parallel ways. Most of the national surveys asked about the activity and influence of low-income housing groups, renters' or tenant groups, and minority groups in the local budgetary process (table 2.3).

In Finland, the one Nordic country with survey results, mayors rated responses to the other social justice groups in the survey the highest on average of any group. At the same time, even more than unions, the activity of these groups was assessed as relatively moderate by comparison with ratings elsewhere. In the United States and Canada, local groups of this kind were assigned somewhat higher average ratings for activity, but this greater activity went along with lower attributions of influence. Among other countries, the wide variations again had little to do with national rates of participation in these organizations. Japanese mayors ascribed these groups the highest levels of participation and influence in the survey, even as the levels of popular participation remained the lowest of any country. France could claim to have among the higher levels of participation and influence, while Italy had among the lowest.

Clearly, different national patterns of local influence go along with the cross-national contrasts in mass participation. In the United States and Canada, mobilization in other forms of civic associations exceeds levels in unions or social justice organizations, and both social justice organizations and the unions for which data is available are quite active at the local level. Yet the local influence for these groups remains moderate (figure 2.2). Finnish and Norwegian unions are by a wide margin the most mobilized in terms of mass participation and exercise some of the strongest influence in local politics. Other social justice groups in these countries, although less mobilized, face similarly favorable conditions for local influence. Moreover, higher ratings for influence than for activity also suggest highly institutionalized opportunities to exercise that influence. In other countries, where mass participation in unions as well as other social justice and civic groups stands at lower levels, local influence and activity vary widely.

■ Table 2.3 Other social justice groups: Mayoral ratings of activity and influence in local politics (100-point scale), with national rates of membership and voluntary work

	UNITED STATES	CANADA	AUSTRALIA	BRITAIN	FINLAND	NORWAY	SWITZERLAND	JAPAN	KOREA	FRANCE	ITALY	HUNGARY[b]
Other disadvantaged groups local activity (general) (SD)	42.14 (23.09)	39.06 (17.45)	28.70 (22.00)	28.47 (19.79)	37.85 (18.10)		38.45 (29.97)	61.65 (22.09)		42.00 (24.41)	17.00 (27.75)	
Other disadvantaged groups local influence /response (SD)	39.40 (20.63)	34.26 (22.96)	31.25 (27.28)	42.94 (28.22)	56.18 (13.91)		40.06 (24.05)	51.42 (24.08)		45.25 (22.66)	22.75 (34.00)	10.12 (15.51)
Aggregated other disadvantaged groups local influence[a] (SD)	40.77	36.66	29.98	35.71	47.02		39.26	56.54		43.63	19.88	
Social welfare service organization membership (voluntary work) (%)	9 (6)	8 (6)		7 (5)	11 (8)	11 (4)	9	2 (2)	6 (7)	7 (5)	4 (3)	2 (2)
Community action organization membership (voluntary work) (%)	5 (3)	5 (4)		4 (1)	3 (3)	3 (1)	3	0 (1)	13 (3)	3 (3)	2 (1)	1 (2)
Average membership (voluntary work) (%)	7 (4.5)	6.5 (5)		5.5 (3)	7 (5.5)	7 (2.5)	6 (3)	1 (1.5)	9.5 (5)	5 (4)	3 (2)	1.5 (2)

Sources: Membership and voluntary work rates from World Values Survey 1990–1993. All other data from Fiscal Austerity and Urban Innovation Mayoral Surveys, 1985–1999.

Note: Groups in this category include low income or housing groups (United States, Canada, Australia, Britain, Finland, Japan), renters or tenant groups (Switzerland, France, Italy), and minority or ethnic rights groups (United States, Canada, Australia, Britain, Finland, Norway, Switzerland, Japan, Hungary).

[a]Aggregated data: (Activity + Influence / Response)/2

[b]Hungary does not have "Activity" data.

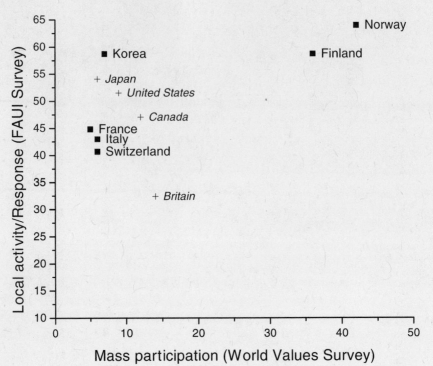

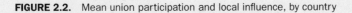

Note: + indicates FAUI averages for "municipal employees and their unions"; other FAUI values are for unions in general.

FIGURE 2.2. Mean union participation and local influence, by country

---

PROBING THE ECOLOGY OF LOCAL INFLUENCE

These differences in mass mobilization and in the local structure of political opportunity undoubtedly affect the strategies and coalition-building approaches of unions and their allies in the community (Sellers 2005). How much influence unions can wield depends on what types of coalitions they build both with other social justice groups and with other types of civic, business, and governmental actors. The FAUI survey enables a cross-national, local test of the types of local contexts that have fostered greater union influence in the budget process. At the same time that these results reveal common cross-national tendencies, they confirm significant variations between national local contexts. Both the local and the national variations have significant strategic consequences for union strategies.

Multivariate models show that the activity of unions along with combined variables that measure the activity and influence of other actors help to account for variations in union influence on local budgets (figure 2.3). The three countries selected for this analysis represent the main national types of local contexts identified earlier: the United States,[4] figure 3(a); Finland, 3(b); and France, 3(c). To further measure the influence of unions and other social justice groups, the diagrams include significant independent coefficients from regressions that modeled the determinants of influence for each of the other local groups and institutions listed. Arrows denote the directions of influence in these models. Although the union variables take a somewhat different form in each country, and in the case of public employee unions cannot be taken as a measure of unions as a whole, the results reveal a great deal about the strategic commonalities and differences in these settings.

For the United States, the results need to be considered in light of the relatively low mobilization of both unions and other social justice organizations and the limited local influence these groups exercise. The public sector unions that are the only type of union represented here derive no apparent advantage from alliances with social justice groups or even the public-regarding civic groups. Instead, their influence waxes in contexts in which local administrators and more narrowly organized interest (in this instance, elderly) groups also exercise greater influence. They also contribute to the strength of business and clientelist interests, a relation that suggests reliance on narrow interest-group strategies. Social justice groups (see table 2.3) rely on a very different network of civic and political support for influence. Both the religious and the more general civic groups that are most mobilized in U.S. cities contribute to the strength of social justice groups. Democratic Party control of the local government contributes as well. Had the U.S. FAUI survey included a category for the unions that have sought to repre-

---

4. OLS regressions of the FAUI data furnish the means to test effects from the efforts of unions and other social justice groups themselves alongside an entire range of additional influences that included the main actors in local civil society, governments at various levels, and local contextual conditions. Successive regressions took the average response to or influence of each social justice classification (all categories in the survey responses that referred to unions, then another category for the other social justice groups compiled in table 2.3) as the dependent variable. As independent variables the regressions included the average of activity for that type of actor, the average of the influence and the activity for each other type, and the indicators of local social and cultural context. Additional FAUI responses permitted a rich array of additional groups to be considered in this fashion: higher level governments, local administrators, dominant local political parties (measured as left, right, or neutral/nonpartisan), general civic groups, clientelist civic groups, taxpayer and property-owner groups, religious groups, and neighborhood groups. Carried out separately but in parallel fashion for each national context, the models amounted to a comparative local ecological test of which actors were likely to depend on which others for influence. These could then be compared between the different national samples. Each regression also included several local contextual characteristics as controls: population size, manufacturing in the workforce, persons aged 18–35, and years of education.

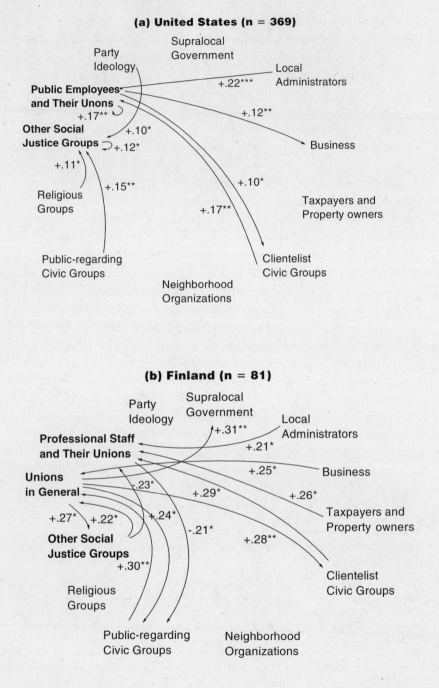

(a) United States (n = 369)

Supralocal Government

Party Ideology

Local Administrators

+.22***

Public Employees and Their Unons

+.12**

+.17**

Other Social Justice Groups

+.10*

+.12*

Business

+.11*

+.10*

+.15**

Religious Groups

+.17**

Taxpayers and Property owners

Public-regarding Civic Groups

Clientelist Civic Groups

Neighborhood Organizations

(b) Finland (n = 81)

Supralocal Government

Party Ideology

Local Administrators

+.31**

Professional Staff and Their Unions

+.21*

+.25*

Business

Unions in General

-.23*

+.29*

+.26*

+.27*

+.22*

+.24*

Taxpayers and Property owners

Other Social Justice Groups

-.21*

+.28**

+.30**

Religious Groups

Clientelist Civic Groups

Public-regarding Civic Groups

Neighborhood Organizations

(c) France (n = 115)

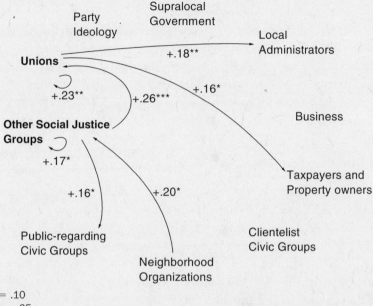

*p = .10
**p = .05
***p = .01

Note: Public-regarding civic groups include the generic category "civic groups, sports clubs, and youth associations" (Finland), ecologists (France), "civic groups" (United States); clientelist civic groups include elderly groups (Finland, United States), youth associations (France), retiree associations (France), and "users associations" (France); taxpayers and property owners include homeowners (Finland, United States) and property owners (France). Results based on imputations of missing values carried out using the program Amelia.

FIGURE 2.3.   Influence by and upon unions and other social justice groups: significant OLS regression coefficients

sent disenfranchised immigrant and service workers, it seems likely that these unions would have benefited from similar movement-based coalitions. Consistent with the greater strength of civic associations in the United States, the relation of these to social justice groups is asymmetrical. The civic groups that support social justice groups do not depend on them for influence. Still, public sector unions and the other social justice groups that are more active secure more local influence.

In the Finnish sample, the many significant regression coefficients highlight how the powerful unions there face a political opportunity structure that offers multiple avenues for greater influence. A further indication of how institutionalized this context is may be found in the lack of a relation between the activity and influence for either type of union or for other social justice groups by themselves. In contrast with both the United States and France, the high influence of these groups in local politics is assured regardless of how much they strive by themselves to enhance it. Even a left party orientation in the local government makes no significant difference for local variations in the influence of these groups.

Finnish general unions rely on a host of other actors and even institutions in the community to enhance their influence. The synergistic relation with the strength of other social justice groups is especially clear. Each contributes to the strength of the other. Unions also do better when more general civic groups are more active and influential, and vice versa. Most distinctively, union influence in this corporatist context depends to some degree on local corporatist alliances. The influence of business and commercial organizations bears a significant ($p = .10$) positive relation to responsiveness to unions in local governance. Alongside these dependencies, unions exercise stronger influence on the effectiveness of other groups and institutions than in other national settings. In a further indication of institutionalized power, union strength in local governance brings a stronger role for officials of the national government. Even the clientelist groups (in this case the elderly) do better where general unions are stronger.

As the U.S. analysis also suggested, the local government professionals and related unions in the Finnish settings depend on very different configurations of local influence. Indeed, the influence of these unions bears a negative relation to that of social justice groups and even works as a negative influence on the power of civic groups. Though associated with the strength of other categories of local administrators, the strength of these unions bears no significant relation to that of unions in general. Strong middle-class groups with more specific material interests in local governance, including homeowners and elderly groups, enhance the power of these unions.

In France, despite the low mobilization and moderate influence of unions and civic associations, local initiatives of unions and social justice groups themselves make a difference that they do not in Finland. Even more strongly than their own activism, unions depend on the local strength and mobilization of other social justice groups (here, renters' associations) for influence in local governance. In contrast with the Finnish category of unions in general, this relation is not reciprocal. Renters' associations in turn derive greater influence from stronger neighborhood associations. The influence of unions in local politics bears fewer relations than in Finland to the influence of other groups and institutions. Perhaps indicative of local clientelist relations, union strength contributes to stronger roles for local administrators as well as property-owner groups.

Several local sources of union influence are common to all three national contexts. Regardless of how high the national rates of union density were or how institutionalized the opportunities for local union influence, unions benefited in the local process from the strength of other civic, political, and institutional actors in the community. Unions in general benefited when other social justice groups were also stronger. Public employee and professional unions, often more middle class in orientation than unions in general, have a narrower, more privileged set of connections to the community and the state than do unions in general. But even these unions depended on commonalities with local civic, governmental, and business interests. Consistent with the thesis of a difference between older industrial regions and newer, service-based economies, union influence in all three countries was higher in cities with higher proportions of the workforce in manufacturing. At the same time, the U.S. as well as the Finnish patterns show the importance of national infrastructures of institutions and organizations for local patterns of influence. In the U.S. context of strong, influential civic associations, the political opportunities for general unions to build civic coalitions are likely to be as asymmetrical as the opportunities for their social justice allies. This stands in clear contrast to the institutionalized, more symmetrical opportunities in the Finnish context.

TAKING LOCAL GOVERNANCE AND POLITICS SERIOUSLY

The survey data examined here stop short of detailing the precise comparative dynamics of local coalition building in different contexts. But examination of union influence in the politics of local governance clearly opens up an illuminating new perspective on the strategic possibilities for unions and their allies. Firm-centered accounts of the strategic possibilities for unions will be complete only when they take into account the possibilities for coalition building in local politics and local civil society. Coalitions at the urban level around agendas of social justice, built on common interests with other social justice advocates and even more general civic and religious groups, offer a means to enhance union influence in local political processes. If pursued with the appropriate partners and agendas, coalitions in local politics can advance the interests of unions within local firms as well as those of workers more generally.

Comparative analysis also illuminates the differences that infrastructures of political, economic, and civic institutions can make for local union strategies. Although largely national in scope, these infrastructures can also reflect variations between regions or cities within countries. The evidence here points to three distinct patterns:

(1) A *civic-localist* infrastructure like that of the United States leaves gover-

nance at the local level more reliant on widespread mobilization among social justice groups and within civil society more generally. In this instance the influence of social justice groups depends both on their own activism and on the outcome of coalition building and asymmetrical struggles for influence with other civic organizations.

(2) Under a *nationalized* infrastructure like that of the Finnish setting, unions and other organizations both mobilize the disadvantaged extensively and have institutionalized chances for influence in local politics and policy. Nationally organized and politically engaged representative organizations assure high levels of participation by these groups. In this context, unions can count on alliances with organized business and even with state governmental representatives implementing national policies, as well as with social justice groups and local civic organizations. But the local initiatives of unions themselves have less effect on their own influence.

(3) In a *clientelist* type of infrastructure like that of France, mass mobilization is limited. Unions and social justice groups also have the opportunity to gain influence through local activism. Beyond bonds among one another, these community alliances around social justice can still achieve influence through relations with local officials.

Local coalition building has special significance for the civic-localist setting. Unions in the nationalized setting can fall back on institutionalized channels of influence within the government, on structured avenues for participation within the community, and on a large mass base of membership. But in the civic-localist setting of the United States, unions face stronger imperatives in favor of community alliances. At the same time that unions lack as wide a social basis of their own, more mobilized and more influential civic associations offer the prospect of powerful coalitions. Unions that can build these alliances can benefit. Those that cannot are likely to face more powerful local civic opponents than elsewhere.

3

ORGANIZING FOR EQUITABLE ECONOMIC DEVELOPMENT

The Significance of Community Empowerment Organizations for Unions

Ron Applegate

In response to the pervasive pursuit of low-road economic development strategies, several local unions have taken the lead in devising high-road strategies for their local economies. Unions are known for their involvement in economic development at firm, industry, and national levels, but initiatives to recast the economic development process at the community level constitutes a departure. Through its endorsement by the Working for America Institute, the departure has gained the support, if not financial backing, of the AFL-CIO. Given the newness of these initiatives, their potential impact remains to be determined. However, examining the organizations already operating on this urban terrain, community-based development organizations (CBDOs), affords a useful perspective for assessing the implications of the newest union tactic for advancing economic development goals.

Based on their historic roles in the New Deal system for governing U.S. economic development, unions and CBDOs are logical allies. Although their respective dates of incorporation into the system differ—unions, beginning in 1935; CBDOs, beginning in 1964—the government's rationale for their inclusion was the same: to include within the economic development governance structure institutions that were dedicated to ensuring the system's equitable operation. Unions were responsible for gaining justice for wage workers; CBDOs, for achieving justice for residents of low-income neighborhoods. The terms of incorporation did not preclude the institutional agents most responsible for reproducing inequality from undercutting union and CBDO efforts to advance equality. Businesses and governments, even when paying lip service to the importance of unions and CBDOs for expanding equality, repeatedly hampered their "junior partners" from carrying out their designated roles.

Despite their commonalities, unions and CBDOs are known for their differences. This circumstance is also tied to their participation in the New Deal economic development system. Within the system's governance structure, unions and CBDOs were positioned apart from each other, defined by the ways in which the interests of their respective constituencies diverged rather than by their constituents' common interest in expanding equality. This disconnection was reinforced by the New Deal system's mode of operation. The government charged different collective agents with controlling different dimensions of development to achieve economic stability, security, and equality. However, in the absence of governmental coordination to realize these public purposes, the system's more powerful agents disregarded the public's interest where it conflicted with the pursuit of their private interests. In a system whose commitment to eradicating inequality proved to be more nominal than real, unions and CBDOs were left to frame separate strategies for advancing equality.

Impediments to the work of advancing equality have only increased with the system's "neoliberal" restructuring, whereby government has outsourced ultimate responsibility for governing economic development to markets. Because market outcomes are shaped by the power differentials among market participants, the government's restoration of market governance has restored the power imbalances that the New Deal governance system was intended to overcome. In addition to sacrificing the governance role of unions and communities to that of businesses, the government's retreat from "mixed" governance since the 1980s has also entailed abandoning economic equality as a public policy priority. By undermining the high-road foundations that supported the creation of a broad middle class, neoliberal policies have fostered a dramatic reversal. Low-wage jobs and increasing inequality are once again defining characteristics of the U.S. economic system.

Union efforts to deal with the current system have primarily focused on counteracting its inegalitarian effects. But these efforts have also led a growing number of unions to address the system configuration responsible for these effects. Unions have challenged public and private versions of neoliberal economic development, while actively seeking a new basis and new partners for restoring a high-road approach. To the extent that unions are engaged in restructuring their organization and operation to assert control over economic development, they are replicating the approach taken by leading CBDOs over the last two decades. As a result, the historic differences between unions and CBDOs are increasingly overshadowed by their convergence on parallel empowerment strategies for advancing equality.

Union-CBDO relations are also being altered by a second dimension of the union response to neoliberal economic development. Seeking to regain power lost in the turn from New Deal to neoliberal governance, local unions are turning to their communities. More precisely, unions are returning to the communities whose interaction with the "new unionism" of the 1930s created the political power base responsible for New Deal labor reform and union inclusion in the economic development system. Unions are repositioning themselves on the urban terrain that enabled unions to frame workers' demands for justice as a social demand and to embed workers' organizations within a social movement. Even as they echo the past, union efforts to reground their reempowerment in their "home" turf alter the present. In many cities, the union turn to communities means that unions are operating in the same communities as CBDOs. In addition to their convergence on parallel empowerment strategies, unions and CBDOs are operationally aligned in ways that foster their collaboration in implementing these strategies.

The prospects for union-CBDO collaboration are increased by the mutual benefits that full collaboration would make possible. Collaboration to control economic development for equitable outcomes would establish a new organizational foundation for unions and CBDOs to carry out their historic roles of expanding equality, enabling both institutions to expand the capacity and reach of their individual programs. Collaboration would necessarily reconfigure the governance framework responsible for undermining union and CBDO efforts. Instead of debating how to begin reconfiguring the existing governance structure, attention could shift to expanding collaboration to other community partners for maximum reconfiguration.

These possibilities are only significant to the extent that the present moment constitutes a turning point in union-CBDO relations. It is equally true, however, that much of the potential contained in the present juncture is derived from constructive interaction between unions and community organizations at similar junctures in the past. In other words, the union-CBDO relationship is the most recent iteration of a longer relationship between unions and community organizations, and the long-term relationship features collaboration. Moreover, the content of previous collaboration has been the common pursuit of empowerment: working in concert to create organizations capable of altering the existing economic development power structure and exercising control over the economic development process. The present moment is auspicious because the obstacles to collaboration in the recent past are no longer operative, and both partners are focused on empowerment agendas that are community based.

To assess the potential of the growing convergence between unions and CBDOs on empowerment agendas for economic development, in this chapter I survey current union-CBDO relations from the perspective of their neglected history. This perspective suggests why the relationship has been dormant and highlights how changes in the community side of the relationship enable the relationship to be established on a new footing. Due to their extensive practical experience in community-controlled development, CBDOs bring to the relationship an unprecedented capacity to promote equitable economic development.

ORGANIZING TO CONTROL COMMUNITY DEVELOPMENT: THE CBDO EXPERIENCE

As the term implies, CBDOs are a specialized category of community organization, focused on increasing community residents' share of the benefits derived from economic development by involving residents in the development process. The term is relatively recent, originating with the community development corporations (CDCs) established since the 1970s to conduct economic development projects in, and for the benefit of, impoverished communities. To acknowledge the fact that CDCs are not the only community organizations functioning as bottom-up development organizations and to encompass the variety of organizations in this category, I follow the convention of using the broader term, CBDO.

Origins: The Empowerment Model of Community Organizing

Viewed from the perspective of the history of community organizing in the United States, it is evident that some community organizations inhabited the CBDO category before it was enunciated. Particularly relevant to the prehistory of CBDOs is the "empowerment" model of community organizing. The invention of the empowerment model effectively reinvented community organizing in the United States, by adding a political activist approach to the social work and neighborhood improvement traditions. As first enunciated by organizer Saul Alinsky, the model responded to the unequal incomes and living standards in many U.S. communities, by locating the roots of their residents' inequality in the unequal control they possessed over their lives and building community organizations with the power to overcome their inequality and powerlessness. Successive iterations of the community empowerment model have informed the community organizing that accompanied the labor organizing of the 1930s, the social movement organizing of the 1960s, and the urban organizing of the 1970s and 1980s variously described as "citizen action" or "new populism" (Fisher 1994, 46–59, 91–109, 121–52; Frost 2001, 71–117).

The community empowerment model's construction and evolution is central to this chapter for more specific reasons. First, the model has union roots. Because unions were central to the model's birth in the 1930s, the empowerment model of community organizing was significantly influenced by union conceptions of empowerment. Second, the empowerment model's continuing reliance on the human resources provided by community residents—in Alinsky's words, on "people power"—led to a conception and practice of community empowerment that includes elements not present in the union version. Community organizing to empower residents to gain the benefits of economic development initially imitated, even as it elaborated on, labor organizing: mobilizing residents to bargain with and compel concessions from those controlling the development system. However, in the face of unyielding opposition to these efforts, some community organizations expanded their empowerment agenda to include residents gaining direct control over the development process within their communities.

The bargaining-to-control transition was not a simple progression, nor was it continuous. One of the community organizations in Alinsky's organizational network first established community-controlled development in the 1960s, but the achievement proved to be temporary. Community organizations were able to reestablish community-controlled development in the 1970s and 1980s, by merging the empowerment model of community organizing with the CDC model of community development to form an "empowerment CBDO" (my term). Recurrent union efforts to make the move from exercising indirect control over economic development to gaining direct control are well known. But so are the unsatisfactory results. The union record imparts additional significance to identifying the dimensions of the community empowerment model that have enabled CBDOs to make the move.

Alinsky's Contribution: Community Organizing as Labor Organizing

The empowerment model's beginnings date to Alinsky's work in the 1930s to build a new type of community organization. As a University of Chicago graduate student, he participated in sociology department programs to create community organizations to combat the "community disorganization" afflicting poor ethnic neighborhoods. The program was based on the assumption that disorganization was rooted in cultural differences that these neighborhoods sustained, creating conditions of "cultural deprivation." Accordingly, the purpose of community organizing was to foster the social integration of community residents by facilitating their cultural assimilation (O'Connor 2001, 26–53). Alinsky became critical of the program's emphasis on cultural sources of disorganization to the exclusion of political sources—in particular, the power that businesses and governments exercised over neighborhood residents' lives. Through his contact with

CIO unions, which were organizing in the same working-class neighborhoods, Alinsky discovered an organizing approach that addressed his concerns. He was particularly drawn to CIO organizing techniques that empowered workers to function as a union on the shop floor before the union was formally established or recognized by the employer. Exposure to the CIO model of labor organizing inspired Alinsky to recast the Chicago sociology model of community organizing, by locating the issue of power—specifically, the need for the powerless to confront the powerful in order to gain control over their lives—at its core (Alinsky 1972).

The union influence on Alinsky's initial experiment with organizing for empowerment was as direct as it was profound, prominently featuring collaboration with the Packing Workers Organizing Committee (PWOC). To create the solidarity required to force Chicago's Big Four meatpackers to bargain with their workers, PWOC's Herb March sought to connect PWOC's organizing efforts with community organizations that did not reinforce workers' ethnic divisions. Since such organizations were both scarce and confined to providing youth programs, Alinsky responded by forming a new organization. Founded in 1939, the Back of the Yards Neighborhood Council (BYNC) sought to unify Polish, Slovak, Lithuanian, Bohemian, and Irish residents behind the goal of improving their collective welfare. Since the income of most households came from working in the meatpacking plants, translating this general purpose into the immediate goal of pursuing wage increases was not difficult. Identifying the basis for unifying all ethnic groups behind this goal was. The obvious cultural connection, the Catholicism that the ethnically defined groups held in common, was routinely linked to ethnicity in ways that reinforced division. As a result, BYNC organizers appealed to workers' common religious bond, but in carefully chosen terms. Working with younger priests, they focused the community's religious attention on *Rerum Novarum,* the papal encyclical that endorsed the right of workers to organize in order to improve their working conditions and living standards (Horwitt 1989, 55–71; Slayton 1986, 189–211).

By successfully articulating a shared purpose and rationale, the BYNC was able to bring about unprecedented collaboration between the neighborhood's two most important institutions, the Catholic Church and the meatpacking union. With representatives of the churches and the PWOC constituting the new organization's core, the BYNC garnered widespread support from residents. By engineering the joint appearance of Bishop Bernard Sheil of the Chicago diocese and the CIO's John L. Lewis at a massive public rally for the PWOC, the BYNC dramatically demonstrated its distinctive contribution to working-class solidarity. By extending their reach to include city hall support, the BYNC served as the pressure group that brought meatpacking companies to the bargaining table. When the companies conceded to demands that were as much the community's as the union's, there was no doubt about the BYNC's capacity to confront Chicago's power structure by building a community form of institutional power (Alinsky 1972; Fisher 1984, 51–54; Horwitt 1989, 71–81).

In 1940 Alinsky established the Industrial Areas Foundation (IAF) for the purpose of building "people's organizations" like the BYNC in working-class neighborhoods of other industrial cities. He envisioned the IAF as a national movement of community organizations working in collaboration with the labor movement to gain justice for working-class Americans. IAF organizations became known for their success in adapting labor organizing tactics—strikes, pickets, boycotts, sit-ins—to community situations and in devising new techniques for exerting pressure, from mass disruption of business operations to public embarrassment of officials to proxy voting at annual stockholder meetings. The aim of these tactical innovations, as in the CIO organizing model that inspired them, was empowerment through confrontation. In Alinsky's community version of compelling justice from the power structure, confrontations were staged between the communities experiencing inequality and the institutions capable of redressing their unequal status. In practice, such confrontation entailed mobilizing a community's institutional resources within a single community organization. The resulting "organization of organizations" assumed the responsibility for defining and implementing an action program focused on targeting "enemies" of justice and pressuring them into a negotiating posture (Alinsky 1971; Fisher 1984, 47–51).

Alinsky's structuring of a community organization as an "organization of organizations" was central to his vision of constructing a "people's organization" capable of generating "people power." A structure for realizing community control could have been established by making membership individual rather than organizational. But an individual-membership organization contradicted Alinsky's CIO-shaped assessment of the organizational form required to empower disenfranchised communities. Because communities were controlled externally by institutions that exercised their power by working in collaboration, challenging this power structure required communities to create a parallel institutional power. Deeming a coalition of community institutions to be necessary from the inception, Alinsky built collaboration into the new community organization. His organizational structure imitated the structure of national CIO unions, rather than that of union locals, since he sought to create within communities the power that CIO unions exercised within industries. The resulting organization was meant to provide for communities what the CIO was providing for workers: the same means of empowerment possessed by business and political elites (Betten and Austin 1990, 152–61).

TWO's Contribution: From Indirect to Direct Control

In 1959, at the urging of black community leaders, Alinsky formed the first IAF organization in a black slum neighborhood, The Woodlawn Organization (TWO) in Chicago. Alinsky was initially hesitant about crossing America's color line, concerned that the racial divide might prove an insurmountable obstacle for the organization to overcome. But TWO proved to be another IAF success story, winning the customary IAF victories: empowering Woodlawn's residents to secure jobs from businesses along with job training programs, affordable housing, and improved services from the city. In the end, TWO not only inspired the creation of additional IAF organizations in other black neighborhoods but added new elements to the IAF model. The additions resulted from TWO's ability to turn an "urban renewal" program into an opportunity for a community-defined version of comprehensive community redevelopment. TWO members successfully insinuated their organization into the development process by establishing TWO's capacity to function as part of the system controlling development. TWO thereby became the first community organization to assert control over the planning and implementation of its systematic revitalization (Alinsky 1972; Horwitt 1989, 363–449).

TWO's organizational development altered the IAF's economic development horizon. By the 1950s, IAF organizations were well known for their incremental approach to economic development, starting with the lowest common denominator issues and progressively setting and achieving more expansive goals. TWO's achievements recast the endpoint of the organizing process: not simply aiming to compel justice from those outside the community controlling the allocation of development resources but also seeking to acquire direct community control of resource allocation to ensure justice. TWO's alteration of the IAF model was itself incremental, making successive additions that extended the model to its logical conclusion. But the impact of arriving at the conclusion was transformative. Before TWO, the community control exercised by IAF organizations over economic development was indirect, pressuring institutions possessing control to do the right thing. To the IAF repertoire, TWO added direct instruments of control. After TWO, community empowerment encompassed possessing the power to plan and implement development inside the community, along with the having the power to compel concessions from those possessing the power to plan and implement development outside the community.

From the perspective of what came before, TWO represented the culmination of Alinsky's attempt to make altering power relations into the crux of community organizing. From the perspective of what was to follow, TWO provided a CBDO version of the empowerment model before CBDOs officially came into existence. However, in the 1960s TWO's impact was defined by immediate considerations, not long-term perspectives. In the face of opposition from city government, TWO's success proved to be temporary. In the face of co-optation from the federal government, the empowerment model of community organizing was transformed in ways that obstructed, rather than fostered, the achievement of community control.

Complication: Government Co-optation

Great Society Sponsorship

In the 1960s the appeal of community empowerment as a solution to problems facing impoverished, disenfranchised communities was not confined to new social movements but extended to the federal government's response to these movements. When the civil rights movement succeeded in pressuring government to resume the New Deal assault on inequality, government officials identified community organization as a primary means for conducting their War on Poverty. Through the Community Action Program (CAP), and an army of local community action agencies (CAAs) to implement the program, the new Office of Equal Opportunity (OEO) effectively incorporated community organizations into the nation's economic development system. CAAs were established as the system's community-level agents, charged with extending the system's benefits to citizens who remained outside its reach, by transforming the neighborhoods in which these citizens were concentrated. As a central feature of the Johnson administration's Great Society agenda, community organizations reached an unprecedented status, officially tied to the nation's economic growth machine.

In the summer of 1964, when the government adopted an empowerment model of community organization, Alinsky and the IAF were the object of media attention. *Fortune* editor Charles Silberman first thrust them into the limelight when his *Crisis in Black and White* championed TWO as the solution to the racial problems festering in cities outside the South. Favorable publicity led civic groups in Kansas City and Buffalo to invite the IAF to their cities, as did citizens in Rochester after a summer riot, and the preparations garnered more publicity. When the OEO turned to an empowerment model, however, it was not the IAF model. The OEO looked instead to empowerment programs operated by the President's Council on Juvenile Delinquency under Robert Kennedy's supervision. The aim of these programs was to improve community conditions to the point that younger community residents could acquire the skills needed to attain economic opportunity. This life-altering experience, whose conclusion was marked when young people relocated from their blighted communities, was defined as individual empowerment. These programs represented the further evolution of the social work programs that Alinsky had rejected in the 1930s; some of which were carried out by his peers and successors. To distinguish his model of empowerment from theirs, and to rebuff any appearance of accepting a backhanded compliment, Alinsky referred to the version of empowerment incorporated into the CAP as "political pornography" (Halpern 1995, 89–105; Horwitt 1989, 445–82).

While Alinsky distanced himself from a program guilty of sacrificing community empowerment to individual empowerment, others did not see the situation so starkly. CAP was an amalgamation of several programs, and activists targeted various elements with the potential to foster community empowerment. The most well-known instance was the authorization given to CAAs to assert community control over antipoverty programs by facilitating the "maximum feasible participation" of community residents. Above all, because the "community action" framework provided a new means for pursuing community-provided solutions, and because the CAP's creation apart from other government agencies was designed to facilitate experimentation, many activists chose to see CAP as a program whose content was yet to be determined. The result was an intense contest to determine the outcome (Halpern 1995, 106–18).

The UAW Role: Facilitating Unintended Consequences

Among those looking to shape the government's new involvement in community organization, and better situated than most to have an impact, was Walter Reuther of the United Automobile Workers. Under Reuther's direction the UAW was already involved in providing support for a new wave of community organizing efforts undertaken by a new generation. Along with the PWOC's successor union, the United Packinghouse Workers of America, UAW leaders had close personal and financial connections with the direct-democracy, community organizing projects of the Student Nonviolent Coordinating Committee (SNCC) and Students for a Democratic Society (SDS). UAW leaders supported these community projects as part of their ongoing political project to build a broad-based political coalition for renewing reform. Their specific aim was to continue the New Deal's restructuring of U.S. political economy to achieve democratic controls over industry and economic development. Consequently, when Lyndon Johnson decided to make reform the hallmark of his presidency and turned to Reuther for support, UAW leaders heralded the moment as a long-awaited opportunity to fulfill the New Deal's unfulfilled promise (Boyle 1995, 158–84; Frost 2001; Lichtenstein 1995, 381–89).

Seeking to define the new situation in accordance with long-standing UAW aims, Reuther and his staff threw themselves into their distinctive mediating role: convincing Johnson to use the War on Poverty as the means to reembrace the neglected goals of maximum employment and purchasing power, while forming the Citizens Crusade against Poverty to unify their reform coalition behind an agenda calling for democratic economic planning, full production, and equitable income distribution. They made it their special mission to provide the coherency missing in the piecemeal, compartmentalized antipoverty programs. The chosen vehicle was their plan for an "urban TVA." The UAW's Demonstration Cities (DC) proposal realigned the CAP with a planning and reconstruction program to rehabilitate the central cores of American cities. Whereas CAP focused on a neighborhood crisis, DC addressed a broader urban crisis. CAP focused on service provision in neighborhoods that were predominantly black and low income, while DC connected neighborhoods with downtowns and addressed housing and public services for blacks and whites, both low and middle income. DC would pull together the divisions that the CAP patchwork continued, while demonstrating the practicality and rationality of democratic planning for urban redevelopment.

As they did during the industrial mobilization of World War II and during the postwar construction of industrial peace, Reuther and his staff were again setting forth a proposal whose ultimate aim was to create broad social-democratic controls over economic development. What they got, as they did before, was something less. Reuther and other UAW officials were central players in the presidential task force to define a national urban policy, and their results were remarkable: the creation of a new Department of Housing and Urban Development (HUD) with their own proposal, renamed Model Cities, as its inaugural program. But they did not succeed in their ambitious efforts to relocate CAP to HUD and have Reuther named the first head of HUD, so they could effectively direct the War on Poverty. Due to the compromises exacted as the price of putting any urban policy in place, Model Cities ended up looking more like CAP than not: ultimately offering no challenge to existing governance relations, while replicating the residential, race, and class divisions that DC was framed to overcome (Boyle 1995, 184–92, 200–205; Halpern 1995, 118–26).

As UAW leaders discovered in their efforts to seize Great Society opportunities such as CAP, they were caught up in a singularly brief moment. Despite advancing plans that outlined a sequence of change, in order to carry out the many facets of needed reform, they found that second rounds were rare—unless they involved a retreat. The social movements to which these reforms were a response had aroused degrees and varieties of activism to which government was not prepared to respond. Moreover, the administration was preoccupied, more focused on figuring out how to respond to the war in Vietnam than to the War on Poverty.

By increasing demands on government attention and funds, while eliciting increased opposition to the administration among reform proponents, war policy undermined any chance that the parties interested in reform could negotiate their differences over the pace and direction of reform. Given the magnitude of his hopes, reinforced by his new access to the power structure, Reuther chose to defend Johnson's reform record. In the end, reforms were decisively marked by the government's rapid shift away from responsive engagement to disengagement.

Because the restructuring process that Reuther envisioned was not completed, his social-democratic aims were more perverted than realized. From the more critical perspective of community activists, Reuther's chosen approach to serving as a Great Society architect was part of the problem. They saw his emphasis on government-sponsored community organization as following from his focus on gaining national-level acceptance for community empowerment to the exclusion of building the local-level power required. His preference for top-down solutions was not incidental to the top-down approach that ultimately prevailed. When Reuther was unable to deliver the ongoing reconstruction process he envisioned, community organizers were left to contend with the restructuring that had occurred: a government role in directing community organizations that was unprecedented, and community organizations that manifested an unprecedented dependence on government for their existence and agenda.

The union-community organization relationship unraveled in the face of the gap between the situation that communities faced by 1968 and the situation that Reuther perceived in 1964. Within the ensuing splits, unions and community organizations tended to end up on opposite sides of liberalism's divide, as the new generation of community organizers were drawn to and influenced by the period's social movements. The uncivil war that pitted new social movements against the labor movement—civil rights and women's groups pursuing legal actions against unions, with unions defending discriminatory practices; unions opposing the antiwar movement, with New Left attacks on unions as being part of the racist, imperialist Establishment—only deepened differences between labor organizing and community organizing. The disruption of union-CBDO relations in the 1960s generated lasting wariness, if not outright distrust, on both sides.

Government-Posed Dilemmas for Community Empowerment Organizing

Beyond making clear to community organizations that having powerful Washington allies on your side wasn't enough, CAP's restructuring clarified fundamental features of their unprecedented circumstances. Three years after CAP officials authorized "maximum feasible participation," Congress required each

CAA to obtain local government authorization to operate and each CAA board to draw their members in equal numbers from elected officials, private-sector representatives, and community residents (O'Connor 2001, 167–73). Top-down, local-level control over operations was joined with top-down, federal-level control over programming. Together, these formed the ultimate terms under which community organizations were incorporated into the economic development system.

The community dimension of the power that remained in CAAs was defined as the power of community self-help: residents' capacity to improve their living conditions and foster their human development by working together to maximize their collective use of federal funding and technical assistance. Mobilizing aggregate demand for services among residents while simultaneously providing the demanded services—that is, functioning as a community service agency—became the condition for CAAs to receive continued funding. The government formally acknowledged the reality in 1974. Consistent with previous actions that declared the urban crisis to be over and shelved the Model Cities program, the Nixon administration replaced the OEO with the Community Services Administration (Halpern 1995, 124–26).

The services that CAAs (the CAA name continued to be used under the Community Services Administration) provided were far from negligible and met substantive needs. But the limits of their provision and the sources of their derivation were inscribed within the CAA framework, not subject to ongoing revision by community residents. To independent community organizations whose purpose was to continue to challenge these limits and sources, CAAs posed a substantive challenge. CAAs provided a nonthreatening alternative for businesses and governments seeking to avoid the demands of traditional community empowerment organizations. With a CAA in town, targets of community pressure campaigns no longer felt the same compulsion to provide community-demanded services, much less concede control over development to the affected communities.

The government's presence in the arena of community organization generated recurrent problems for independent community empowerment organizations. Many of these problems were experienced as technical problems of coexistence: surviving against a more numerous and well-funded adversary. However, the underlying political nature of these resource problems was brought out more starkly with the government's increasing use of community organizations as economic development organizations, and not simply as service agencies. Beginning in the 1970s, the government funded community development corporations (CDCs) to increase the number of community-level physical development projects—housing, commercial, and infrastructure—in communities unable to attract private-sector developers. As empowerment organizations recognized, the program offered access to the technical power required to realize full community empowerment. As designed, however, the program did not disseminate expertise among community residents, relegating them to a secondary, advisory role in the CDC development process. Since program participation was offered on government terms that undermined full empowerment, the program confronted independents with an impossible choice: foregoing access to needed development expertise to preserve their empowerment approach, or sacrificing empowerment organizing to acquire the expertise.

Resurgence: Community Restoration of the Community Empowerment Model

Community-Government Conflict over Community Empowerment

Since their introduction, CDCs have expanded dramatically in number, as governments have identified these community organizations as the receptacle for the remnants of antipoverty and urban programs. Although these program assignments have been accompanied by limited funding, they have carried large amounts of rhetoric extolling their importance for economic opportunity and individual empowerment. Consequently, CDCs have proved to be the mechanism for bringing the differences between the rival programs of community-based empowerment to the fore. For example, Jack Kemp's contribution to Reaganomics was to empower the poor by turning CDCs into marketing agents of government resources: turning the poor into homeowners by selling them their HUD housing units; promoting jobs for the poor by reclassifying their communities as "enterprise zones" (EZs) and giving tax breaks to businesses willing to operate within their boundaries. The Clinton administration, by adding traditional community programs into the mix along with more subsidies, sought to enhance the alignment between markets and poor communities. To drive home the potential of making communities more marketable sites for investors, while better preparing residents to participate in markets, EZs were renamed "empowerment zones."

Because successive government-defined empowerment programs have largely failed to stimulate community economic development, they have drained political meaning from the public's perception of "empowerment." But independent CBDOs seeking to empower their communities to control their development have had a very different experience. Against their own definition of empowerment, these CBDOs have had to contend with government programs whose rationale has ignored and devalued what these community organizations seek to achieve. Community-defined empowerment programs have sought, at a minimum, to counteract the harm caused by market-controlled development. Maximally, they have sought to compel alterations in the operation of market controls or to replace them with community controls. For communities, market-controlled development has been the problem to be overcome through organization. Conversely, from the government side, market-controlled development has either been allowed to provide the decisive solutions or has been championed as providing the best possible solutions. Consequently, government-defined empowerment programs have narrowly focused on preparing community residents, and other community resources, for market inclusion. As the latest iteration of government-defined community development highlights, the enduring relationship is one in which the government's logic of community development effectively stands the logic held by CBDOs on its head.

The Emergence of Empowerment CBDOs

Some CBDOs have yielded to the pressures of working in a government-dominated arena, eliminating organizing for empowerment as the price of continuing to function as a development organization. Others have taken the opposite approach, continuing to base their organizations on community mobilization for empowerment. These CBDOs have upheld the primary significance of organizing, even though mounting pressure campaigns to secure their ultimate development objectives of community control had to be placed on hold. A third type of CBDO has managed—in a trial-and-error fashion, to be sure—to adhere to Alinsky's model of combining organizing and development. Crucial to their success has been their use of Alinsky's tactics of constructive confrontation to shape their relationship with government community development programs.

CBDOs in this category—the organizations I am referring to as empowerment CBDOs—have acted to compete with government programs: meeting the community needs addressed by government-sponsored CBDOs, while creating programs whose levels of comprehensiveness and innovation surpass government efforts. They have effectively turned the government's invasion of their terrain into an ongoing contest: mobilizing against government program limitations and for program reforms, even as they successfully fight to use existing programs for their own purposes. They have sought to use the government's weak program of empowerment wherever possible to enhance their own strong program, building community activism and control into development programs where the government has sought to exclude such activism and control. At the foundation of their stance is their rejection of the dichotomy that government has sought to impose on the arena of community organization: the dictum that those organizations working to change the existing system cannot also work within the system but must choose one path or the other. Through their combination of empowerment organizing and development activity these CBDOs have persisted in operating in both domains. The measure of their achievement, in accordance with the community version of community development logic, is that these organizations constitute the logical extension of TWO. In the face of the government's installation of a rival conception and practice of empowerment within government-sponsored community organizations, these groups have responded by providing an enhanced version of the model that the government shunted aside in 1964 (Bruyn and Meehan 1987).

A Reconstructed Foundation for Empowerment Organizing

Experienced in working to change the development system as they operate within it, empowerment CBDOs—the Dudley Street Neighborhood Initiative in Boston, the Coalition for a Better Acre in Lowell, East Brooklyn Congregations in New York, and others—have successfully instituted a comprehensive organizational approach. Their emphasis on combining activities that suffer from separation has brought together agitation and implementation, community-provided services and community-controlled economic revitalization, the human development of residents and the physical development of communities. The key to advancing their broad agenda has been their attention to, and success in, creating new institutional capacity within their communities: using the community's existing institutions as the foundation for building new institutions focused on development. By relying on the community's human and institutional resources, these CBDOs have built the new institutions required to control each phase of the development process: mobilizing for participation, resident training in the development process, multilevel planning from neighborhood to project, program administration and project implementation, and ownership and management of the social and physical assets developed. These CBDOS have strengthened community institutions externally as well, building coalitions across cities to collaborate on programs across neighborhoods, to expand political education efforts, and to form broad pressure groups when pressure is required (Gittell 1992; Medoff and Sklar 1994).

To advance their empowerment agenda, these CBDOs have begun forming regional networks of their peers. The Massachusetts Association of Community Development Corporations has explicitly focused their collective efforts on enabling member organizations to be structured and operate as CBDOs with the capacity to combine organizing and development. Empowerment CBDOs have also collaborated extensively with supportive foundations. As empowerment

CBDOs have benefited from the practical experience gained since the 1970s, so have the foundations that have supplied the funds for community economic development experiments. Foundations have become vital partners in establishing, and advancing, comprehensive community organizations. In sum, empowerment CBDOs have been engaged in constructing a viable organizational infrastructure in the community arena of national economic development, one with the capacity to contribute significantly to the national system's reconstruction (Sirianni and Friedland 2001, 56–66).

Because the disruption generated by the government's adoption of community empowerment extended to the relationship between community organizing and labor organizing, unions have been more bystanders than participants in the contest over who defines the content of community empowerment organizations. But this situation, too, is changing. The existence of empowerment CBDOs is particularly relevant for unions engaged in restructuring their organizations to become active in economic development, while confronting the need to restructure the economic development system in order to succeed. They provide a model for moving forward, manifesting that restructuring along alternative lines can be successfully pursued, despite concerted efforts to co-opt and derail the alternative. Empowerment CBDOs also afford an experienced partner in the double restructuring process. The potential of that partnership has yet to be realized, but its outlines can be glimpsed in the relationships forged in living wage campaigns between participating unions and the Association of Community Organizations for Reform Now (ACORN). Most important, a solid foundation for realizing the partnership is being constructed as unions replicate the recent experience of empowerment CBDOs, bringing together empowerment organizing and economic development activity within the boundaries of a single organization.

EMPOWERMENT CBDOS AND UNIONS

The vantage point of the present—with the community restoration of the community empowerment model and the revitalization of the controls involved in community-controlled development—highlights the importance of possessing the organizational capacity to promote equitable development on two fronts. On the first front, CBDOs successfully organized to acquire the power required to gain concessions from those possessing ultimate power: the power to allocate resources, to decide where human, material, and financial resources are invested, and, thereby, who benefits and who doesn't. On the second front, CBDOs successfully organized to place ultimate power in community hands. To possess the capacity to exercise both direct and indirect control over development is to possess the power to create as well as compel equitable development outcomes.

The difficulties that CBDOs have faced in acquiring and exercising this double capacity have implications for unions that run in two directions. First, because the consistency in changing government policy toward community empowerment organizing has been its adherence to an opposed mode of promoting economic development, empowerment organizing involves creative engagement with government. Although the details obviously differ, the incorporation of unions into the governance structure of the national economic development system has been as disruptive for unions as for CBDOs. The terms of incorporation enabled unions to exercise more control over development than CAAs, but unions have their own version of diminished controls that require recapture. Of particular significance, the actions of Congress and the National Labor Relations Board (NLRB) have placed on indefinite hold union efforts to use collective bargaining to address businesses' exclusive possession of ultimate power over business operations. Conversely, because unions possessed enough control to affect the exercise of business power they have emphasized defending that control when the government has reneged on its commitments or has transferred the government's share of control to markets that were, in turn, largely controlled by corporations.

The second implication is highlighted by the first: to engage creatively with government, along with private-sector opponents of community-controlled development, CBDOs must build the community power base required to prevail in these confrontations. The necessary focus on national-level neoliberal governance regimes cannot come at the expense of attention to community-level coalition building. Walter Reuther's example spells out the consequences of such neglect. To the extent that unions have turned back to community power building, they not only exhibit their grasp of this point but also their actions signal a pivotal moment in the union response to the spread of low-road strategies—the turn from defense to offense.

It is in the arena of the union shift from defense to offense—in union actions to restore lost controls and create new controls—that community experiences with empowerment resonate with union experiences. The clearest connection has been generated by labor organizing to retain and expand the power to compel concessions from employers in collective bargaining. Not only have unions framed "corporate campaigns" that utilize tactics long used by community organizations but unions have solicited and received the participation of community organizations in the successful conduct of these campaigns. On the basis of having jointly resisted management cost cutting in the workplace, unions and community organizations have joined forces outside the workplace, collaborating to counteract the community effects of the inequality generated by a one-dimensional exercise of corporate power.

A less visible connection is the one derived from union organizing to gain direct power over economic development. These efforts are less visible because they are taking place outside the workplace power contest. But their construction and evolution on the community terrain makes them highly visible in their local communities. That is why the union-community connection can be glimpsed in stories told elsewhere in this book. For example, when unions in western New York decided to become more directly involved in promoting high-road economic development, by becoming the developers of an energy production facility and affordable housing units, they not only took on CBDO functions, they made the leap to forming a union-controlled development organization. As the foundation for their leap, the unions that formed the Economic Development Group built on their years of exercising control over development through collective bargaining. To add a second dimension to their development initiative, the unions formed a regional development partnership with their historic bargaining partners. The unions have thereby inserted labor-management relations into their version of community-labor collaboration for high-road development (Fleron and Applegate 2004; see also Greer, Byrd, and Fleron, chapter 6 in this book).

In California, Silicon Valley unions, under the leadership of the South Bay Labor Council, formed Working Partnerships USA (WPUSA) to mobilize the community to demand political accountability in the administration of public development funds. By allying union members with unorganized immigrant workers and community organizations in a broad community coalition, WPUSA succeeded in directing funds for community-defined purposes. Their initial success provided the platform for seeking direct control over public development funds. First, WPUSA coalition activists became the public decision makers, by successfully running for public offices. Then, other activists formed businesses that, by successfully bidding for public funds, implemented publicly funded development. In sum, when unions needed new partners in order to play a new role in economic development, they created a new community organization. WPUSA, in turn, took the lead in expanding the economic development agenda, including sponsoring other community organizations as needed (Muller et al. 2003).

In cities across the country, local unions have worked collaboratively with a variety of community organizations to enact and implement living wage laws (see Luce, chapter 1 in this book). To facilitate local campaigns, unions have also worked closely with a national-level community empowerment organization, ACORN. By coordinating local efforts and providing critical support, ACORN's Living Wage Resource Center has played a significant role in making separate living wage campaigns into a national movement. It is important to note that these coordinating skills were not developed for the occasion. ACORN's contributions are rooted in its long history of fashioning a community development agenda in dozens of cities and hundreds of chapters, while coordinating the work of these organizations so that their agenda has influence at city, state, and national levels. It is equally important to recognize that union collaboration with ACORN existed well before the living wage campaign, and in a most distinctive fashion. ACORN's comprehensive approach to community empowerment led organizers to mobilize their members to gain power at their workplaces as well as in their communities. In the 1980s these efforts culminated in the creation of two Service Employee International Union locals covering workers in four states: SEIU Local 100 (Louisiana, Arkansas, and Texas) and Local 880 (Illinois). As the continuing collaboration between these union locals and ACORN chapters makes clear, they provide a model in which the union-CBDO connection is established on the basis of affiliated, and not just allied, organizations (see ACORN website, http://www.acorn.org; for ACORN history, see Delgado 1986).

Whereas WPUSA found it necessary to sponsor community organizations to carry out its union empowerment agenda, ACORN found it necessary to sponsor union locals to carry out its community empowerment agenda. Together, they demonstrate that the connection between unions and community organizations runs in both directions. In the terms of the metaphor used to describe alternative approaches to the neoliberal development model, these organizations have constructed the two-way thoroughfare on which the high road can be rebuilt.

These examples only begin to tell the full story, but they underscore the convergence taking place between unions and CBDOs in their efforts to create new institutional means for gaining control over economic development. Because union innovations do not simply replicate community experience, the means are multiplying. Because the political environment is unfriendly to their agendas, unions and CBDOs are both working with broad community coalitions to create the political opportunity structures required to push ahead. If these examples accurately represent the current direction of the evolving relationship between unions and community-based development organizations, then the long-delayed moment of their full collaboration may finally be at hand.

4

BUILDING COALITIONS FOR REGIONAL POWER

Labor's Emerging Urban Strategy

David Reynolds

Urban politics scholars have long realized that the governing power structure of a city or urban area encompasses far more than elected officials and public administration (see, e.g., Stone and Sanders 1987; Stone 1989; Clavel 1986; and Clavel and Wiewel 1991). Because local government capacity and authority are limited, public officials must ally with private groups that can offer knowledge and resources necessary to affect the region's economic future. Typically, urban politics in the United States revolves around various alliances between local government officials and private business. Such regimes have governing "power" in the sense that they are able to set the terms of public debate and practice in regional economic and social development. Recently, however, labor and its allies in a small but growing number of urban areas have begun to put into place systematic strategies for establishing alternative progressive power. They aim not simply to elect progressive majorities but to establish the broader resources and knowledge base that will allow new coalitions to govern a region by defining the public debate over its economic and social future from inside and outside the halls of government. I refer to this general strategy as regional power building.

In this chapter I draw on case studies conducted in seven cities that identified six defining components that make regional power building a distinct strategy: deep coalition building, aggressive political action, economic development agendas, "think and do" tanks, leadership development, and growing organizational capacity. By "region," I mean a greater metropolitan area—a core city and its surrounding suburban rings.

The author would like to thank members of the network, especially Barbara Byrd, Kent Wong, Stephanie Luce, Mark Nelson, and Tom Karson for their comments on this chapter. Editor Dan Cornfield also provided excellent feedback on several drafts.

REGIONAL POWER BUILDING IN SEVEN CITIES

In 2003 the AFL-CIO's Field Mobilization Department, the AFL-CIO Central Labor Council Advisory Committee, and the United Association for Labor Education's Central Labor Council Task Force launched the Building Regional Power
Research Network (http://www.powerbuilding.wayne.edu) to document and
promote self-conscious power-building work by central labor councils. Our cases
draw from those experiences identified by key activists and staff as the best examples of power-building work under way in the country.[1] The seven cases available at the time this was written were San Jose, Los Angeles, Denver, Houston,
Seattle, Cleveland, and Buffalo. I offer a snapshot of each before exploring in detail the common forces at work and the six components of common strategy.

San Jose offers a well-established case that has served as a model for others.
Although citizen movements of the 1970s shaped the area's moderate-liberal governing regime, organized labor traditionally had not had strong political influence. At the same time, the much-touted economic growth in Silicon Valley has
had a significant dark side. An explosion of low-paying service jobs and contingent work has been combined with a high cost of living. Following the election
of Amy Dean as its president in 1994, the South Bay Labor Council began to build
a capacity for labor and its allies to shape the future direction of the valley's political economy. Organizers describe their strategy in terms of three legs: labor-
community coalition building, aggressive political action, and developing a
capacity for policy research and development. Building these legs has entailed increasing political coordination among union affiliates and key community allies,
founding a nonprofit "think and do" tank called Working Partnerships USA,
building an active interfaith committee, and launching a series of city and county
policy campaigns. Ten years later leaders point to concrete victories in such areas
as living wage campaigns, a children's health initiative, and affordable housing.
The ability to enact local government reforms in these areas reflected a growing
electoral capacity that has produced pro-labor majorities in San Jose and suburban Sunnyvale.

Faced with a Republican-dominated state government and an affiliate base of
only fifty thousand members, Denver Area Labor Federation (DALF) leaders
drew self-consciously on San Jose's three-legged strategy.[2] Following the 1998

---

1. The full papers on all seven cases, as well as other materials, are available at http://www.power
building.wayne.edu. The papers on Los Angles, San Jose, Denver, and Houston were originally published as the December 2004 issue of *Working USA* (see Bryd and Nari, Frank and Wong, Luce and
Nelson, and Karson). The project will document new cases of regional power building as they emerge.

2. For decades Colorado Republicans had dominated state politics. Indeed, for years labor stood only

election of Jobs with Justice staff person Leslie Moody as DALF's only full-time paid officer, the council revamped its political program. Rather than each union running its own operations, DALF convinced affiliates to place staff and rank-and-file members under its direction. These personnel were fed into the core electoral activities of intensive voter registration, education, and get-out-the-vote work. This increasingly effective electoral work delivered a string of successes (along with some defeats) for school board, city council, and state legislative races. In 2004, these seeds produced the first Democratic Party–controlled state legislature in forty years in addition to two Democratic U.S. House and Senate victories. DALF launched the Front Range Economic Strategy Center to help develop effective policy campaigns. FRESC has grown from one staff member to six and a budget of $450,000 in three years. Growing electoral and policy capacity has allowed DALF to pursue coalitions for intervening in regional economic development decisions. A successful living wage campaign was followed by a three-year DALF and FRESC-led alliance that secured a community benefits agreement with the $1 billion redevelopment of the former Gates Rubber factory site. Partners in this later campaign include ACORN, 9 to 5, and Save Our Section 8. The early 2006 victory paved the way for a new era of activism around local economic development.

Power-building components came together differently in Los Angeles, originating in two separate but complementary developments. In 1993, Hotel Employees and Restaurant Employees (HERE) Local 11 launched what is today called the Los Angeles Alliance for a New Economy. Now with two dozen staff members, LAANE builds a progressive voice for regional economic development decisions through research, policy development, and coalition building. LAANE, for example, has done extensive research and monitoring of the city's economic development programs. Los Angles leads the nation in generating poverty-wage jobs. The second development came in the mid-1990s when the Los Angeles Federation of Labor began to revamp and reenergize its political program under the direction of Miguel Contreras. Today, the federation coordinates hundreds of full-time precinct walkers supported by many more weekend volunteers during elections. A number of alliances have proven key to the federation's growing influence. The new Organization of Los Angeles Workers (OLAW) brought together labor and Latino groups to increase Latino voter participation in targeted, typically Republican-represented districts.[3] A similar coalition with Action

a few Republican swing votes away from passage of a right-to-work law. Even without a full right-to-work law, unions in Colorado must win a second election in order to establish a union shop.

3. By 2000, Los Angeles County's population was 45 percent Latino. Like labor, the Latino communities traditionally had little influence in regional politics.

for Grassroots Empowerment and Neighborhood Development Alternatives (AGENDA) increases turnout in black and brown neighborhoods. Today, the Los Angeles City Council and several suburban communities have pro-labor majorities. Growing progressive political strength was reflected in the ability of the federation's former political director, Fabian Nuñez, to not only win a California legislative seat in his first time as a candidate in 2002 but to quickly become the speaker of the California Assembly, making him one of the most powerful Democrats in the state. LAANE's policy development has combined with the labor federation's political capacity to produce a rich experience of coalition building around model living wage enforcement efforts, pioneering community benefits agreements, and several large-scale immigrant rights campaigns.

Our four other cases show leaders starting on a power-building path by developing one or more components, although not necessarily a complete or self-conscious long-term project. In late 1999, Seattle became known worldwide for the massive demonstrations and direct action against the World Trade Organization. The large crowds in part reflected years of innovative coalition building by the King County Labor Council beginning in 1993 when Ron Judd was elected the council's executive secretary. Previously, as president of the Seattle–King County Building and Construction Trades Council, Judd had worked to overcome years of tensions with minority communities by building alliances to increase minority and women apprenticeship opportunities and the use of union labor in public construction work. Throughout the 1990s the council worked to build union and community mobilization capacity around such key labor battles as the 1995 and 2000 strikes at Boeing. Using national AFL-CIO funds the council launched Seattle Union Now as an ambitious plan to support worker organizing. When Steve Williamson succeeded Judd in 2000 he placed a greater emphasis on the council's electoral program, including helping to elect a pro-labor Seattle mayor. The new millennium has also seen increasing coalition work around public economic development efforts and support for union organizing and bargaining within the city's huge port and airport facilities.

With its massive deindustrialization Cleveland is a classic rust-belt city. Following his election in 1987, Cleveland labor council executive secretary John Ryan worked to revitalize the area's labor-backed United Way affiliate (the United Labor Agency) by not simply renewing its traditional community service work but by expanding the organization's scope into such areas as a dislocated worker program, a community hiring hall for displaced and homeless workers, support for minority union-apprenticeship training in the building trades, housing renovation, and a nonpartisan voter registration project. The council has also worked with affiliates to better coordinate political endorsements and campaign work. A 2001 school bond issue and a living wage campaign are among its successes. The

United Labor Agency and the Cleveland AFL-CIO also provided seed money to launch Policy Matters Ohio as a nonprofit institute that conducts research on economic and policy issues in Cleveland and Ohio. The council also established a full-time position to support multiunion organizing.

Unlike Cleveland and Seattle, labor has never had a strong presence in Houston. An exploding immigrant population could have been seen as a threat by the area's largely Anglo union movement.[4] Yet, when elected to the leadership of the Harris County AFL-CIO in 1995, Dale Wortham and Richard Shaw saw an opportunity to reach out to the Latino community around several initiatives. The council helped build a Justice and Equality in the Workplace Partnership to bring together government, labor, and community groups to build awareness among immigrants of their legal protections at work and to strengthen governmental enforcement of these rights. The council also supported the new Mayor's Office of Immigrant and Refugee Affairs, staffed by an immigrant rights activist. As in many of the cases, the Houston council was an active sponsor of the 2004 Immigrant Worker Freedom Rides. The council also developed an active "street heat" capacity in the form of an annual Justice Bus that delivers a busload of union and community activists to confront hostile employers. More recently, the council has begun to enter into economic development debates and is working with affiliates and a local interfaith organization to expand its Community Services Program into a more comprehensive worker center.

Buffalo, by contrast, has traditionally been one of the most unionized cities in the county. Yet, like Cleveland, it has witnessed deindustrialization and declining union density. Beginning in the 1970s these challenges produced strong efforts at labor-management cooperation to save existing industrial jobs through high-performance workplaces. What makes Buffalo notable, however, is how this workplace activism grew into broader community projects that have positioned labor as a major player in regional economic development decisions, connecting unions with a rich array of coalitions within the community. Today the union-driven Economic Development Group serves as the project coordinator for several major public-private initiatives including electricity relicensing, a downtown biomass heating system, and a minority jobs training initiative. The joint labor-management Champions Network promotes the area's skilled, high-performance unionized workforce as an advantage for would-be investors. At the same time, through the work of the Coalition for Economic Justice, unions have linked up with community groups to block the alternative "low road" in which employers compete by increasing the direct exploitation of their workforce and the com-

---

4. In 2000, 38 percent of the city's population was of Latino origin and 31 percent, Anglo.

munity. Unlike the other cases, this has taken place largely outside the local labor council and without a major transformation of union political action.

COMMON FORCES AT WORK WITH LOCAL LABOR MOVEMENTS

Although our cases vary in their urban scale, traditional political climate, economic makeup, and the level of development of their power-building work, they share several characteristics common to power-building innovations.

With the exception of Seattle and Buffalo, our case cities have traditionally not been known as labor strongholds. Even in Seattle and Buffalo declining union fortunes have played out in a way that has established a critical mass of local unions looking to confront a challenging future through new collective responses. In nearly every case, traditional union political activity, which sought insider access with individual officeholders, reached an impasse. Instead, the agenda driving government policy had shifted firmly onto the neoliberal ground of privatization, tax cuts, and "free market" economic development. Faced with a shifting local political framework, progressives generally are less able to pursue individual policy goals without both joining forces with other groups and seeking to move the overall terms of the regional debates back onto questions of social justice and corporate responsibility.

The cases also point to the growing importance of local (county, city, and municipal) politics for union political action. Several forces are at work. First, devolution from the federal government onto the states and from state governments onto the local level has pushed responsibility downward. At the same time conservative and neoliberal dominance at the national level and within many state governments has made the local level the terrain most favorable for developing progressive policy responses. Second, despite the much-publicized forces of globalization, localized factors such as regional labor markets, workforce development, infrastructure and energy costs, community quality of life, and regional consumer markets play major roles in firm success and investment decisions. Companies that pursue "high road" strategies typically rely on cooperation and resources that develop at a regional level. At the same time, a region's political economy strongly influences the relative availability and attraction of low-road alternatives. Finally, in contrast to national and often state action, intervention in a region's political economy does not necessarily involve confronting the corporate power structure head-on. The on-the-ground opponents of regional power-building work are typically not an alliance of big corporate players but developers, retailers, hotels, and entertainment businesses that have a vested interest in both local economic development policy and low-wage business strategies.

Finally, innovation has generally followed from changes in labor council leadership. This pattern in part reflects the rise of a new generation of leaders coming out of specific local unions or allied groups (such as Jobs with Justice chapters). For these leaders, even the most effective organizing and servicing by individual unions is not enough for labor's rebound. Organized labor's difficulties are rooted in the basic power imbalance between America's democratic potential and runaway corporate power. Only by becoming a core force in building a revitalized progressive movement for political and economic change can unions hope to experience the kind of upsurge that occurred in the late nineteenth century or the 1930s.

With our cases we are also seeing a critical change in the importance attached to central labor councils as a position attractive to innovative leadership. Traditionally, central labor council positions have not served as centers of power in most local labor movements. Therefore the ambitions of rising and dynamic local leaders naturally tended to focus elsewhere. By contrast, within most of our cases key gifted activists had come to view holding central labor council office as a position from which they could exercise important and meaningful leadership in their region.

SIX COMPONENTS OF POWER BUILDING

Collectively our cases point to an emerging six-part model for regional power building (see table 4.1, which summarizes how each case fits into these six components). All six strategies are necessary to sustain successful progressive regional power building over the long term. Indeed, together they produce a sum that is far greater than the parts.

From Single-Issue Alliances to Deep Coalition Building

In our cases, coalitions have formed around a range of issues including living wages, affordable housing, workers' right to organize, health care, immigrant rights, and job access. Labor's community partners have spanned the spectrum from low-income to interfaith to civil rights to environmental to immigrant rights groups. While labor-community coalition experiences in general have increased over the past two decades, the work found in our case studies stands out for combining three distinct characteristics.

Table 4.1 Summary of power-building work

	BUFFALO	CLEVELAND	DENVER	HOUSTON	LOS ANGELES	SAN JOSE	SEATTLE
Council Name and Staffing	Area labor federation added to central labor council[a]	Cleveland AFL-CIO Federation of Labor—7 staff	Denver Area Labor Federation—3 staff	Harris County AFL-CIO—4 staff	Los Angeles County Federation of Labor—20 staff	South Bay Labor Council—8 staff	King County Labor Council—5 staff
Principle Affiliates and Overall Affiliate Base[b]	CWA, IBEW, IBT, SEIU, USWA, public sector, IAM, OPEIU, PACE, UFCW, UAW 85,000 members	AFSCME, UFCW, SEIU, AFT, CWA, Building trades, Firefighters, UNITE HERE Over 140 affiliate locals	UFCW, CWA, SEIU, AFT, IAM, APWU, AFGE 50,000 members	CWA, PACE, IBEW, AFT, UFCW, ILWU, 70,000 members	SEIU, AFT, UFCW, Entertainment industry unions, UNITE HERE, IBT 700,000 members	SEIU, UFCW, UNITE HERE, AFSCME, Building trades 110,000 members	IAM, SPEEA/IFPTE, UFCW, Building trades, SEIU, IBT, UNITE HERE 150,000 members
1. Deep Coalition Building[c]	Minority training Labor-management partnerships Early childhood education	Minority jobs access: community hiring hall, construction pre-apprenticeship program Housing revitalization School bond	Living wage, Immigrant Worker Freedom Ride	Immigrant rights including Justice and Equality in the Workplace Worker Development Center Justice Bus	Immigrant-labor voting bloc Ethnic media outreach Immigrant rights Economic justice campaigns Anti-Wal Mart	Children's Health Initiative Inclusionary zoning—affordable housing Smart growth	WTO protests Boeing strikes Housing issues Building trades—minority apprenticeships
2. Aggressive Political Action	Voter registration and GOTV	Voter registration Affiliate-council coordinators	Staff and lost timers from affiliates Candidate briefing program	Labor-to-Neighbor	Staff and lost timers from affiliates Aggressive labor-community precinct operations and phone banks	Staff and lost timers from affiliates Officeholder policy education sessions	Labor-to-Neighbor Strengthen endorsement process Strategic targeting of port and council races

	Col 1	Col 2	Col 3	Col 4	Col 5	Col 6	Col 7
3. Economic Development Agenda	Living wage Champions Network Energy relicensing Downtown heating High toad business attraction	Living wage	Living wage Community benefits agreement Reports on regional economy and public policy	Unsuccessful minimum wage Broker PLA	Living wage Community benefits agreements Reports on regional economy and public policy	Living Wage Community benefits agreement Reports on regional economy and public policy	Port expansion Leverage development agreements—building trades and hospitality
4. "Think and Do" Tank—and Staff	Economic Development Group—expand to 5 staff Cornell ILR Champions Network—2 staff	United Labor Agency—35 staff Policy Matters Ohio—4 staff	Front Range Economic Strategy Center—6 staff	Worker Development Center	LAANE—20+ staff	Working Partnerships USA—20 staff	Worker Center—7 staff
5. Leadership Development			Piloting Civic Leadership Institute			Labor-Community Leadership Institute	
6. Sample of Building Core Partners (not included in the above)	Coalition for Economic Justice Champions Network Economic Development Group	Union Construction Industry Partnership Jobs with Justice Day Laborers Organizing Committee Full-time organizing coordinator	Jobs with Justice ACORN Leveraged political and community support for organizing	Immigrant work with faith groups and SEIU City of Houston Building trades—immigrant work ACORN	Incubate SMART and Clergy and Laity United Leveraged political and community support for organizing by SEIU, UNITE HERE, and others	ACORN—Labor council partnership Interfaith council Leverage political and grassroots support for union organizing and bargaining	Jobs with Justice Church Council of Greater Seattle Environmental alliances Leverage political and grassroots support for union organizing and bargaining

a In Buffalo power building was not initiated out of the central labor council.

b Affiliates list the situation prior to July 2005.

c Deep Coalition Building also includes the partnerships behind the projects listed under Economic Development Agenda.

First, groups are not simply supporting each other's organizational agendas. Coalition activity can include, for example, community support for union organizing and contract campaigns. However, the overall basis for alliance building lay in a process by which labor and community groups have developed new mutual agendas that often transcend their traditional activities. This transcendent character can be seen in such efforts as living wage campaigns, community/labor benefits agreements, the Children's Health Initiative in San Jose, and labor protections for immigrant workers. In each case, the direct organizational interests of key partners became embedded in a larger community cause around which the campaigns were organized.

Second, although the coalition work can involve a broad range of groups that vary from campaign to campaign, the power-building cases also involve deliberate efforts to establish deeper relationships among a core of partners. In San Jose, for example, cooperation between the labor council and ACORN around renters' rights and affordable housing produced a more formal partnership. In the summer and fall of 2003, a joint grassroots organizing team combining labor and ACORN organizers conducted door-to-door neighborhood visits in poor, predominantly immigrant neighborhoods in support of a community benefits initiative campaign. This partnership produced new ACORN members, greater community support for the initiative, and a stronger electoral base for labor. The labor-Latino political alliance in Los Angeles similarly reflects deep coalition building. Union organizing and political action has become a path for Latino empowerment, and in turn Latino political development strengthens labor.

Third, every case includes some form of significant outreach by labor specifically to minority communities—African American, Latino, and immigrant. At least three logics appear to be at work. The low-income organizing of specific unions, such as SEIU and UNITE HERE, has enmeshed them in minority communities. Alliances around broader community issues reflect these unions' organizing campaigns, which have involved significant community outreach. In the process, joining unions becomes framed as a key dimension of community development. As a general rule, minority workers are particularly receptive to unionization (Bronfenbrenner 1998).

New coalition work has also set out to address past tensions between organized labor and minority communities. For example, the preapprenticeship training and minority hiring programs seen in several cases respond to a history of conflict over job access between the building-trades unions and African American and Latino communities. Over the past twenty years nonunion contractors have used their base in residential construction to move into the core areas of union industrial work. They have sought to draw on African American, Latino, and immigrant workers as a source of both skilled and unskilled labor (Linder 2000). Either the building-trades unions find ways to build alliances in such communities or these workers provide a weapon for employers to use against organized labor.

Finally, the new connections between labor and minority communities reflect a common dilemma of local political marginalization or declining influence. For minority communities the local regime has either locked them out altogether or their representation is dominated by business-oriented, middle-class elites. Basic math on potential voter numbers naturally suggests political alliances—neither labor nor specific minority communities alone have the strength to achieve electoral power.

New Alliances for Aggressive Political Action

As with coalition building, grassroots electoral activism by itself signifies nothing new. However, our cases point to a decisive shift in the goal and scope of this work. Put concisely, power building aims not simply to elect endorsed candidates or enact specific policy reforms but to establish a capacity to govern. This capacity has several aspects.

First, power building requires an expanded scale of electoral mobilization. During the 2001 Los Angles mayoral race, for example, OLAW fielded 150 full-time precinct walkers six weeks before the election. In addition, the federation mobilized twenty-seven hundred volunteers. In most of the cases, labor and its allies have developed some form of systematic electoral program that strategically examines an area's voting patterns and then marshals the resources needed to raise voter turnout among targeted populations.

Second, increased scale is possible due to greater political coordination among key partners. Power-building central labor councils have assumed a more central role in coordinating and directing union political work. Most significantly, in many cases they have taken over directing union members brought out of their workplace and placed on "lost time" (union pay) by their locals. Control over this resource has been traditionally well guarded by individual unions.

Third, power building places the electoral mobilization in the context of a more coherent and coordinated progressive message. Although in no case has a power-building project been able to produce a comprehensive blueprint for regional change, over time the many electoral and policy reform campaigns have articulated a greater common sense of progressive values, given more priority to a messages of social and economic justice, and raised questions about corporate power.[5] Issues such as job creation move from the neoliberal focus on raw num-

---

5. Working Partnerships USA did attempt to develop a blueprint for change among its partners. Al-

bers and a "better business climate" to questions of job quality and overall community well-being.

Fourth, because of its other components, power building connects the general
themes and issues raised during election seasons to practical grassroots organizing and legislative policy campaigns that are year-round. With its emphasis on individualized candidate campaigns, such connections are rare in U.S. politics.[6]

As electoral work and policy development takes on new life, power building
begins to change the relationships that labor and its allies have with candidates.
Traditionally, labor and community groups endorse candidates by seeking their
positions on a range of specific issues. By contrast, power-building politics seeks
a greater role in developing both candidates and their messages. In cases such as
Denver, labor and its allies now require candidates to go through training in their
core concerns. In San Jose, the development of current and future officeholders
is one of the outcomes sought by the Leaders Development Institute.

Power building can lead to confrontations with centrist Democrats. Ongoing
policy campaigns highlight the gap between progressive champions and the more
limited horizons of centrist Democrats. This contradiction worked itself out in
Los Angeles in 2001 when the L.A. County Federation of Labor backed Hilda Solis in a successful challenge to Marty Martinez, a long-term centrist member of
Congress. Solis had led the fight in the California Legislature in 1996 to successfully raise the state's minimum wage. By supporting her, the federation sent a
message that working people need "labor champions" and "labor warriors" in
office.

Where the Private Economy Connects
with Public Decisions

By themselves, the above two components do not lead to the kind of sustained
and coherent effort that grows progressive power over time. Elections are
episodic, and rarely do coalitions live beyond the issue or campaign that pulled
the groups together. Sustained power building requires a focal point that connects

---

though the process produced several successful efforts around specific issues, it failed to produce the
kind of overarching and comprehensive progressive agenda that organizers had sought.

6. In theory political parties should provide a bridge between what is said during elections and the
pursuit of concrete policy changes. However, in the United States weak party structures lead to a much
more diffuse process. Candidates traditionally develop their own individualized campaigns that tend
to focus on personality and general themes. Party structures play little role in policy development
or debates—these functions instead grow out of the byzantine world of interest group lobbying.
Through power building, activists are essentially establishing many of the functions that a strong party
system would provide.

the many different efforts over time. This need highlights the significance of the emphasis placed on regional economic development policy found in all of the cases. Economic development provides an arena where private employer decisions connect with public authority and resources. Local policy tools include tax abatements and public financial assistance, zoning regulations, the public acquisition and selling of land, government contracting, local workforce development programs, and leases at public facilities such as airports and ports.[7]

By its very nature, local development policy connects specific projects with ongoing questions about a region's long-term future. It also provides an arena in which a modest investigative effort can unearth a compelling case for change. In Los Angeles, for example, LAANE's research into two major local economic development programs found millions of dollars in public subsidies being spent with little effective criteria for community well-being. Job quality, for example, was not a criterion used in either program. Public efforts were not targeted specifically toward underserved communities. Indeed, the city had no coherent strategy targeting key industry sectors but, rather, focused its energy on attracting individual firms. The reports recommended far less emphasis on retail and much greater attention to smaller projects. The research fed successful campaigns around living wage policies, labor-peace compacts, and community-benefits agreements. The lax standards shown in Los Angeles are all too typical. Given the business-driven nature of the process it comes as no surprise that such community-destroying employers as Wal-Mart enjoy lucrative economic development assistance from communities across the country.

The economic development arena offers activists the opportunity to organize around specific and winnable local reforms that nevertheless speak to larger issues of concern to labor and community groups. This dual nature can be seen in the success of living wage campaigns—identified in six of the seven cases in table 4.1. On the one hand, requiring companies that receive public funds to pay a living wage is a fairly clear step that local governments generally have the power to enact. Because battles over local living wage ordinances usually do not draw in large corporate players, local campaigns can prevail over the opposition of local chambers of commerce and their local business allies. On the other hand, while the reach of living wage laws—in terms of the portion of an area's working poor covered—is quite modest, living wage campaigns speak to big questions about poverty wages, public spending, and the role of local government in private eco-

---

7. The specific strategy of providing subsidies to attract business investment has grown markedly over the past few decades. In 1977, for example, only twenty-eight states had programs to grant businesses property tax abatements, via local governments, for machinery and equipment. By 1993, forty-one states had such programs. Eight states allowed local governments to offer loans in 1977; forty-five did so by 1993. The numbers are from the clearinghouse Good Jobs First—http://www.goodjobsfirst.org.

nomic decisions. Indeed, the tendency of the opposition to speak of living wage ordinances as if they were across-the-board minimum wage laws or some even greater attempt at "government control over the economy" reflects the broad issues embedded in this very specific reform.

As table 4.1 suggests, four of our cases have also produced what is likely the next step in economic development intervention beyond accountability measures: the community-benefits agreement.[8] These take the form of legally binding documents signed between a grassroots coalition and the developer of a specific large-scale project. The developer commits to such measures as building a certain percentage of affordable housing in developments, living wage requirements for leasing businesses, space and funds for child-care or youth centers, resources for community development projects, local hiring, prevailing wage construction, and neutrality and card check recognition for worker organizing drives. A potentially broad range of union and community partners can build their goals into such agreements. In return, the developer receives the support of the coalition in moving through the public approval process. Community benefits campaigns take advantage of the fact that time is money for developers. The support or opposition of a grassroots coalition can have a major impact on both the speed and final outcome of the public process.

While living wage campaigns and community-benefits agreements seek to raise standards, the kinds of high-road economic development found in Buffalo point toward complementing work to better support and reward desirable company practices at a regional level. Today, most public economic development focuses on attracting outside investment on an isolated firm-by-firm basis. By contrast, power building develops alternative agendas that focus far more on locally grown and integrated resources, collective business success, and shared community prosperity.

The rich campaign work in the economic development arena contrasts with the notable lack of energy in our cases involving local public social spending—a second potential source of glue for the long term. The notable exception is the Children's Health Initiative in San Jose, which provided health care for the area's 70,000 uninsured children. Here, however, leaders took advantage of a specific opportunity when city and county governments faced a decision on how to spend tobacco settlement funds. By contrast, our power-building cases have not produced a clear response to the fiscal crisis facing local governments. For the past twenty-five years neoliberal reforms at the state and federal level have set up the steady starvation of the public purse. The question of why no clear progressive

---

8. Indeed, our two most developed regional power-building movements, Los Angeles and San Jose, are also national leaders in this emerging arena.

agenda for reestablishing fair taxes and adequate social spending has emerged at the municipal level offers a promising avenue for exploration that is, however, beyond the scope of this chapter. Part of the answer may lie in the fact that while local economic development may be constrained by larger forces it nevertheless involves clear local levers with real impact. By contrast, taxing and spending by local governments has been increasingly constrained by state and federal actions. In addition, tax reform and local public spending does not appear to speak as directly to the organizing interests of unions such as SEIU, UNITE HERE, and the building trades in the same way that economic development policy does.

Creating a Cross-Movement Capacity for Research and Policy Development

All of our power-building projects involve either founding new 501(c)3 "think and do tanks" or building a similar capacity out of existing resources. Coalition building, economic development work, and aggressive political action require a capacity to understand the detailed workings of the local political economy and to develop specific progressive policy reforms that can then be fought for. As indicated in table 4.1, the staffing resources of these nonprofits typically exceed those of the central labor bodies, often by significant margins.

Although each have their own particulars, three nonprofits—the Los Angeles Alliance for a New Economy, Working Partnerships USA (San Jose), and the Front Range Economic Strategies Center (Denver)—represent a common model. All pursue two research prongs. They produce general reports on the state of working people within their regional economy that highlight trends of growing inequality. They also conduct detailed investigations of local economic development programs that both identify the local levers of decision making and the lax standards and corporate welfare currently involved. Such understanding allows for focused and effective campaigns for living wages, subsidy accountability, and community benefits agreements.

These nonprofits, however, do not simply engage in applied research; they also participate in organizing. Nonprofit staff help build policy coalitions. Indeed, where coalition partners have limited staff resources, the organizing capacities of these institutions can prove critical. Working Partnerships USA and LAANE both served as incubators for developing regional interfaith coalitions focused specifically on worker issues.[9] LAANE also fostered a grassroots membership organi-

---

9. Called the Interfaith Council on Race, Religion, Economic, and Social Justice and Clergy and Laity United for Economic Justice.

zation called Santa Monicans for Responsible Tourism (SMART) that fought for a zone-based living wage ordinance and has supported worker organizing and contract efforts in the city's booming hospitality industry. The general "think and do" model reflected in these three nonprofits have produced such spin-offs as the East Bay Alliance for a New Economy in Oakland and the Center for Policy Initiatives in San Diego.

The other cases have attempted to generate a similar capacity in different ways. In Seattle, leaders have struggled to redefine the work of the existing Worker Center to incorporate greater power-building work, especially economic development campaigns. With an eye to enhancing immigrant rights work in Houston, the labor council and its allies are working to put a worker center in place. In Cleveland, council leader John Ryan helped found Policy Matters Ohio. Because it generates some of its funding by providing research support to local unions and because it supports progressive policy efforts at the state level, Policy Matters Ohio has grown as a more strictly research organization. In Buffalo, the innovative economic development efforts have drawn heavily on the capacities of staff at the Cornell-Buffalo School of Industrial Relations.

The Partnership for Working Families began as a network of the key power-building nonprofits in California. In 2005 it brought on new staff to support power-building efforts across the country. By 2006 the partnership was supporting efforts in at least a dozen cities outside of California to establish community-benefits and similar economic development campaigns and to found, staff, and fund nonprofit "think and do" arms.

Establishing Collective Leadership Development and Bridge Builders

As a decadelong strategy, power building must both expand the ranks of current leadership committed to the concept and ensure replacements for the current core leadership. In San Jose, the Labor-Community Leadership Institute brings together primary and secondary leadership from labor, religious, community, and political groups in a seven-session program that develops their understanding of the South Bay political economy and the potential for progressive change. The program links to the other power-building components. Working Partnerships' research and policy materials allow participants to talk about the regional economy and the levers of public authority at a very concrete level. This shared understanding and the individual relationships that participants develop with one another strengthens the groundwork for coalition building. The curriculum includes a class project that plugs participants in to some existing campaign. The institute recruits political leaders as participants, and the program explores in detail the roles of both elected officials and appointed boards in the regional political economy. Thus the institute helps generate knowledgeable progressive champions among the pool of existing and future officeholders and candidates. It also produces bridge builders—activists with backgrounds and experiences that span different types of social movements.

Although table 4.1 has many blank entries under leadership development, this absence will likely change in the coming years. The importance of generating a network of leaders who share a common vision of regional change is reflected in efforts to replicate the Labor-Community Leadership Institute model in other cities. The new nonprofit Building Partnerships is working to establish civic leadership institutes around the country. Still in its infancy, this project is developing a general curriculum adaptable to local conditions.[10] Pilot civic leadership institutes were held in late 2005 and early 2006 in Denver, Boston, and Atlanta. Several of our other cases provide likely sites for future expansion.

Building Each Core Partner's Organizational Capacity

Because local government's authority and resources are limited, changing the composition and agenda of public authority alone is not sufficient to govern a region. Power building must develop the capacities of nongovernmental actors to support the public agenda and to organize for economic change directly. The "think and do" tanks are expressions of this capacity. However, power building must also develop the capacities of its core grassroots players.

A virtuous cycle must be established between political action, coalition building, and union organizing. Unions provide crucial resources for engaging in electoral action, enacting policy, and building coalitions. Yet ever since the AFL-CIO launched Union Cities in 1996, central labor councils have struggled to define a direct role in worker organizing. In Seattle, Los Angeles, and Cleveland the central labor councils have raised resources to support organizing staff. Defining their precise role has proven a difficult task. Should labor council staff view their role as organizing support for existing union efforts or developing innovative cross-union campaigns?

The links between power building and union growth have also emerged through three more indirect links. First, by establishing a capacity to intervene where public authority connects to private employers, power building provides

---

10. The author has served as the developer for this curriculum. For more information contact David Reynolds at aa2589@wayne.edu.

leverage for deactivating antiunion campaigns and securing card-check and neutrality agreements or project labor accords. In Los Angeles, for example, living wage work fed directly into agreements with employers that helped SEIU and HERE build significant strength at the city airport and among area hotels. In Seattle, a coalition campaign helped secure local hiring, minority apprenticeship slots, and union labor at the city's large stadium project. DALF's ability to help elect two new school board members directly resulted in 125 part-time custodians being able to join Communication Workers of America (CWA) Local 7777. Political and coalition leverage was also crucial in the unionization of forty-six hundred graduate students at the University of Washington in Seattle.

Second, the coalition partners formed around power building also become allies for worker organizing and contract campaigns. Clergy and Laity United for Economic Justice, for example, has provided direct aid to HERE and SEIU efforts in and around Los Angeles. The Denver Building Trades Council worked with the revitalized Denver Federation of Labor and FRESC to successfully support efforts by Colorado University students to require strong union-supporting wage, benefits, and apprenticeship standards on $400 million in campus construction. The Labor-Community Leadership Institute curriculum includes discussions that build awareness among community leaders of the role and importance of unions for community change.

Although political leverage and coalition allies have made a clear difference for organizing by specific unions, the overall numbers remain modest. Organizing gains in general come in units of hundreds and the low thousands. However, as many labor historians have observed, the labor movement has never grown incrementally. Rather, individual gains lay the groundwork for major upswings when broader social and economic conditions foster a period of social awakening (Clawson 2003).[11] Seen in this context, power building produces a less measurable but no less important effect in changing the way in which unions are perceived within the broader community. In explaining his immigrant rights work to a local union representative, Houston labor council leader Richard Shaw commented, "We aren't going to organize unions for him [the union representative] . . . but by the time he gets to the parking lot the workers will know who the hell he is and what he is there for."[12] By pursing power building, central labor council and key union leaders are fostering a broad regional movement for social and economic justice that has labor at its center. In the process sectors of the community come to see joining and organizing unions as a central vehicle for community advancement.

---

11. Also Nelson Liechtenstein, personal conversation.

12. From an interview with Richard Shaw conducted by Tom Karson, November 2003.

Building organizational strength is not restricted to union organizing. Like unions, ACORN is a membership-driven organization. The joint organizing team formed between the South Bay Labor Council and the local ACORN chapter expresses in a formalized way a more general commitment shared by both labor and ACORN elsewhere to build mutual organizational capacity.

Power building also grows the capacities of regional labor bodies. This can take the form of direct organizational growth. The Los Angeles County Federation of Labor, for example, has grown to nearly two dozen staff members. Looking only at direct personnel, however, risks missing the main dynamics of growth. In Denver, for example, Leslie Moody remains the only full-time elected officer. Growth in many councils' organizational capacity has taken place in two areas outside year-round staff. First, foundation funds have allowed a noticeable staffing expansion in the "think and do" nonprofit organizations. Working Partnerships USA has over twenty staff members while FRESC and Policy Matters Ohio have between four and six. Second, councils have developed deeper relationships with core affiliates. Traditionally, local unions have viewed council activities as external to their core operations. Through participation in power-building work individual locals begin to integrate this council-driven agenda into their internal planning. In addition, unions become more open to sharing resources and capacity. The willingness of unions to place their staff and lost-time members under the control of the labor council during election seasons, for example, represents a major shift in the relationship between council and local unions.

CHALLENGES FOR EFFECTIVE POWER BUILDING

As ongoing experiments, the cases reveal several challenges that leaders who pursue regional power building are likely to encounter. An examination of the most active players in our power-building cases makes clear that this work must connect to the direct self-interest of the organizations involved. Labor and community leaders do not build power for its own sake or become active in coalitions because it is the right thing to do. They do so because establishing alliances, passing specific government policies, or growing political influence over the long term helps them to address the central goals of their organizations. This does not mean such connections must be defined narrowly or simply in immediate terms. Indeed, participation in our cases can reflect a significant broadening by an organization in its understanding of the scope and time frame of its core interests. Thus, developing a constituency for power-building efforts involves a twin process of defining the work to speak to different partners' core goals while at the same time encouraging them to rethink what those self-interests involve.

Related to the above, in most of our cases manufacturing unions are noticeably marginal players in power-building work. This is especially noticeable in Cleveland and Seattle, which have had traditionally strong unionized manufacturing industries. In part this may reflect the different geographical scope of employers. Building owners and hotels operate in regional markets while large manufacturing firms define their operations in national and international terms. Buffalo, however, stands out as an exception to the above pattern. Why? The Buffalo-Niagara region enjoys relatively high union density based in manufacturing. As a way of saving jobs, manufacturing unions like the UAW pursued significant experiments in labor-management cooperation, worker training, and other innovations to produce high-performance workplaces. Although such high-road strategies are not unique to Buffalo-area unions, the case stands out for how a workplace-restricted experience spilled over into activism around public economic development policy and community coalitions. The extent to which power building can connect to regional manufacturing revival strategies elsewhere represents a topic for greater investigation.[13]

Tensions can occur between labor councils and their affiliates. While power building may incorporate the growth strategies of the most active affiliates, other local unions may be only secondarily involved with the council's agenda. Leaders of these latter unions may have varied opinions about the wisdom of allocating movement resources to power-building work. Work among immigrant and minority communities, in particular, can generate differences among affiliates, since the full virtues of such connections are hardly universally accepted within the U.S. labor movement. The same is true of economic development work. Our cases include examples in which economic development coalitions helped forge new alliances between building trades unions and minority and immigrant communities and examples of how ongoing tensions between the two groups has worked to undermine such work. Economic development campaigns can offer new opportunities for building trades unions to connect to such communities while generating greater leverage over public construction. However, such campaigns can also seem to threaten traditional strategies that have sought project labor agreements on their own.

When initiative for power building first comes out of individual unions and allied groups, such as Jobs with Justice, tensions can develop with a more tradi-

---

13. With its innovative manufacturing partnership (the Wisconsin Regional Training Partnership) and its dynamic and active labor council, Milwaukee offers a particularly promising potential case study in this regard. For a discussion of the Milwaukee experience, see Reynolds 2002, chap. 8, and Eimer 2001.

tional or less capable labor council. In one case not covered in this chapter, the prior leaders of a local labor council attempted to shut down a Jobs with Justice chapter that they saw as a direct threat to their leadership position. An opposite dynamic is also a danger when groups such as Jobs with Justice have traditionally filled mobilizing roles not provided by a central labor body. As a previously moribund council becomes more effective, it may draw in many of the roles and resources previously held by an active Jobs with Justice chapter. In several of our cases the new leadership of the council came directly from Jobs with Justice. Ironically, subsequent power building by the council led to a crisis of purpose for the Jobs with Justice chapter.

Finding greater resources represents an ongoing challenge. To avoid saturating national foundation sources, power building needs strategies to cultivate regional funders. The ability of the Economic Development Group in Buffalo to become the managing body for major economic development initiatives offers an intriguing dimension of self-funding. Although many union affiliates face declining resources, full labor council affiliation by area unions (or some form of resource sharing where affiliation may not be possible) could represent an effective way of steering scarce resources into a pooled capacity. Certainly, council reorganization around power building provides a context for raising this question. Furthermore, the labor movement still raises large sums of money for electoral action. Even when such funds go to ground operations rather than candidate campaign coffers, the episodic nature of elections leaves behind a weak organizational legacy. By contrast, regional power-building work offers an ongoing framework conducive to maintaining and utilizing political capacities between election cycles.

The need to redeploy existing resources can present other challenges. What happens to a long-time employee when a council redefines its mission at the expense of traditional work that an individual may have dedicated his or her work life to? The changes in the mission and work of the Worker Center in Seattle and the United Way agency in Cleveland point to a related challenge at an organizational level.

Finally, leaders in several cases explicitly identified strategic planning as a central need. Indeed, our cases vary considerably as to whether work in individual campaigns and power-building components connects to a self-conscious vision of building power over the long term. Even when such a strategic perspective exists among key leaders, how many affiliate unions and allied groups share this vision? The leadership institute model clearly aims to broaden the ranks of leaders with a shared long-term vision. Similarly, the AFL-CIO Field Mobilization Department has pursued leadership development that promotes greater strategic planning around regional power building.

THE PROMISE OF REGIONAL POWER BUILDING

While power building puts into place the tools, relationships, and capacity to govern at a regional level, it can also provide the incubator for generating strong progressive movements for contesting state and national power. The 2004 Colorado electoral victories, the changes within the California Democratic state legislative caucus, and Hilda Solis's win in Los Angeles all illustrate that since most electoral districts are a local geographical area, regional power building can also influence state and national politics. As was demonstrated in the period leading up to the New Deal, policy agendas first developed locally can be translated into state and national politics even when local reforms are blocked by interventions from higher levels.[14] Regional power building also allows progressives to develop messages and a vision that resonates with the public and candidates whose political careers are built around championing progressive change. It also should strengthen the grassroots infrastructure for progressive change by growing the capacities of participating organizations and communities.

Finally, the transformation of central labor councils around power building raises the question of a similar potential for state labor federations. The work of the Colorado state federation in 2004 to take over the election mobilization capacities first established by the Denver Area Labor Federation provides one example of innovative work. Certainly, all of the six components outlined in this chapter have relevance for state-level power building. And thanks to U.S. federalism, building a capacity to govern states opens the door to fight for such reforms as comprehensive health-care reform, tax fairness, new public investments, and other potentially exciting and history-in-the-making agendas.

---

14. Indeed, most of the federal policy reforms that progressives generally support, including most of the New Deal, historically had precursors in pioneering state and local laws. Similarly, Canada's single-payer health system was born out of a system first established in a single province. The hoped-for ability of community-benefits agreement work in California to move from city to state policy provides an example of the same dynamic.

Part II

UNION TOWNS

5

THE POLITICS OF LABOR IN BOSTON
Geographies of Union Renewal

Heiwon Kwon and Benjamin Day

Recent union revitalization efforts are associated with the need to rebuild a labor-community alliance in order to advance a progressive urban agenda. Along with a growing emphasis on organizing the large pool of unorganized low-wage workers, who are mostly women, people of color, and immigrants, coalition building with communities becomes central for successful organizing campaigns. In other words, social coalitions with local communities are today a primary resource on which labor unions are drawing in trying to revitalize the labor movement.

In this context, labor scholars have recently begun to shed light on union renewal efforts at the urban level. But most studies have not paid full attention to distinctive geopolitical factors, including the locally specific social movement infrastructures that facilitate or block innovative union strategies. While labor unions in some cities have built strong movement infrastructures and social coalition networks among unions and various labor and community organizations, unions in other cities—where history and strategy have inclined unions toward political unionism—have failed to do so, or have been slow in laying a groundwork for strategic labor-community alliances.

In this chapter we will try to address the question of why unions in Boston have developed a predominantly top-down, political strategy for organizing and campaigning by highlighting the geographical scope of the local labor movement rather than taking an undifferentiated approach toward labor movement revitalization. We first look at labor movement strategy and reform in its geographic context: How have union strategies over time interacted with the changing politics of metropolitan governance? How have labor groups interacted with the often more visible politics of community organizing around urban development, rent control, and public schooling? And how has the reorientation of many unions toward organizing new members since the mid-1990s dealt with fragmented political geographies and the geographic strategies of union and nonunion corporations?

These questions relate to the embedded characteristics of local unionism, highlighted by a political insider strategy that moves labor organizations toward "political collective bargaining," in which unions will often trade short-term political support for politicians in exchange for their interventions in bargaining or organizing efforts. Political bargaining, or short-term electoral coalitions, cast locals in a mold of political unionism. In its reliance on political coalitions, political unionism often undermines unions' ability to build stronger and broader social coalitions. This political bargaining approach has espoused top-down organizing methods while neglecting grassroots campaigns built on wider labor-community coalitions in the suburban areas. This strategy has failed to effectively counter the business strategies of capital relocation to nonunion suburban areas. Thus, the restructuring of the suburban labor market as an unregulated, nonunion, and low-wage market has gone relatively unchallenged.

Unions' political strategies have created strained relationships with communities, and this has impeded labor-community alliance. In Boston, politicians at both the state and city levels cultivate relations with certain unions while undermining and opposing unions in other sectors. Since some unions' political strategies often set them at odds with other community groups and other unions, the resulting weakness of labor-community alliances has made labor revitalization on a wider geographical scale slow and halting.

By considering the specific local character of unionism with its distinctive organizational bases and community resources, our analysis avoids taking a "best practices" approach to labor studies. As Steven Henry Lopez has noted, "Existing case studies suffer from a tendency to tell success stories—ascendant narratives romanticizing workers' solidarity and downplaying internal obstacles, struggles, and difficulties" (Lopez 2004, 12). Instead, we look at how union strategies interact with local politics and how embedded local labor characteristics have fostered obstacles and limits to broader social coalition building. However, the identification of obstacles is not intended to present a pessimistic view for local labor movements. The analysis of specific problems connected to the embedded features of local unionism indicates points of intervention for local unions and directions for further innovation. In this respect, we hope this chapter has some significant practical implications for union revitalization.

ELECTORAL COALITIONS AND POLITICAL UNIONISM IN BOSTON

Although fairly unified at the level of national elections, Massachusetts labor organizations are much more fragmented in gubernatorial elections and in central-city politics. At both the state and local levels, many of Boston's largest unions often work at cross-purposes to community organizations and minority groups' political activism.

This is linked to some unions' strategic approach, what urban labor historians have termed "political collective bargaining," in which unions eschew party affiliations and agree to support whatever candidates will offer them the most appealing "deal" (Schneirov 1998). A number of Boston unions take a "political collective bargaining" approach to state or city politics, and some important locals have supported Republican candidates for governor. This strategic orientation, however, tends to involve short-term deals with politicians in exchange for short-term loyalty and often promotes candidates who govern at the expense of community groups and other local unions.

Examples of political fragmentation and short-term political bargaining that undermine labor's social coalitions with other labor and community organizations can be found on many occasions. Among others, the 1998 election shows how Republican affiliation fits with the pursuit of a narrowly defined interest for some unions. In that election, Republican candidate Paul Cellucci ran against former state Attorney General Scott Harshbarger, a Democrat. The unions that backed Cellucci included Local 26 of HERE, SEIU Local 254 (the janitors' union), Teamsters Local 25 (the largest Teamsters local in Boston), the Boston Carmen's Union Local 589 (bus and subway drivers), the Boston Firefighters, the Massachusetts Laborers District Council, and the Iron Workers District Council of New England.[1]

The Hotel Employees and Restaurant Employees (HERE) Local 26 had become renowned under President Domenic Bozzotto for organizing the backrooms of hotels across the city and for militant and successful strike actions during bargaining campaigns. However, in 1990 HERE stunned the local labor movement by backing Republican candidate Bill Weld and by agreeing to attend a party fund-raising event with Bob Dole or George Bush at the nonunion Westin hotel. Local 26 continued their support for Republican governors, and current Local 26 staffers have explained that this is due to the conservatives' support in securing card-check neutrality for newly built hotels:

> We supported Governor Celluci who ran against the Democrat Harshbarger back in the late '90s. Celluci was Republican. Celluci signed on to our organizing program. Harshbarger did not. Harshbarger in fact had his campaign events in nonunion hotels. So the choice was clear to us. Now the rest of the labor movement was behind the Democrat, but that has not been the major consideration for us. The major consideration for us was what's gonna move our organizing program forward.[2]

---

1. Jordan, *Boston Globe*, March 23, 1999; and Walker, *Boston Globe*, September 20, 1998.

2. Interview, HERE Local 26 staff, March 18, 2004.

Boston's Carmen's Union, Boston Firefighters, and the Teamsters also bargained with Cellucci for the protection of their members' interests in exchange for their political support. In this way, the Carmen's Union and the Firefighters obtained generous wage settlements and protective contracts.[3] The Teamsters also gained state funding for a large truck-driving program. When asked whether the funding was Cellucci's reward for political support, George Cashman, Local 25's president—later federally indicted for embezzlement of union funds—replied, "You'd have to ask him. I asked for it, he gave it to me."

In sum, these cases show the entrenched practices of political collective bargaining that trade short-term political support for the pursuit of union members' narrow interests, regardless of where the support comes from. Because unions that favor political bargaining often support candidates antagonistic toward other unions, this widens rifts with other unions pursuing party-loyalty strategies. And while a group of unions have backed Republican gubernatorial candidates in exchange for contract, legislative, or organizing gains, the long reign of the right wing in the governor's office has seen, among other moves, the abolition of the state's secretary of labor position; the reduction of maximum benefits for workers' compensation, which is now the lowest of all fifty states; the opening and growth of privatized career centers to replace the state's public employment services, which has led to plummeting assistance for welfare recipients; and a more recent wave of closings of offices of the state's Department of Social Services.[4] Public service unions and the communities of color they both hire and serve have been hit the hardest. As a measure of this, union density in the public sector began a clear downturn in the early 1990s when the Republicans first won office: union density in the public sector was 60.9 percent in 1990 and then decreased to 58.8 percent in 1995, 54.2 percent in 1997, and 50.8 percent by 1999 in Boston and the surrounding metropolitan area.[5]

---

3. Cellucci agreed to write into the contract of the Carmen's union a moratorium on any proposals to privatize the bus lines for the next five years (see Jordan, *Boston Globe*, March 23, 1999, and Palmer, *Boston Globe*, October 26, 1998). The support of the Boston Firefighters union was also more or less explicitly negotiated. Cellucci agreed to restore binding arbitration, which the Firefighters had lost in 1980. Second, Cellucci agreed to increase the state's Student Awareness of Fire Education (SAFE) program by $1 million, which provides a significant source of overtime pay for firefighters who are hired to visit schools while off duty. Third, Cellucci agreed to provisions raising the wage increase earned by Firefighters completing postsecondary degrees in their field by as much as 25 percent (Jordan, *Boston Globe*, March 23, 1999; and Phillips and Lehigh, *Boston Globe*, March 15, 1999).

4. Cassidy, *Boston Globe*, September 1, 1998; Lewis, *Boston Globe*, October 28, 1997; Globe Spotlight Team, *Boston Globe*, May 11, 1997; Zuckoff, *Boston Globe*, May 21, 1997; Grunwald, *Boston Globe*, November 20, 1996.

5. Source: http://www.trinity.edu/bhirsch/unionstats.

THE ORGANIZING IMPERATIVE AND POLITICAL BARGAINING

Increasingly, unions that rely on political and legislative mechanisms for pursuing organizing or contract goals tend to parlay political influence into top-down campaign strategies, pressuring employers into acquiescence instead of organizing unorganized workers.

HERE Local 26, for example, uses its political clout as a bootstrap into the hotel development process, putting pressure on hotel developers to sign on to card-check neutrality agreements. Local 26 has as many as five researchers dedicated to analyzing the development process and environmental laws, identifying key political forces as well as the sources of financing for development projects. They approach developers and offer their support in building the hotels if they will sign on to an agreement. When developers refuse, the union applies political pressure through their Republican allies, as one HERE Local 26 staffer explained:

> We actually are very active politically. And it has been very useful, particularly in our campaigns with new hotel developments, because the agencies through which the hotel developers have to get approvals are controlled by political people: mayor, governor, to a lesser extent city councilors. And so for the last seven years we tried a very similar program in our political endorsements. And there've been specific ways that politicians can demonstrate their support for card-check neutrality agreements. And we have been very pragmatic in that we endorsed whoever supports organizing. And some people take issue on that. Some people say you must have a broader political vision. But as long as the labor movement is hovering at around 10 percent, we're not gonna have an impact on that broader political vision. So we have to be focused on organizing.[6]

Yet the dilemma of union decline appears when, despite the increasing use of the political coalition strategy for organizing, unions in the greater Boston area have the lowest membership density of any large metropolitan area in the country outside of the right-to-work states. In 2000, union density in Boston was 13 percent compared to 31.3 percent in Buffalo, 23.3 percent in New York, 18.9 percent in Seattle, 17.4 percent in Philadelphia, and 14.9 percent in Los Angeles.[7] Why then have unions in Boston failed to increase their membership?

Grassroots coalitions among unions and other labor and community organi-

---

6. Interview, HERE Local 26 staff, March 18, 2004.

7. Source: BNA Compilation from the *Current Population Survey 2001*.

zations in both the central city and suburban areas can offer significant resources for successful organizing. A number of studies point to the role that community support and grassroots activism has played in successful labor campaigns (Delp and Quan 2002; Milkman 2000; Milkman and Wong 2000; Hurd, Milkman, and Turner 2003). Those successes were built on a combination of the labor movement's support for local organizing efforts and network mobilization. In the latter case, the bottom-up organizing of immigrant workers and labor's social coalitions, rooted in community networks, has been the cornerstone of strategic victories.[8]

In contrast, a number of key unions in Boston largely neglect to build grassroots coalitions in the suburbs and rely mostly on their political insider connections for organizing. The central characteristics of this approach expose a bias toward top-down organizing and the lack of broader social strategies grounded in coalitions with other working-class organizations and communities. This has made it difficult for unions to challenge antiunion employers in the suburbs, where labor lacks political insider status. The weak political position of labor in the suburbs has rendered the top-down organizing approach ineffective and vulnerable in these areas and has exposed a need for grassroots campaigns built on broader community coalitions. But unions in Boston have paid little attention to the latter, leaving businesses' geographical strategy of fleeing to nonunion suburban areas relatively unchallenged.

Many key unions in Boston, such as the janitors union, hotel and restaurant employees union, and building-trades unions, have their membership density heavily concentrated within the central city, although their jurisdiction extends over thousands of unorganized workers in the suburban areas and other outlying central cities. Boston's central city is extremely small relative to other major metropolitan areas, with a little over 10 percent of Boston's residential population living in the city. In particular, the highway belt circumventing Boston— Route 128—has long been a center for a vehemently antiunion and politically far-right-wing high-tech industry, around which office parks and suburban development have exploded. The virtual saturation of development along Route 128 has more recently led to rapid growth along Route 495, a second outer highway that circles the city.[9] In attempting to extend their organizations into the sub-

---

8. For example, the home-care organizing in California involved extensive grassroots organizing prior to any legislative victories. According to Delp and Quan, SEIU Local 434B in Los Angeles organized a massive outreach program, going to senior citizen's centers, doctor's offices, markets, and churches. And through extensive calling and door-to-door outreach, the local was able to sign up twelve thousand workers in less than six months in 1987–88—before the existence of a public employer of record. See Delp and Quan 2002, 1–23.

9. For the politics of Route 128 businesses, see Saxenian 1989, 25–70, and Jonas 1996, 617–34. For the growing move of business development into the Route 495 area, see Horan 1996.

urban markets, unions have sought to parlay their political influence and central-city density into card-check agreements.

Staff from the Carpenters New England Regional Council, for example, have commented on using their downtown clout to force double-breasted contractors into unionizing out-of-town subsidiaries:

> Organizing strategy builds on both top-down pressure and bottom-up mobilization, but the top-down approach is very effective. And there's one single difference from the past. The Boston market was highly unionized, and unions had tremendous political power. So if a contractor wants to come to Boston, he has a perception that he needs to sign a union agreement. Otherwise he has to face all kinds of corporate campaigns that will have negative effects on them. So they think they need to sign on to the agreement in order to avoid the risks. The difference now is that we say, "If you want to come to Boston, you have to sign a state agreement that will cover the New England region."[10]

It is precisely in the suburbs, though, particularly in residential construction—which is now almost completely nonunion—that the building trades have been most soundly defeated by the open shop movement. "Over the course of the 1970s and 1980s, this so-called 'open shop movement' spread from city to city by establishing a foothold in suburban areas and then targeting union strongholds in the center cities" (Safford and Locke 2001, 9). Open shop contractors have had much greater success breaking union hiring halls in the relatively depoliticized, regulation-thin outlying areas and construction markets, where the restricted reach of unions' central city influence represents a real limit on new organizing.

The Justice for Janitors (JfJ) campaign in Boston is another example of union weakness in the suburbs. During the JfJ strike in 2002, SEIU Local 254 members in downtown Boston won a much more substantial pay and benefits increase package than suburban janitors, few of whom were mobilized during the strike. This was the opposite of contracts won for janitors in Los Angeles during a 2000 strike, which provided for larger increases for suburban workers. Perhaps most significantly, the JfJ strike in Boston does not seem to have led to any significant new organizing of janitors in the suburbs, as it has in Los Angeles and in the suburbs of northern New Jersey, where SEIU Local 32BJ has been successfully organizing in order to defend New York City union jobs from capital flight.[11]

The JfJ campaign in Boston has shown the enormous potential for labor community alliances. The Greater Boston Interfaith Organization played a crucial role

10. Interview, Carpenters New England Regional Council staff, October 13, 2003.

11. Blanton, *Boston Globe*, October 25, 2002; Agreement between Maintenance Contractors of New England and SEIU Local 254, *Handbook of Local 254;* and Erickson et al. 2002.

in "bridging" labor and religious organizations and in helping the local union to reach out to church members during the strike. Jobs with Justice played a similar role in linking the union with other community, immigrant, and student organizations. The campaign also gained substantial support from businesses, politicians, and the clergy in pressuring cleaning companies. Community mobilization during the 2002 strike was all the more spectacular because the relationship between the local union and the communities had been hostile under the local's previous leadership. Yet, the historical legacy of the janitors union's entrenched leadership put constraints and limits on the outcome. Because of the long reign of a corrupt leadership, Boston's JfJ campaign was ten years behind many other cities.[12] Thus, while L.A. janitors could win a contract that reduced the initial interregion wage differentials and "equalized pay in several non-core areas" in 2000 (Erickson et al. 2002, 549), which built on their previous gains in 1990 and 1995, Boston's 2002 contract retained and even exacerbated city-suburban wage differentials. Secondly, JfJ strikes have often been translated into organizing drives, particularly in the suburbs. Within half a year of the 2000 strike in Los Angeles, "SEIU had unionized 2,000 workers in nearby Orange County and negotiated new contracts with Silicon Valley's high-tech giants."[13] New York's 32BJ has launched massive organizing drives in the suburbs of New Jersey, winning contracts in most counties there.[14] In contrast, Boston's Local 254 has remained relatively weak in the suburbs, particularly in the antiunion high-tech belt. And two years after the Boston strike, grassroots organizing efforts in the suburbs were still absent. Although the local has stated that their primary goal was organizing the suburban ring that surrounds Route 128, when asked whether there have been efforts to reach out to nonunion workers and to build coalitions with community organizations in targeted suburban areas, staff members reply that such efforts are nonexistent and that they have just started to research who the biggest building owners and contractors in the area are.[15]

A common theme that emerges from these suburban campaigns is that Boston unions are severely constricted by the reach of their political influence. In Boston, HERE has come to rely on the regulation process through which hotel development passes to turn the screws on new building owners, using both political in-

---

12. SEIU Local 254 previously had a corrupt leadership under Eddie Sullivan, which had been an impediment to grassroots mobilization and labor-community alliance. In April 2001, Sullivan was indicted and SEIU's national headquarters placed the local under trusteeship. The backwardness and the initial limits and difficulties of JfJ campaign can be understood in that light, because the local union could launch its JfJ campaign only after the trusteeship.

13. Gaither, *Boston Globe,* October 15, 2002.

14. Barbanel, *New York Times,* September 3, 2003.

15. Interview, SEIU Local 615 (previously Local 254) staff, March 16, 2004.

fluence and the threat of disruptive corporate campaigning. The Carpenters union, likewise, look to unionized downtown developers operating separate nonunion operations in the suburbs as perhaps the most viable targets, due to their political vulnerability in the central city. And perhaps the most significant and successful labor action in Boston for decades, the 2002 Justice for Janitors strike, actually increased pay and benefit inequalities between downtown and suburban office workers and has had no spillover into suburban organizing that might pose a challenge to downtown firms increasingly outsourcing office operations to Route 128 and Route 495 locations. All these cases show that major unions in Boston downplay the importance of building broader social coalitions to overcome their political weakness in the suburbs. Yet, the prevalent political organizations reach the end of their influence in the suburbs. Suburban political bodies, high-tech manufacturing firms, Route 128 office park realtors and building maintenance contractors, and open shop building contractors cannot easily be leveraged from above. Whatever tendrils may link the suburban periphery to its urban core are eagerly grasped, but not all corporate roads lead to Boston, leaving a vast nonunion wasteland of lower-wage jobs with worse benefits outside of the central city.

LABOR POLITICS IN THE CENTRAL CITY

At the level of central city politics—mayoral and city council—labor is not divided along party lines (most city elections are nonpartisan in any case), but a significant division has persisted for many decades between the interests of the building trades and the public sector unions and communities of color. The building-trades unions in Boston typically wield vastly greater resources per member than unions representing low-wage and public sector workers, and a number of the building trades are deeply rooted in the old immigrant communities of Boston, particularly Irish South Boston and the Italian North End (although this has changed dramatically in some of the trades in recent years). Both factors have tended to lend construction unions a much greater voice in local politics and to create a ladder from which officers or representatives of the building trades sometimes move into political office—a ladder that does not exist for other unions in the city. However, the building trades—which over the course of the twentieth century have lost almost all representation in residential construction—are heavily dependent for their existence on public and downtown commercial development projects. Their political orientation has been toward job creation, and they have traditionally formed an important component of the city's "pro-growth coalition" (Mollenkopf 1983)—with an officer from one of the building trades usually the only labor representative on the Boston Redevelopment Authority.

Unlike the 1960s, when neighborhood and community organizing efforts focused on urban renewal in cities like Boston with a severely eroded infrastructure and often unhealthy, unsafe urban environments, community organizing in later decades—after the boom in downtown development and skyrocketing real estate prices—has to a great extent shifted toward new issues: in particular, to resisting the pressures of gentrification and fighting for job access for city residents (Van Meter 2004). Both of these pressures are particularly sharp in Boston, which has one of the highest costs of living in the country due to rent inflation and one of the most suburbanized populations of any large metropolitan area. This has created a commuter economy with extraordinarily high unemployment rates for central city residents, particularly for minority communities. Given this shift, the orientation of community organizations and unions organizing public services and minority-dominated occupations in the city has not always been well aligned with that of the building trades. Minority communities have resisted gentrification or commercial development from infringing on residential areas that might drive up rents or lead to displacement, and organizers from minority neighborhoods have fought to open up construction work to greater employment of nonwhites and Boston residents, a fight that has been carried out both through cooperative efforts and through lawsuits. Although the building trades and the Boston Central Labor Council have tended to dominate city council elections, in recent years community organizers have begun to make inroads in seating local activists as councilors for wards representing communities of color. Both of the recent successful campaigns run by community groups—the election of Chuck Turner of the Greater Roxbury Workers Association and Felix Arroyo of the South End—were won without the support of the construction unions, because of the candidates' history of campaigning for minority job access or opposing certain development initiatives.[16]

Ironically, the one Boston community that has had the greatest success in *opposing* development initiatives that might create gentrification pressures, traffic pollution, or displacement has been Irish South Boston. Time and again, projects planned for Southie have been abandoned when neighborhood politicians brought their weight to bear, while those in other communities have gone forward, even sometimes at the cost of entirely uprooting neighborhoods (Silderberg 1998). This makes the pill of growth-oriented labor politics especially hard to swallow for minority communities and the issue of discriminatory unemployment all the more pressing.

This is not to say that there have been no improvements in labor-community

---

16. Interview, Chuck Turner, March 25, 2004; and conversation with Patrick Keeney, Felix Orroyo's campaign manager, July 23, 2004.

alliances. Organizations such as Jobs with Justice and the Campaign on Contingent Work have made sustained efforts to build bridges between communities and the local labor movement: they played pivotal roles in mobilizing community networks and linking local unions with the minority communities in such campaigns as JfJ and other workers' rights mobilizations.[17] These organizations have not only helped unions in participating in ad-hoc coalitions but have also provided a more permanent basis for labor-community links around such issues as health-care justice, affordable housing, and immigrant workers' rights.[18] Some local unions have started to recognize the need for broader social coalitions and have begun turning toward more strategic alliances with communities. For example, IUE-CWA (International Union of Electronic, Electrical, Salaried, Machine and Furniture Workers–Communications Workers of America) and the Essex County Community Organization jointly created a machinists' training program called E-team "in order to build a strategic alliance between the movement of immigrants and other people of color with the labor movement," and it also "tried to build an alliance with immigrant communities—largely Dominicans who will be affected by hotel construction projects—to get both freedom of organizing when hotels will be built and union construction when they build hotels."[19] The health care union, SEIU 2020, has also started to work in a more sustained fashion with the Greater Boston Interfaith Organization on an affordable housing campaign,[20] and the Bricklayers union has worked with communities of color to open up their membership to minorities and to initiate and support affordable housing initiatives in the Roxbury area. The Painters union recently made some progress in building a coalition with communities of color.[21] But these examples have been exceptions and the labor-community relationship has remained a contentious and strained one. Often, many local unions that have been strongholds of local labor power have not had a strong history of coalition politics outside of their ranks or social movement–style activism, except when their interests are directly threatened. Labor has a great deal of power in Boston, but it is by no means monolithic at the local level. In general, the unions that have had the greatest political influence at the local level have downplayed the importance of sustained grassroots community coalitions and leaned more toward a "political insider strategy" to exert their power.

---

17. Interview with Elaine Bernard, director of the Harvard Trade Union Program, March 18, 2003.

18. Interview with Russ Davis, director of Massachusetts Jobs with Justice, October 15, 2003, and with Jason Pramas, Campaign on Contingent Work, October 17, 2003.

19. Interview with Jeff Crosby, president of IUE-CWA and North Shore Central Labor Council, October 15, 2003.

20. Interview, SEIU Local 2020 staff, March 13, 2004.

21. Interview, Chuck Turner, March 25, 2004.

Why has the labor movement in Boston relied on a political coalition strategy and not made greater strides toward progressive revitalization? If elected officials present an "opportunity structure" for unions, why do they appear not to have taken advantage of that opportunity? First, some unions have based their political power on strategic alliances with otherwise antiunion and unquestionably antiwelfare politicians. Some have adopted such political alliances as their primary organizing tool, while others, not oriented toward organizing, have used them as leverage for contract bargaining. But this pursuit of the "issues"—so narrowly defined—has contributed to a long Republican reign along with its hostile labor policy, deregulation measures, privatization, tax cutting and retrenchment on social spending, fragmenting the local labor movement.

Second, the neoliberal climate in Massachusetts has put constraints on many public service unions and communities of color, undermining organizing efforts that require expansion or defense of the public sphere. These unions instead have fought defensive battles against privatization and cuts in social services and welfare.

Third, and particularly at the city level, there is often a division between labor organizations with "political power" and unions oriented toward social organizing. This is not only true among unions but between communities of color and certain unions. These divisions have revolved around the politics of urban growth and the lack of any mechanism for addressing dramatically discriminatory unemployment levels in the central city.

Virtually all unions have adopted the rhetoric of revitalization, along with the organizing imperative preached from the AFL-CIO since the election of John Sweeney. Unions such as SEIU Local 2020 are following their international unions' guidelines for allocation of organizing resources:

> In 1999–2000, we switched a lot of our resources. We were probably thirty staff and we had one to two organizers back in 1998–99; only 5 percent of our money went towards organizing. In 1999–2000 we made decisions to move to 10, 15, 20, so now 23 percent of all my staff and resources goes towards organizing. So it's a conscious commitment and that's why you see the growth because we put the money towards organizing. . . . We have eight full-time organizers out of thirty staff.[22]

When asked what their primary goal is, almost all union leaders and staff interviewed answer unanimously that it is "organizing." Why then haven't there been any significant organizing gains recently? Are there any particular aspects of organizing strategies that differentiate Boston locals from others? Again, does it have something to do with Boston's politics of labor?

---

22. Interview, SEIU Local 2020 staff, March 13, 2004.

At this rhetorical level we find what Voss and Sherman label a "new tactical repertoire" in this region, too, including the use of card-check recognition, strategic targeting, corporate campaigns, disruptive direct action, and community alliances (Voss and Sherman 2000). This "tactical revitalization" has often been praised as a mark of "rank-and-file member activism." But most unions that have put greater resources into organizing have not necessarily shifted these resources toward bottom-up strategies. In "reinvesting in organizing," many unions in Boston have shifted organizing resources into *research* capacity, for purposes of strategic targeting, which reflects the top-down strategic orientation toward organizing dominant in the area.

The prevalent organizing model in Boston still involves pressuring strategically targeted employers to sign on to union agreements and offering to support the employers' political and developmental goals in exchange for neutrality or open support. In this picture, grassroots membership organizing is only secondary and sporadic, concentrated during contract campaigns if at all.

FOCUS ON GRASSROOTS ORGANIZING AND CAMPAIGNING

We have tried to understand the particular characteristics of the Boston-area labor movement by examining how local unions have strategically interacted with the politics of metropolitan governance. We have emphasized specific problems connected to the embedded characteristics of regional unionism.

First, we found that many unions have increasingly turned to "political collective bargaining" practices, which involve short-term deals with politicians, often at the expense of public sector unions and the communities of color that have suffered under the governance of elected officials because of privatization and the retrenchment of social welfare. Such practices have long characterized a number of the building trades, but a much broader range of national unions have begun supporting political bargaining strategies among their locals. The group of unions that in 2005 split from the AFL-CIO and formed a parallel Change to Win federation share this political orientation. At roughly the same time, the leadership of the AFL-CIO supported moves toward a political bargaining approach, in part to secure support from the Firefighters union at the biannual convention at which the competing national union groups were expected to contest the AFL-CIO presidency.[23]

---

23. On the Change to Win coalition, see Hurd 2004, 5–25; on the AFL-CIO, see Josh Gerstein, "AFL-CIO President Vows to Reach Out to Republicans," *New York Sun,* June 7, 2005.

Second, we examined how local unions have combined this political strategy with a strategic orientation toward top-down organizing. The experiences of other regional labor movements have shown that grassroots organizing methods were central to the success of suburban organizing. In Boston, however, unions have downplayed the importance of organizing at the periphery and have largely abandoned the suburban areas to an unregulated, nonunion, lower-wage political economy. Although some unions have made organizing the suburbs a goal, most lack the grassroots approach that we believe will be essential for successful organizing at the periphery.

Third, the tension between organized labor and Boston community and minority organizations has slowed the emergence of innovative initiatives aimed at progressive revitalization with a wider geographic focus. This has led to a disjunction between the need for a sustained labor-community alliance and organizing that relies heavily on a top-down political approach that often hurts the communities needed as allies. Grassroots community and worker mobilization, while having shown its potential for revitalization, has still largely remained sporadic.

To rebuild a local labor movement on a progressive urban social agenda, we need to turn our attention to these problems of geography, business strategy, and the potential for labor and community groups to undermine one another in developing fight-back strategies. For unions, intensive grassroots organizing and campaigning seem to have shown the potential for overcoming many of these obstacles of the metropolitan political landscape, from penetration of the suburbs to sustained community mobilization around social campaigns.

6

TWO PATHS TO THE HIGH ROAD

The Dynamics of Coalition Building
in Seattle and Buffalo

Ian Greer, Barbara Byrd, and Lou Jean Fleron

Labor-community coalitions are not a new concept. Unions approach such coalitions now, as in the past, as one way to enhance their bargaining power with an employer. Such coalitions are temporary and often issue based. In recent years, however, some local labor movements have begun to look at coalitions more broadly, as a means of improving their public image and building power in the political arena. This broad-based approach requires the development of coalitions for the longer run, not just for temporary expediency. In this chapter we develop the notion of a high-road social infrastructure as a way to understand how union leaders develop and sustain coalitions and find the resources they need to succeed in shaping economic development priorities for the region.

We define the "high road" as a path of economic development that provides a high level of worker rights, skill investment, and wages and benefits. Ideally, high-road businesses thrive by producing high-quality products and services. In exchange for high productivity and a commitment to innovation, employers have to pay high wages, provide good benefits, and invest in training. The low road, by contrast, is a pattern of employer behavior that seeks competitiveness by lowering wages and shifting costs and risks onto workers. Because businesses do not usually pursue high-road strategies on their own, unions and public policymakers have to establish a framework of rules and organizational structures to regulate economic development in a way that closes off the low road and builds the high road.

Case study evidence suggests that union efforts to promote high-road regional economic development are widespread in the global North. David Reynolds, for example, draws on the European experience to make sense of labor's high-road projects in U.S. urban regions (2002). Bruce Nissen (2004) takes the concept further in his discussion of the politics of coalition building, with an argument that unions should establish independent structures to carry out local high-road projects that, to some extent, allow the community to take the lead. Others have discussed central labor councils (Ness and Eimer 2001) and labor educators (Fricke and Totterdill 2004) as advocates of the high road. These studies emphasize the importance of organization building outside the structures of local unions as helpful in using coalitions to shape economic development.

Individual unionists acting as political entrepreneurs play a central role in most stories of coalition building. Fred Rose (2000) calls the leaders that stitch together coalitions "bridge builders." These leaders are comfortable in activist situations outside of the union's organizational boundaries and, in many cases, have personal histories in other social movements. Coalition work does not require a "natural" community of interest; instead, it requires that leaders reframe issues and strengthen their personal relationships with activists in other social movements, in order to build coalitions across class, race, and other lines. This process requires a "strategic choice" of union leaders.

Union leaders, however, tend to move on, and coalitions are too often temporary. Typically, the shared work of social action in committees or joint campaigns is the glue that holds coalitions together, and thus these coalitions survive only as long as all sides perceive the need to work together on concrete ongoing issues. Labor's lasting contribution to a region, however, can be sustained when coalition work becomes institutionalized. This is more likely to occur when unions and their partners set up organizations with paid staff to develop and administer projects to coordinate the shared work. Such semiautonomous organizations work outside the structure of unions and can therefore carry out projects that would be impossible if a single union were in charge. The common work of steering the organization through a governing board and carrying out the organization's ongoing projects provides the glue that keeps labor together with its community allies.

Institutionalizing coalition activity is important because it creates a basis for further work through what Lowell Turner calls "spillovers" (2004a). Observers of social movements have shown that campaigns, revolutions, and other popular mobilizations occur in causally connected sequences (Tarrow, McAdam, and Tilly 2001). For example, the 1999 protests in Seattle against the World Trade Organization brought activists together in new ways. Over the next few years, they organized a series of international demonstrations and domestic campaigns. In local politics, different events or campaigns are likewise interrelated. Individual protests or campaigns can have spillovers on their own; organizations, with full-time staff managing projects, carrying out research, writing grants, lobbying, and maintaining community ties, can create spillovers over a long period by launching projects and carrying out long-term relationship building. This cycle of organization building and spillovers, catalyzed by individual union leaders, is the process through which high-road social infrastructures emerge.

Can sustained coalitions contribute to rebuilding the labor movement? Can they help overcome well-known problems of uninspired leadership, lack of concern for new organizing, and blindness to broad community concerns? The literature on union revitalization has documented exceptions to the rule, where unions have reoriented themselves around organizing (Fantasia and Voss 2004; Voss and Sherman 2000; Bronfenbrenner et al. 1998) or broad community concerns (Frege, Heery, and Turner 2004; Milkman 2002). Although these studies pose the problem well, they have either lacked a normative dimension (revitalization for what?) or treated coalitions as part of the intuitively powerful but hard-to-define phenomenon of revitalization. In this chapter, we find unions building infrastructures to engage with the economic development problems of their regions, in a way, however, that does not address the problem of declining membership.

In the rest of the chapter we will examine this process in two very different cities: Seattle and Buffalo. Seattle is an affluent, politically progressive city struggling with the contradictions of growth; Buffalo is a politically paralyzed city facing deindustrialization and population decline. Barriers to success, such as a past of labor-community conflict, a one-sided probusiness orientation in local government, and the problems of racial segregation and deindustrialization, exist in both cities. Nevertheless, unionists, with an eye to coalitions and organization building, have reframed these barriers as problems to be solved. Drawing on cases from our earlier work (Greer and Fleron 2005; Byrd and Greer 2005), we conclude by discussing the parallels of infrastructure building in the two cities. The Seattle-Buffalo comparison shows that infrastructure building can work as a response to very different economic development challenges in very different political contexts.

SEATTLE

Seattle is a growing urban region with major concentrations of aerospace, transportation, and research-related jobs. The metropolitan area has added about two hundred thousand jobs during the past ten years, mainly in the service and transportation industries, spurring an explosion in nonunion work. The University of Washington, the Port of Seattle, Boeing, and Microsoft have been the central hubs of economic activity, serving as employers and attracting other firms. The largest unions are the International Brotherhood of Teamsters, Boeing unions (International Association of Machinists [IAM] and Seattle Professional Engineering Employees' Association [SPEEA], which is part of the International Federation of Professional and Technical Engineers), public sector unions (NEA, AFSCME, SEIU, and IFPTE), construction trades unions (IBEW and others), and service unions (SEIU, UFCW, and UNITE HERE). In recent years, new locals have emerged to organize the growing precarious workforce, including graduate employees (UAW), home-care workers (SEIU), and technology workers (CWA-WashTech).

Although the economy as a whole has grown substantially in recent years, the manufacturing sector, especially waterfront-oriented industries such as shipbuilding, have struggled. In many of the growing industries, temporary, part-time, and low-wage work has replaced unionized, full-time, middle-income jobs. The challenge for unions has been primarily to retain "good" jobs and to organize the new work that employers have created. They have been doing so primarily through a revitalized central labor council, the King County Labor Council (KCLC), which has engaged in coalitions around immediate union fights (initially via Jobs with Justice and eventually via its own internal Union Cities program), around economic development policy (via the Worker Center, AFL-CIO), around global justice issues (via the WTO protests and subsequent fair trade efforts), and around local elections (in coalition with environmental and other groups). Although the effect on union density has been modest at best, the effect on politics and policymaking has been dramatic (Byrd and Greer 2005).

Seattle is historically an AFL town, with both strong conservative and progressive currents. Old AFL unions continue their predominance in service, construction, transportation, and manufacturing industries. Progressivism stretches back to the Seattle Central Labor Council of the early twentieth century, which operated a daily newspaper and organized the 1919 general strike. Despite heroic moments, the events played into the hands of a right-wing populist mayor and left the labor movement deeply divided between progressivism and a rising tide of business unionism. During the 1920s, Seattle native Dave Beck began to organize workers in transport and related sectors into Teamsters locals throughout the West, using control over deliveries to win recognition. Beck formed close ties with the business community to "stabilize" sectors where union members worked and distributed the proceeds of the local monopolies as higher wages. Conservatism continued to dominate through the civil rights era, as AFL-CIO leaders joined the building trades to resist demands for racial equality in hiring (from the community, from federal judges, and from the Republican governor and county executive).

The waves of union defeats and plant closures during the 1970s and 1980s, however, created a political will for change. Slowly, nonprofits organizing around environmental and civil rights issues emerged, engaging unions as adversaries or setting up worker organizations outside the unions. In 1993, Ron Judd assumed leadership of the KCLC. Having served as an organizer for the local electricians union (IBEW Local 46) and then head of the local building trades council, Judd already had experience dealing with difficult issues through coalitions. At Local 46, for example, he had worked with environmentalists to halt a major nonunion factory construction project.

As head of the building trades council, Judd worked to heal relations with the minority community and participate in economic development using the mechanism of the project labor agreement (PLA). By building a coalition involving owners of projects, community groups, and unions, supported over time by the KCLC, he began to engage the minority community around issues of job access. With support from the Port of Seattle, a long process began in which the building-trades council built cooperation between community groups, craft unions, governments, and employers to desegregate the trades. Public owners of projects, such as the port and the city of Seattle, found that they could introduce new regulations into project labor agreements that would facilitate connections between public works and raising purchasing power in low-income neighborhoods. The hiring rules in the PLAs provided employment opportunities for unionized workers and shut out contractors without apprentices, while making exceptions for nonunion minority contractors (and, they claimed, the opportunity to organize these contractors). By the early 2000s, project labor agreements requiring minimum levels of apprenticeship labor, and setting targets for female and minority hiring were common on large public and private projects. The same activists who had sued the building trades in the 1970s over discrimination were now working with the trades to enforce apprenticeship and diversity standards.

Within a year of joining the KCLC, Judd coordinated a series of high-profile actions in conjunction with Jobs with Justice. In May 1993, he led a demonstration at the local NLRB office against the board's ineffectiveness in enforcing labor law, in which he was arrested. Soon thereafter, the KCLC threw its weight behind a contract battle at Alaska Airlines using CHAOS (Create Havoc in Our System) sickouts, a campaign that included the arrests of twenty-five activists at the firm's Seattle headquarters. The council's attention then turned to U.S. Senator Slade Gorton, who supported legislation making it easier for companies to permanently replace striking workers. One hundred activists, including several "permanently replaced" flight attendants, disrupted the opening ceremony of his new local office. In March 1994, the council cemented its reputation by organizing two hundred activists to invade a business-sponsored celebration of the North American Free Trade Agreement (NAFTA). Jobs with Justice and KCLC continued this pattern of "street heat" throughout the 1990s, by supporting a pair of enormous strikes at Boeing, a musicians' strike, and the WTO protests (Rosenblum 2001).

Judd also incorporated the Worker Center into the KCLC, which came to serve a lobbying and policy development function. The WC had been organized in 1986 by a coalition of labor, religious, and other community groups to fight plant closures and layoffs in the wood products and shipbuilding industries. Judd saw it as a vehicle for policy development and research on issues of economic and workforce development. Promoting a vision for giving economically disadvantaged workers increased opportunities in the unionized sector, Judd won support from existing WC funders and the national AFL-CIO. With the building trades, the WC has helped to develop apprenticeship utilization and project labor agreements at the Port of Seattle and elsewhere. More recently, the WC helped a coalition of port unions respond to the port's threat to end a decades-long policy of multiemployer collective bargaining covering nine hundred HERE members. The WC produced a study arguing for an employment policy for the 6,740 employees of subcontracted service providers at the airport, including expedited organizing campaigns, job security, stable contracting relations, wage minimums, training, and career ladders. The port eventually agreed to retain collective bargaining. Clean energy has also been on the WC's agenda, and it has supported Washington's Apollo Alliance, a coalition of unions and environmental organizations that promotes job-friendly ecological energy policies.

Perhaps the high point of the Judd years came with the 1999 World Trade Organization protests, conducted by a massive coalition dealing with much bigger issues than the previous campaigns (Levi and Olson 2000). The coalition included the full spectrum of organizations critical of the one-sided business orientation of the world's trade regime. Rather than taking on a specific employer, politician, or public agency, these protests targeted the WTO as a symbol and agent of globalization. The KCLC's decision to push for massive labor involvement in the protests grew out of the ongoing concern of the WC and the KCLC about the impact of international trade on jobs and working conditions in the highly trade dependent Seattle area. In a strategic move that won practical assistance as well as credibility from the national labor movement, Judd convinced the AFL-CIO leadership in Washington, D.C., to commit substantial staff and financial resources to the effort. To do so, he had to convince the AFL-CIO that the community coalition itself was a legitimate organization in Seattle and worth supporting, even though at times labor would have to bend to the will of the larger group.

The opportunity to work with other organizations in preparing for the protest was seen by Judd and others as a way to solidify existing coalition-building activities. Beginning in the early summer of 1999, meetings of interested organizations took place at the KCLC's headquarters building. The Direct Action Network, the Ruckus Society, the Sierra Club, the Citizen's Trade Campaign, the Labor and Employment Law Office (LELO), and the Church Council of Greater Seattle all worked together in the months leading up to the meeting. They honed the message and organized the logistics for a fifty thousand person demonstration, which eventually turned into a gathering of almost one hundred thousand demonstrators from the western United States and Canada.

Despite disagreements over tactics, the anti-WTO coalition made a lasting difference for the KCLC. The planning and the tension-filled week of the protests created durable and long-lasting personal relationships between labor activists and their partners. Involvement in the WTO led the KCLC, for example, to support Jubilee 2000, as a way to deepen ties with activist leaders from the faith community and their congregations. It set the stage for a future blue-green political effort (blue for labor, green for environmentalists) to elect new commissioners for the Port of Seattle. The KCLC's involvement also strengthened its ability to do internal education, to educate its affiliates on trade issues, to mobilize large numbers of activists, and to build leadership skills among its staff.

After Judd's departure in 2000 to become Western Regional Director of the AFL-CIO, Steve Williamson took over as the KCLC's leader. Williamson had been an organizer for SEIU and the Teamsters prior to becoming active in the KCLC during the WTO protests. His contribution was to refocus the council's coalition activities around political campaigns. Although the labor council had been politically active during the 1990s and supported such initiatives as the 1998 statewide minimum wage increase, Williamson refined the council's candidate endorsement and member mobilization practices to involve more members. He hired a political director, first from the Nevada AFL-CIO, then from Washington Conservation Voters. The KCLC's new approach, coordinated with the state AFL-CIO, emphasized more systematic member mobilization for voter turnout, targeting of union members in canvassing, alliances with environmental groups in political campaigns, and more accountability for endorsed candidates.

The KCLC first tried out the new political strategy in the port commission and mayoral races of 2001. Tensions between labor and the port had become apparent over organizing rights and outsourcing fights. At the same time, environmental groups were coming into conflict with the port over its construction practices. As a labor-management partnership unraveled, the port commission began to oppose labor's initiatives on a regular basis. The KCLC responded by targeting normally uncontested port commissioner races. Using a new approach designed to develop a consensus of affiliates, KCLC held candidate interviews with rank-and-file union members, who unanimously rejected the incumbents. Lawrence Molloy from Washington Conservation Voters won labor's support with his advocacy of a new airport runway as part of his sustainability platform. Molloy won the KCLC endorsement and, with the support of unions and environmentalists, beat his opponent by a narrow margin. Molloy became the first reliable labor vote on the commission, and the KCLC's support for him reinvigorated labor's ties with the environmental community. In 2003 the council repeated this performance, electing Alec Fisken. In 2005, in an effort to win a third seat on the commission and therefore exercise a majority, the president of the Building Trades Council, Peter Coates, sought one of three open slots. Unfortunately, Coates was eliminated in the primary.

The 2001 mayor's race was a clear victory for KCLC and its allies. In the primary, the council endorsed challenger Greg Nickels for mayor over incumbent Paul Schell and City Attorney Mark Sidran. This endorsement lacked the consensus within the house of labor that had characterized the port commission race, since unions of city workers had good relations with Schell. After Schell lost in the primary, leaders of these unions viewed Sidran as more likely to carry on Schell's cooperative labor relations approach. Other KCLC affiliates opposed Sidran, who as city attorney had prosecuted anti-WTO protestors and had allegedly ignored claims of unfair treatment by women workers in the city attorney's office. The KCLC threw its muscle into the race behind Nickels, who won the runoff election by a razor-thin margin, which he credited to labor. Nickels subsequently began pushing initiatives in cooperation with the KCLC and its affiliates, including promotion of affordable housing, cooperation with the Immigrant Workers Freedom Ride, advocacy of project labor agreements, and a letter of support for striking grocery store workers.

As of mid-2006, Seattle's economy seems, once again, to be booming. Due to years of reforms and the electoral success of the Democrats in 2004, labor now has unprecedented access to public officials at the city, county, and state levels. It remains to be seen, however, how unions will take advantage of their channels of insider access in the state legislature and county and city councils. Furthermore, it is unclear how this new power can be sustained, much less translated into a regionwide strategy, given the 2005 split in the national AFL-CIO and subsequent loss of affiliates by the KCLC. Finally, the political gains are hardly a sure thing, even when the infrastructure is in place, as illustrated by the defeat of labor's third candidate for the port commission in the 2005 primary, amid a backlash from the business community. The KCLC has also faced another shift in leadership: In late 2005, Steve Williamson resigned to work for the UFCW local. Dave Freiboth, the former President of the Inland Boatman's Union, has taken his place and faces the challenge of rebuilding the KCLC's political program with a smaller affiliate base and renewing and further developing its coalition work.

The biggest limitation of the KCLC's efforts has been the link to organizing. Judd and Williamson tried to connect the coalition-building work of the KCLC, Worker Center, and Jobs with Justice to organizing new workers. In 1997, the national AFL-CIO created the Union Cities program, and Seattle found itself a center of the new organizing push. Leaders identified the role of the KCLC in supporting organizing as mobilizing members to support affiliate campaigns and research and training. The KCLC executive board hired a full-time Union Cities organizer who worked with affiliates to build their capacity to turn out allies and union members in support of campaigns. It also created a multiunion organizing body called Seattle Union Now, which lasted a bit over two years but folded amid interunion squabbles around the time Judd left. Despite the many successes, such as the stronger ties to the broader community and the improved access to local government, as well as Judd's personal role in advocating a shift of resources to organizing, the central labor council and its associated structures never spurred any push into the new economy that attracted many members, with the exception of a few specific worker groups such as graduate students at the University of Washington.

Seattle's high-road infrastructure is a case of organized labor coming to terms with the local politics associated with the globalization of manufacturing, services, and distribution. The KCLC has played a central role by organizing around these substantive issues and thereby winning new channels of influence in the region. In workforce development, unions used the building boom to heal their relations with the minority community and innovate in neighborhood economic development policy. In electoral politics, unions have strengthened both membership involvement and community cooperation; the successful outcomes have created new channels of insider influence. These coalition-building efforts are not merely ad hoc marriages of convenience but are part of an overall growth of organizations and relationships that, because of ongoing spillover effects from one project to another, has lasted nearly two decades. With no end in sight to Seattle's development boom and a string of visible payoffs from coalition work, organized labor is positioned to play a role in shaping the city's future.

BUFFALO

Buffalo is a union town facing a crisis due to job loss, social polarization, and population decline. Between 1956 and 2000, Buffalo lost 125,000 out of more than 200,000 manufacturing jobs, including the region's largest private employer, Bethlehem Steel, which employed 20,000 workers at its peak. The machinists, steel, textile, printing, and chemical unions were hit especially hard. With these industries virtually gone, the most important employers are in the public sector, health care, and several large auto plants. The largest unions are thus in these sectors: AFSCME, American Federation of Teachers (AFT), CWA, SEIU, Teamsters, and the UAW, plus the building trades.

In response to failed economic development policies, unions have stepped in and built several organizations to fill the vacuum. Buffalo's unions have pursued both community coalitions and labor-management partnerships to deal with economic decline. Mobilizing against plant closures and cooperating with management to keep plants competitive are the two dominant union strategies, at times used simultaneously by the same unions. The new initiatives discussed here emerged not through the central labor council but largely as a spillover from social movement unionist and labor-management partnership initiatives.

Most of Buffalo's major unions were organized during the CIO upsurge of the 1930s. Before the decade of the Wagner Act and sit-down strikes, Buffalo had a reputation as a nonunion town. The weakness of AFL unions outside of the skilled trades and transport sectors helped attract such major employers as Bethlehem Steel, Westinghouse, Ford, and General Motors. After a tumultuous period of organizing, marked by violent clashes between employers and workers (McDonnell 1970), Buffalo became one of the most strongly unionized cities in the country. The 1949 Bell Aircraft strike was a victory of nationwide importance in labor's drive for employer-provided pension benefits, and by the 1970s Buffalo was also one of the most strike-prone cities. During the 1980s, Buffalo's union leaders played a leading role in the national Solidarity Day protests against the Reagan administration.

Buffalo's chief problems are deindustrialization and population decline, and neither politics nor free enterprise has served Buffalo very well in dealing with them. The "Queen City of the Great Lakes," once an economic powerhouse and the country's tenth biggest city, is reeling from global competition, shifts of population and jobs to the Sunbelt, and state policies that fail to stop the hemorrhage. Since 1970, the Buffalo-Niagara region has lost two hundred thousand residents, and since 1950 Buffalo's population has declined by more than half. In the public sector, a declining tax base has forced the city and county governments to lay off thousands of workers, despite a growing need for public services and good jobs. As the population has dispersed into the suburbs, social inequality has deepened. A racially diverse urban core with high unemployment and poverty rates has emerged, as the relatively affluent and overwhelmingly white suburbs have grown. This polarization and decline (Goldman 1983; Taylor 1990) has led to a search for public investment from the state and federal governments and a colorful local politics of Rockefeller Republicanism, tax revolts, and economic nationalism.

Union-driven high-road economic development projects have a different flavor in Buffalo than in Seattle. Rather than emerging from a vibrant CLC interested in challenging corporate globalization, Buffalo's projects are driven by a network of pragmatic activists fighting for jobs. Job retention has involved contentious campaigns, such as the one in the late 1980s to prevent auto parts maker

Trico from moving its assembly jobs to Mexico, a campaign that led to the creation of the local Jobs with Justice affiliate. Nevertheless, Buffalo also played a pioneering role in the growth of labor-management cooperation. The Buffalo Area Labor-Management Committee, Western New York Employee Involvement Council, and the Cornell University ILR extension have played a role in promoting labor-management partnership locally, especially in large local factories. By the late 1990s, Buffalo had unusually cooperative labor-management relations (Fleron, Stanger, and Patton 2000).

The union leaders who have pushed Buffalo's economic development projects have come out of these community and labor-management initiatives. For example, Kevin Donovan had led a union at a local General Motors owned forge (UAW Local 846). After threats of closure, GM sold the forge, along with several other axle-related plants to a newly formed company, American Axle and Manufacturing. Donovan's local union worked with local managers to make production more efficient, increase local employment, and establish a new facility (albeit under a somewhat lower wage scheme). Another bridge builder is Richard Lipsitz Jr., an antiwar and civil rights activist who had worked for several local unions, including a health care local (which is now part of SEIU) and the Teamsters. He had helped create a local multiunion initiative to provide low-cost health insurance and coordinated an international campaign of the Teamsters to fight job losses in the warehousing sector.

Around the same time, the business community announced a new regional marketing initiative, known as the Buffalo Niagara Enterprise. Along with a broadly representative group of regional labor leaders, Lipsitz and Donovan helped to initiate labor's response, a union-governed economic development organization, the Economic Development Group (EDG). By 2000, the EDG had a full-time coordinator, Phil Wilcox (political action officer of a utility IBEW local), who proposed a series of projects with ambitious goals, big budgets, and multiyear timelines. The projects addressed energy, housing, brownfields restoration, and workforce development issues, and required several years of proposing, planning, and coalition building before implementation. In 2002, the EDG became a chartered nonprofit corporation, hired a professional grant writer as its executive director, and by 2004 was launching some of the proposed projects.

After the formation of EDG, Donovan and Wilcox became involved in a local committee to rework the rules of electricity provision in the region. The New York Power Authority (NYPA) had operated a hydroelectric power plant in Niagara Falls for nearly fifty years. Under the terms of a federally issued license, NYPA had been required to provide inexpensive power to local industry. The authority announced its intention to renew its license in a consensual way, in order to avoid legal fees, sparking a complex set of negotiations. As cochair of the committee,

Donovan worked to build agreement among a wide range of stakeholders (mainly city and county governments, Indian tribes, environmentalists, and business and union interests). At stake were maintaining the flow of cheap power to the region's key employers and distributing NYPA's surplus revenues from the hydropower plant (amounting to $500 million a year) into community development projects and cash-strapped local governments.

Another of EDG's projects, District Energy, aims to reduce costs and pollution while creating local jobs through a new downtown heating scheme. In April 2001, the city government announced its intention to develop a district energy system modeled on a new biomass heat plant in St. Paul, Minnesota, and facilities common in European cities. Buffalo's city council named EDG as the developer of choice for the project. Organizers estimated energy cost reductions of as much as 40 percent for downtown businesses, hospitals, government agencies, the public schools, and housing projects.

Under the new scheme, local farmers would produce energy crops to fuel the plant, which would pollute less than the current system. The new facility was projected to create a handful of skilled jobs downtown in a new nonprofit corporation. By 2006, this promising project remained stalled in political negotiations and its objectives had been scaled down to EDG's attempt to take over the existing downtown energy loop.

Training has also been on the EDG agenda. The local building-trades unions established an urban construction training program under the terms of a PLA for a new billion-dollar state-funded project of the Buffalo public schools. The PLA mandated contributions from contractors on the project into a pre-apprenticeship program that would bring minority youth into the building trades' apprenticeship programs. After a high-profile start, the complexity of the training project proved to be beyond the capability of the building trades. EDG took over the pre-apprenticeship funding attached to the school PLA and renamed the effort the Buffalo Niagara Jobs Initiative. It works as a network, connecting training providers to trainees in minority communities (mainly black and Latino). The craft unions provide on-the-job training in urban residential housing rehabilitation for trainees who then go on to union apprenticeship programs, higher education, or residential construction jobs. The building trades have been pushed by their local community, including other unionists, to change their hiring practices and the racial profile of their membership, in order to boost wages in low-income communities.

Through the EDG, unions created an organization to undertake development projects directly. There is, however, a second aspect of the strategy. Buffalo's unions follow a "two-lane high road" strategy that includes collaboration with willing progressive employers in the region through the Champions Network

(Fleron and Applegate 2004). The network emerged from the 2000 report *Champions at Work* and is organized around specific development projects. The staff of the local Cornell ILR office and two recently retired union officials from the IAM and the OPEIU provide organizational support to the network, which is directed by a volunteer steering committee of labor and management representatives.

Organized by the local ILR office, the *Champions* report presented original survey results and case studies of local employers to augment the regional marketing activities of the Buffalo Niagara Enterprise. The representative survey supported claims that the region's highly skilled, unionized workforce had advantages for potential investors in terms of labor peace and innovative work practices. The report's fifteen case studies were based on extensive taped and transcribed interviews with business owners, human resource managers, and union officials, undertaken by a team of labor and management volunteers under the direction of Cornell ILR researchers (Fleron, Stanger, and Patton 2000). The interview process and supplemental research to complete the case studies created relationships among the employer, union, and university participants, forming the basis of the Champions Network. Funded by the region's delegation to the state legislature, the report was released at a public event attended by civic, business, and union leaders.

In 2003, Cornell ILR staff revived the Champions Network, conducting separate labor and business focus groups to identify common concerns about local economic development strategies. In a subsequent joint meeting, union and business leaders established three areas in which they thought they should work together on the region's challenges. One focus area, headed by an official from the CWA and a manager from a health insurer, concerns economic development policy. They have consulted with heads of the region's industrial development agencies about how to improve economic development incentives. A second project, chaired by a local beverage distributor and the head of the teachers union, promotes voter registration and civic involvement and uses the workplace as a forum to get out the vote and focus political attention on the shared needs of companies and workers. The third arena, on "regional image," is cochaired by a retired representative from the OPEIU and a manager from a large telecommunications firm. They provide support for the "Believe in Buffalo Niagara" campaign, initiated by a local surgeon, to collect one hundred thousand signatures on a letter touting the region's virtues and dynamism. Once collected, organizers plan to send the letter to several hundred consultants and CEOs responsible for investment decisions and to get supporting letters from high-level politicians. This project attracted broad initial support, although without adequate structure for timely implementation, it remains in the signature-collection phase.

Evolving labor-management networks continue to generate new projects.

Cornell ILR recognizes examples of high-road job creation and retention through local in-plant partnership by its annual Champions @ Work Award. The first recipient, in 2004, was the local Ford plant and UAW Local 897, whose jointly governed production improvements brought representatives from all of Ford's North American plants to the area for a meeting of the Lean Implementation Network. The 2005 prize went to a locally based baseball cap manufacturer, New Era Cap, and CWA Local 14177, which, after a nearly yearlong strike and boycott, turned the business around with a labor-management partnership that has improved productivity, developed high-value niche market products, and secured corporate compliance with international labor rights accords.

In partnership with Cornell ILR, the network also plays an educational role, teaching the business community the value of organized labor and promoting a better understanding of mutual concerns. The resulting change in attitude has led, for example, to BNE officials referring prospective investors worried about unionization to union leaders involved in the network. In February 2004, Cornell and the Champions Network hosted a "high-road economics" conference attended by 160 union, community, and business leaders that featured presentations by union leaders from San Jose, Milwaukee, and Pittsburgh as well as the CWA's national president, Morton Bahr. Participants exchanged best-practice ideas from around the country, prompting further debate and enthusiasm and strengthening the relationships with community organizations beyond labor and management.

More recently, representatives from the Apollo Alliance, local unions, interested businesses, environmental groups, and energy experts gathered at a Cornell ILR Champions conference to explore the importance of the renewable energy sector for the future growth of the area's economy. The IBEW utility local continues to build partnerships for innovative energy technologies, collaborating with NRG Energy, Inc., in 2006 on a $1.8 billion investment in a new coal gasification plant at their electric generation facility just north of Buffalo. The United Steelworkers are also taking leadership roles in local blue-green partnerships for sustainable energy and energy conservation.

Alongside the dialogue between labor and business leaders, another channel of influence has emerged to promote mobilization and social justice. The Coalition for Economic Justice (CEJ) originally formed in the Trico campaign of the late 1980s and later affiliated with Jobs with Justice. CEJ organizes community support for union struggles, workers rights, and progressive public policies such as the living wage, health care reform, and accountable development initiatives. Governed by a board of union and religious leaders, its staff connects unions with the region's broader forces of progressivism.

In recent years, CEJ and its Workers Rights Board have supported local and national struggles, including several local strikes. Grievances from local hospitals and from national targets Wal-Mart and textile services firm Cintas were aired at the first Workers Rights Board meeting in 2004. They have assisted in rally turnout, most recently for city workers, nurses, and Adelphia workers. They also supported workers at an Oregon dairy farm owned by Buffalo-based Sorrento Lactalis. The Workers Rights Board awarded Sorrento its Grinch of the Year award for refusing to negotiate with workers. CEJ also supported New Era Cap strikers in 2001–02, in conjunction with a nationwide network of student labor activists, United Students against Sweatshops.

The CEJ led the living wage campaign by building broad support for the measure and getting help from local union activists. In 1999, the Buffalo City Council passed an ordinance mandating that government contractors pay a living wage (now $9.03 an hour with health insurance or $10.15 without). Because of fiscal problems, however, the city never enforced the ordinance. CEJ and Citizen Action of New York sued the city and, in 2003, won new language to delegate enforcement to a living wage commission made up of representatives from labor, business, the religious community, community organizations, and Cornell ILR. With assistance from University of Buffalo law student interns and pro bono attorneys, the commission has won wage increases for over 160 workers of contractors at city-owned parking lots through voluntary compliance agreements with employers. The commission is also reviewing all city contracts for compliance and promoting improved contracting procedures within the city administration, functions that were strengthened early in 2006 when grant funding enabled Cornell ILR and the commission to hire a living wage compliance coordinator.

Unlike the EDG or Champions Network, the CEJ confronts low-road employers in a public and visible way. In the minds of union leaders, the CEJ fits into the overall scheme of labor's local development initiatives, because strike support, living wage enforcement, and mobilizations around plant closures also aim to preserve good jobs. It operates alongside, and in cooperation with, other active coalitions in the region, including Champions and other single-issue coalitions devoted to occupational safety, child care, and "economic self-sufficiency." In addition, it links local activists to national campaigns, such as those against Wal-Mart, Cintas, and Sorrento. CEJ is an example of social movement unionism, in the sense that it mobilizes broad community support for the struggles of workers and their unions.

CEJ also intervened in the 2005 battle over restructuring county government, convening a broad community coalition that issued a report recommending progressive fiscal reform. With strong union support, Democrats swept the 2005 local elections. Maria Whyte, longtime executive director of CEJ, was elected to the county legislature, becoming its majority leader.

As Buffalo's problems persist, union capacities to address them are growing. Firmly rooted in historical legacy and anchored by geographical place, Buffalo's union leaders are demanding a voice and taking a hand in building the industries of the region's finally emerging new economy. Although the population and some of the key manufacturing industries have stabilized in the region as a whole, suburbanization and public sector retrenchment continue. Cuts to city and local government services are especially painful, since they eliminate thousands of middle-income jobs and make it difficult for local government to address persistent social needs. At the same time, the central labor council leadership, which until 2005 was not deeply involved in coalition work, has changed. The new Area Labor Federation (ALF) structure effectively utilized local solidarity charters to prevent the national AFL-CIO split from fracturing regional union bodies. Now led by Change to Win union representatives and staffed by an experienced local CWA leader, the ALF shows promise of giving the collective bodies of the local labor movement a more active role in carrying out local coalition work.

Buffalo's high-road infrastructure is a case of unions coming to terms with the policy concerns associated with the globalization of manufacturing and the decline of a region. Despite differences in the problems unions face in building partnerships, Buffalo's unionists, like those in Seattle, have found ways to institutionalize their partnerships with the broader community. Champions, EDG, and CEJ are only three faces of this evolving development, organizing regional partnerships, development projects, and contentious mobilization. Although social movement unionism may seem inconsistent with labor-management partnership, the same individuals push both approaches. As Buffalo's chronic job crisis persists and moves to the public sector, support within the local labor movement for the high-road infrastructure is growing. Labor's coalition work continues to spill over into ever more ambitious and diverse initiatives.

HIGH-ROAD SOCIAL INFRASTRUCTURES

Although Seattle and Buffalo have different industrial structures, face different policy challenges, and have different labor histories, unions in both areas have built a high-road social infrastructure. We have depicted two paths to the high road: Seattle's, where unions work to redistribute the gains of vigorous economic growth, and Buffalo's, where they seek new solutions when economic development policy has proven ineffective. In Seattle, unions have used economic growth as a lever for addressing problems of inequality, unstable work relations, and threats to manufacturing jobs. Buffalo's unions, in contrast, have built local political will to reverse the course of economic decline.

Differences in local politics matter. Seattle's unions have participated in a progressive local political scene and developed a strategic relationship with local Democratic politicians. Buffalo's unions, by contrast, have worked not only with Democrats and community groups but also with the local business establishment and moderate Republicans. While progressive elements in local government, like the mayor's office, have been central to high-road policymaking in Seattle, Buffalo's financially bankrupt city and county governments have played, with few exceptions, a more passive role to date.

Nevertheless, these infrastructures have much in common. Unions set up a series of organizations to design policies, administer programs, seek funding, lobby, mobilize, and maintain relations with partners. The infrastructures grow from project to project, and each project sets up relationships and raises issues that can lead to more coalition work. In both cities, the policies involve integrating minority workers into middle-income construction jobs in the name of connecting building to a more egalitarian form of economic development. Labor faces the same kinds of opponents in both cities: antiunion contractors' associations opposed to the building trades' market stabilization efforts, organized companies where strikes occur, and nonunion companies where organizing drives take place. While these businesses take on the unions as opponents, others ally themselves with unions. Unionized contractors implementing new workforce development programs (and winning contracts in the process) and the broad labor-management partnership sponsored by the Champions Network are two examples. Individual union leaders play a key role in both cases by finding partners and cementing cooperation by setting up new organizations with staff. Indeed, the political situation in Buffalo seems to be improving as unions, along with other progressive groups such as CEJ and Citizen Action, helped progressive Democrats to win in the 2005 county legislature and mayoral elections.

Organizing of new workers remains missing from the form of union revitalization discussed here, even if being "part of the solution" improves unions' chances of winning the hearts and minds of unorganized workers. Although Seattle is home to many organizing unions, the KCLC has managed to support, but not to initiate, organizing drives. During the 1990s, the KCLC's attempt to create a more proactive multiunion approach to expanding organizing efforts failed. Similarly, in Buffalo, there are organizing unions. At the EDG, however, the link to organizing is absent even in theory, and CEJ activists bemoan the lack of requests to support new organizing. In practice, the infrastructure cannot support organizing if (1) local unions are not organizing new workers, (2) local unions do not approach these organizations for help, or (3) local unions as a whole do not reach a consensus that it makes sense for the infrastructure to support organizing more directly. These, at least, are the obstacles in Seattle and Buffalo.

High-road economic development strategies have emerged in an AFL town on the Pacific rim and a CIO town on the Great Lakes. They amount not merely to single initiatives but to two infrastructures that have supported a series of initiatives over a decade or more. Along with the weight of evidence in this book, these two case studies suggest that community-minded unions can build these structures in a wide range of urban environments and that, with political will and organizational skills, urban labor movements can learn from one another.

7

POLITICAL INSIDERS AND SOCIAL ACTIVISTS

Coalition Building in New York and Los Angeles

Marco Hauptmeier and Lowell Turner

Labor movements in New York City and Los Angeles, as we know them today, emerged from very different historical trajectories. New York has remained a solid union town throughout the postwar period. As in earlier years, labor unions have been a consistently important political force in New York politics, and many social policies in areas such as public housing are products in part of labor's influence (Freeman 2000). The labor movement gained its strength from a highly unionized industrial workforce, which then supported union growth in the public sector. By comparison, Los Angeles throughout most of the twentieth century had a well-earned reputation as a business town with an antiunion climate. Labor in Los Angeles never gained the strength of urban labor movements in large industrial cities in the Northeast and Midwest or up the coast in San Francisco. In part this was because sprawling Los Angeles lacked a concentrated industrial workforce and public sector, but more important because business and political interests marketed Los Angeles as a wide open, union-free environment and made a determined effort to keep it that way.

Today the images presented by these labor movements are reversed. Los Angeles has become a poster child for labor movement revitalization. With innovative strategies and high-profile organizing victories, the labor movement has emerged as a powerful force in L.A. politics and has reshaped the political landscape, advancing progressive policies just as New York's unions did in the 1950s and 1960s. Compared to Los Angeles, New York's labor movement appears aged and traditional today. Still strong in size and political influence, New York unions have lost membership slowly but steadily in the private sector. With stable membership in the public sector, unions still successfully represent the interest of their

This chapter has benefited from a research stay by Marco Hauptmeier and discussions at the New York City Extension office of the ILR School at Cornell University. In particular, Sean Sweeney, Pam Whitefield, and Jill Kubit provided valuable support. We would also like to thank Ben Day, Dan Cornfield, Janice Fine, Ian Greer, Paul Hayes, Ruth Milkman, and Ralph Turner for their advice and useful comments.

members, yet they no longer play a central role as movers and shakers for a broader social agenda beyond their own constituencies.

Why have labor movements in New York City and Los Angeles changed so dramatically? And more specifically, why have the activist social coalitions that revitalized the labor movement in Los Angeles not played the same kind of role in New York? Our research persuades us that the relationship between contrasting coalition types—political and social—is central to explaining the differences. *Political coalitions* refer to cooperation between unions and parties, politicians, and other social actors, focused largely on elections and policy-making processes. *Social coalitions,* by contrast, include labor and other social actors such as community, religious, environmental, and immigrant rights groups, focused on a range of political, economic, and social campaigns.

A comparison of the two metropolitan areas over the past two decades reveals distinct patterns of coalition building in New York and Los Angeles. In New York, the labor movement is dominated by several powerful local unions, often at odds with one another in contending political coalitions. New social coalitions have developed but are not central to organized labor's political action. The focus of most unions on narrow interest representation contributes to a disconnect between social and political coalitions in which the latter dominate. In Los Angeles, by contrast, the significance of social coalition building stands out as the labor movement has coalesced over the past fifteen years. To be sure, labor in Los Angeles participates actively in political coalitions. In contrast to New York, however, political coalitions move beyond narrow union interests, building on social coalitions that broaden the influence of labor as a whole.

Our argument favors two related causal factors. The preexisting position of organized labor in urban political structures and the strategic choices of union leadership together provide an explanation for the differing characteristics of contemporary union coalitions in Los Angeles and New York, as well as for relative gains or declines in union influence. In New York, where the labor movement is dominated by several large locals and entrenched in the political structure, union leaders have to a large extent chosen to participate in political coalitions that in some ways inhibit the development of social coalitions. By contrast, unions in Los Angeles lacked a strong position in industry or city politics, resulting in a sort of "advantages of backwardness" (Gerschenkron 1962; Milkman 2002) that gave a new generation of labor leaders space to experiment with innovative strategies based on new social coalitions.

POLITICAL INSIDERS AND SOCIAL ACTIVISTS

Coalitions organized around specific issues by unions and other social actors are often part of a broader effort by outsiders to break into inner circles of political influence. The irony is that once unions become insiders they find themselves in a position to block future social coalitions struggling to join the inner circles of influence. Thus in New York, a few strong union locals long ago became insiders entrenched in local politics. Although they often fight among themselves and thus weaken overall union influence, their powerful presence tends to close off the space available for a socially activist unionism. Although labor-inclusive social coalitions have emerged over the past decade, this has usually happened outside the dominant framework of union power and to a large extent without the participation of the strongest local unions. Although social coalitions have had some success in particular campaigns, they have remained for the most part outsiders with limited political influence.

In Los Angeles, by contrast, a history of weak unionism characterized by minimal consolidation of local union political power left the field wide open for social coalition building. Thus the story line in the 1990s: Justice for Janitors and other coalition campaigns, spilling over into local politics with a renewed union influence based on social activism. The result by the early 2000s was an unprecedented position of political influence for the central labor council and various union locals, based on a continuing series of social coalition campaigns.

The Los Angeles story thus mirrors the New York story. While in New York City powerful local unions with political insider status and narrow bargaining strategies have limited the influence of emerging social coalitions, labor in Los Angeles, in the absence of postwar consolidation or insider status, has built increasingly successful social coalition campaigns that have led to new positions of political influence. In a context of divergent opportunity structures, unions in Los Angeles and New York made different strategic choices in the 1990s, resulting in significantly different outcomes for labor influence by the early years of the twenty-first century.

LABOR AND GLOBAL CITIES: NEW YORK AND LOS ANGELES COMPARED

Similar in many respects, New York and Los Angeles have been described as the quintessential American global cities (Abu-Lughod 1999). Roughly equal in population, the New York metropolitan area has 8.7 million residents while Los Angeles has 9.3 million. Both cities have served as a major port of entry for immigrants that have become central components of local population and culture. Representing over 30 percent of New York City's total population and 45 percent of the city of Los Angeles, Hispanics are by far the largest of immigrant groups. Other large ethnic populations come from various Asian countries such as China and South Korea (Abu-Lughod 1999), and about a third of the population of each city is foreign born, reflecting the international status of these global cities.

Los Angeles and New York City are agglomerations of great wealth and corporate power. Both cities are central nodes in the global economy, fulfilling important capital market functions. Wall Street's stock exchange is the largest in the world, while many multinational companies locate important business services in one or the other of these cities. New York is home to twelve of the twenty largest international law firms in the world (Yaro, Hiss, and Regional Plan Association 1996). As much as these two cities are centers of power, they are also places of much poverty and social exclusion. With poverty rates of 18.6 percent and 17.7 percent respectively, New York and Los Angeles stand far above the 2003 national rate of 12.5 percent (DeNavas-Walt, Proctor, and Lee 2004). Extremes of poverty and wealth make economic and social inequality a defining characteristic of contemporary New York and Los Angeles.

The transformation of these cities from industrial toward more service-based economies has been more dynamic and encompassing than in most other American cities (Sassen 2001). Different sectors of the service economy, however, have offered vastly different opportunities. Winners of the restructuring process in both cities include professionals in finance, insurance, real estate, business services, and information technology, while workers in low-wage service industries, many of them immigrants, have been the losers, often unable to earn a living wage.

With nine hundred thousand union members, New York's labor movement is the largest in the country. Los Angeles has about six hundred thousand union members. Union density in the metropolitan area in 2004 was 24.5 percent in New York and 15.5 percent in Los Angeles. New York has large public sector unions with a membership density of about 66 percent, while the level in Los Angeles is 53.3 percent. Private sector union density in 2004 was about 10 percent in Los Angeles and 17 percent in New York City. Since the late 1980s, overall membership density in Los Angeles stabilized and then grew modestly in both public and private sectors, while in New York union density in the private sector declined slowly but steadily from 23 percent in 1989 to 17 percent in 2004 (Hirsch and Macpherson 2006).

COALITION BUILDING IN NEW YORK: THE POLITICAL TRUMPS THE SOCIAL

A primary strategy of labor unions in New York is to advance their interests through political coalitions. This has been a highly effective strategy, making labor unions influential players in the political power structure of the city. This is related to the high unionization rate as well the role played by unions at critical moments in the city's history. When the city was threatened with bankruptcy in the late 1970s, unions helped out with money from their pension funds. The most important factor for the political access of unions has been their actual or expected leverage in elections (Mollenkopf 1992). Despite a loss of influence compared to the 1960s and 1970s, unions along with political parties are unrivaled at voter mobilization. With their highly regarded phone banks and organizers, New York City's unions are well aware of their appeal to politicians. After successful contract negotiations for seventy thousand members of SEIU/1199 in 2002, in the biggest collective bargaining agreement ever signed in the U.S. health-care industry, Dennis Riviera wrote in a letter to SEIU members: "We also won this agreement for another very important reason—our political strength. . . . When tens of thousands of our union members volunteer to get out the vote on election day, our elected officials notice. And they respect us."[1]

In standard political exchange arrangements, unions expect politicians to promote labor interests. These interests, however, are defined with considerable variation, including the traditional divide between the interests of public and of private sector unions. Unions in New York tend to formulate their interests narrowly in favor of their own constituencies, often resulting in support for different candidates and a fragmentation of political influence. In the face of powerful local unions, the central labor council is all too often unable to unify divergent positions. In addition, narrow interest formulation and political insider coalitions result in hidden or sometimes open conflict with social groups. Seldom in recent years has a unified labor movement acted as part of a broader social or political movement.

In the Democratic primary for the mayoral election in 2001, unions endorsed four different candidates. The United Federation of Teachers (UFT) supported City Comptroller Alan G. Hevesi. UNITE, UAW, and SEIU/32BJ endorsed Public Advocate Mark Green. Most of the locals in AFSCME District Council 37 backed Council Speaker Peter Vallone, while others such as the cafeteria workers and crossing guards supported Fernando Ferrer—creating conflicting endorsements within the same union (Greenhouse 2001). SEIU/1199 stayed neutral for

---

1. Quote from an undated letter to union members by SEIU 1199 president Dennis Rivera in 2002.

a long time, as Dennis Rivera argued that his union would gain nothing by endorsing a Democratic primary candidate. In the final weeks before the election, however, when Ferrer appeared the likely winner, Rivera made a last-minute endorsement. He bet wrong as Mark Green finished first in the Democratic primary.

Labor's political fragmentation could not be bridged before the runoff election between Green and Republican candidate Michael Bloomberg. Although most unions officially supported Green, the two largest unions, SEIU/1199 and UFT, sent out mixed signals. Neither union mobilized organizers or used phone banks to turn out the vote for Green. The absence of a unified mobilization resulted in a marginal impact for labor and opened the door for Bloomberg's victory (Robbins 2001).

The political fragmentation of the labor movement in New York is a recurrent theme, contributing to the election of Republican Rudi Guiliani in 1993 and 1997. The central labor council's endorsement has little influence on the decisions of the powerful locals. The last time labor united to support a mayoral candidate was in 1989 when a broad liberal coalition with labor at its center swept into office David Dinkins, the first black mayor of New York City.

Lack of unity continued as Governor George Pataki, a Republican, used legislation and policy to win the support of several large New York unions in his 2002 election campaign. Rivera's SEIU/1199 struck the best deal when a state bill allocated $1.8 billion over three years to finance raises and job creation for health-care workers. UFT's Randi Weingarten, UNITE's Bruce Raynor, and Roger Benson's Public Employees Federation also endorsed Pataki, in part because of union-friendly legislation: all three were present when Pataki signed a bill preventing employers from using state funds to fight union organizers. UFT was also able to negotiate an additional $200 million in raises for school teachers (Dewan 2002).

The decision to support Pataki was opposed by rank-and-file members in SEIU/1199 and UFT, and the deals were widely criticized by other unions as well. SEIU/32BJ's Mike Fishman, who endorsed Democratic challenger Carl McCall, said, "Pataki did a great thing for 1199. But that contract was just one issue, just one fight. Our members are some of the newest citizens, with a wide range of needs. They need somebody consistent on all issues, who's consistently pro-union and pro working people" (Meyerson 2002, 28).[2]

Pataki's election victory resulted in part from the unprecedented deal between Governor Pataki and 1199's Riviera, an agreement that helped workers and families in the health-care industry, many of them low-wage workers. At the same

---

2. SEIU/32BJ is the high-profile building services union from which John Sweeney launched his successful campaign for SEIU national president in 1980 and from there to AFL-CIO president in 1995.

time, unions and other social groups opposed this political-insider coalition with a governor who had cut a range of programs for the socially excluded in New York (both city and state). Despite Pataki's election success, however, unions lobbied successfully to raise the minimum wage in the state from $5.15 an hour in 2004 to $7.15 in 2007 (Cooper 2004).

Social coalitions have played a significant but limited role in advancing union goals in New York City, while relationships between labor and community groups have often been contentious. The low point may have been when construction workers attacked antiwar demonstrators during the Vietnam War. The affluent lifestyle of some union leaders—in some cases with Mob connections—has also historically distanced unions from social groups. Confronted with "big labor," social activists have sometimes had trouble seeing labor as a natural ally for progressive forces in New York City (Mantsios 2001).

Despite this history, coalitions between labor and social groups have expanded since the mid-1990s, when new leadership at the AFL-CIO opened up space for new social coalitions. Although such initiatives and the social movement strivings they represent have remained secondary in the New York City labor movement, some promising examples have emerged, including Make the Road by Walking, Workplace Project, Domestic Workers Alliance, and the Taxi Workers Alliance–NY. In addition, the Working Families Party and the local chapter of Jobs with Justice have served as meeting points in various campaigns.

When the new AFL-CIO leadership initiated Union Summer in 1996, UNITE brought campus activists to New York City to work on anti-sweatshop campaigns. From this union-campus collaboration came the United Students against Sweatshops (USAS), which spread quickly to over three hundred campuses around the country. One of the two national offices of USAS is located at the headquarters of UNITE (now UNITE HERE) in New York City. Together USAS and UNITE forged broad coalitions with other groups such as Jobs with Justice and the New York Labor Religion Coalition. One of the goals of such coalition efforts was to get anti-sweatshop legislation passed by the city council, assuring that the $70 million spent annually on uniforms by New York City agencies are not produced under sweatshop conditions. This initiative resulted in the Anti-Sweatshop Procurement Law, passed by the city council in March 2001.[3]

Another coalition effort developed around the greengrocer campaign in 1998, supported by a wide range of groups including the Lower East Side Worker Center, UNITE, Jobs with Justice, and Casa Mexico (Ness 2005). Greengrocers are small retail stores that started out as corner produce stores and over time broadened their range of products. The campaign protested widespread violations of

---

3. Interview with Ginny Coughlin (UNITE HERE), 2003.

minimum wage and overtime laws—with employees forced in some cases to work up to seventy-two hours per week. The campaign attracted media attention and brought working conditions to the attention of the attorney general for the state of New York, Eliot Spitzer. An investigation by his office revealed a widespread pattern of labor rights violations and led to negotiated settlements with individual greengrocers and development of a code of conduct for the industry. Established in negotiations that included store owners, coalition campaigners, and the attorney general's office, the code was subsequently accepted by over two hundred greengrocers.

The Restaurant Opportunity Center (ROC) was set up in the wake of September 11, 2001. The attacks killed seventy-three employees of the restaurant Windows of the World, located at the top of the World Trade Center, and left another three hundred workers without jobs—all of them members of HERE Local 100. ROC was founded by HERE to help the relatives of the victims and displaced workers. ROC helps displaced workers find new jobs and offers training courses for workers in the restaurant industry. ROC and former Windows of the World employees opened a new restaurant called COLORS in January 2006, organized as a cooperative and owned by the workers themselves. ROC has also become a voice for unorganized immigrants in the restaurant industry, in several instances forcing restaurant owners to reinstate workers and pay back wages. However, the relationship between ROC and UNITE HERE has become somewhat fragile, as activists at the immigrant-led worker center have criticized union leadership dominance by white males, despite the great importance of immigrants and women in the hotel and restaurant workforce.[4]

In the fall of 2003, the Immigrant Workers Freedom Ride brought nine hundred immigrants and their supporters from across the United States in caravans of buses, ending in a rally of over one hundred thousand in Flushing Meadow. New York's central labor council, with the support of most member unions, spearheaded organization of the rally, one of the largest and most unified labor mobilizations of the past decade in New York City. The freedom ride was important not only for demonstrating new union support for immigrant rights (codified in an AFL-CIO policy change in 2000) but for possible ramifications for future coalition-based campaigns. Spillover from the mobilization along with massive immigrant rights demonstrations in the spring of 2006 have shown the potential of expanded social coalition activism.

---

4. Interviews with ROC organizer, 2003 and 2004.

THE RISE OF SOCIAL UNIONISM IN LOS ANGELES

Since the 1930s, when workplace and social unrest propelled union organizing campaigns across the country, on the West Coast centered in the port cities of San Francisco and Seattle, Los Angeles has gone a different route. From the current era of global liberalization we can look back on the L.A. experience as what Joseph Stiglitz (2002) has called "market fundamentalism." In a journey that paralleled the "grapes of wrath" migration that transformed farmers from Texas, Oklahoma, and other states into job-seeking foot soldiers for Western fields and factories, Southern California offered a welcome union-free destination for a triumphant "cowboy capitalism."

Although in the postwar period unions organized heavy industry (such as automobiles and aerospace) and eventually reached union density rates comparable to national levels, Los Angeles remained a center of economic development in which unions played only a minor role. A lengthy story can be told (e.g., Gottlieb et al. 2005; Milkman 2006), but the weak-union pattern persisted through the 1980s. Modest union growth in the public sector could not offset the loss of union jobs as large industrial factories closed, and labor continued to play a marginal role in L.A. politics. The difference between this situation and strong union insider status in postwar New York City would be hard to exaggerate.

Quite surprisingly then, a 1990s resurgence of the labor movement has made Los Angeles a prominent case of successful union revitalization. To a national labor movement in crisis, Los Angeles now offers the possibility of union-based solidarity, an unexpected revitalization of social forces in which coalition building is the key ingredient. Although union density remains low in comparison to New York, trajectories of union political and social influence have reversed quite dramatically over the past fifteen years.

In labor circles the contemporary L.A. story is widely known (Pastor 2001; Milkman 2002; Frank and Wong 2004; Gottlieb et al. 2005). The defining moment came in 1990 when several thousand janitors, mostly Latino, joined a union-led comprehensive campaign—with grassroots organizing, mass demonstrations, and other innovative pressure tactics—to win a dramatic strike victory in a decidedly union-unfriendly context. Framed as a battle for social justice, this Justice for Janitors campaign was backed by a broad social coalition including immigrant rights, religious, and community groups, and in the course of the struggle it won widespread public support. In addition to winning significant organizing and bargaining gains for janitors, the campaign mobilized L.A.'s large Latino community and brought together a variety of social groups in coalitions that would spill over in subsequent years into an array of other campaigns (Pastor 2001; Milkman and Wong 2000).[5]

The emergence of a coalition-based social unionism contributed to a succession of organizing, bargaining, and public policy victories—in the health-care and hospitality industries, in transportation, construction, and building services. In health care, for example, SEIU organized seventy thousand home-care workers in Los Angeles, which included a successful campaign for enabling state legislation and then a sustained effort to sign up members. Case-by-case hospital organizing campaigns by SEIU and the California Nurses Association also resulted in breakthrough victories. Catholic Healthcare West, for example, fought unionization campaigns vigorously until key defeats led the company to sign agreements providing for management neutrality throughout its numerous hospitals and health-care facilities. Between 1995 and 2003, the unionization rate in the L.A. health-care industry rose from about 25 percent to over 50 percent.[6] In the hospitality industry, successful hotel organizing campaigns since the late 1980s laid the groundwork for a major strike/lockout victory in 2005. Led by UNITE HERE, the new hotel contracts not only raised wages and benefits for housekeepers and other employees but won a contract expiration date synchronized with New York City, Boston, Chicago, and Honolulu, laying the groundwork for a nationwide "Hotel Workers Rising" campaign in 2006.[7]

In 1996, the Los Angeles County Federation of Labor elected a new president, Miguel Contreras, trained in social movement unionism during his years as an organizer for the United Farm Workers, who brought unions and community groups together in a series of successful campaigns and local political elections. By the turn of the century, the city council was dominated by union supporters, while campaigns in 2001 and 2005 each resulted in the election of a pro-labor Democratic mayor (the second, Antonio Villaraigosa, is a former union organizer).

Specific effects of the spread of social coalition building in Los Angeles include organizational revitalization for SEIU and UNITE HERE locals (among others) and the county federation; institutional and policy change such as the implementation of new minimum wage standards by aggressive living wage boards; and the building of enduring coalition-based organizations for economic development such as the Los Angeles Alliance for a New Economy, or LAANE (Frank and Wong 2004, 173–77). At the same time, however, we do not want to idealize

---

5. Social networks of Mexican Americans and Mexicans, with and without legal status, provided a strong base for union revitalization in Los Angeles. Immigrants from Central America, many socialized in antiauthoritarian struggles in countries such as El Salvador, also played an important role.

6. Interview with SEIU lead organizer, 2004.

7. Talk given by UNITE HERE president Bruce Raynor at Cornell University, October 20, 2005.

the growing influence of the labor movement in Los Angeles. Tensions developed, and remained to be resolved, between unions and a series of new worker centers such as the Korean Immigrant Workers Association, which are run for and by underrepresented immigrant workers (Fine 2006). And a major defeat for striking grocery workers in 2003 indicated both the power of employer countermobilization and the failure of the United Food and Commercial Workers, in a context marked by public support and union solidarity, to mobilize the strategies and coalition efforts necessary for victory.

Nonetheless, the overall pattern of growing labor movement success in Los Angeles stands out as an example of union revitalization in the United States. There were several key ingredients in this transformation. The Justice for Janitors strategy was developed at SEIU national headquarters. Although the traditional local leadership held back (at one point the local was placed in trusteeship), grassroots activists embraced the strategy, mobilizing workers and supportive community groups for the struggle. Framed in terms of social justice for low-wage service workers and immigrant rights, the campaign targeted large building owners (and their contractors), which were sensitive to their public image as stable providers of Pacific Rim offices for multinational corporations. Mass demonstrations and civil disobedience attracted public support (Milkman 2002). And in subsequent years, social actors built on the victory in a cascading series of campaigns that, whether successful or not, contributed to political transformation and the development of a "social justice infrastructure" (Nissen and Russo, chapter 8 in this book).

The unexpected transformation of the past fifteen years shows that significant social and labor gains are possible across a large urban region, in a city closely linked to the global economy, with weak labor institutions at the outset and a long history on the front lines of market liberalization. Beyond the fact of transformation, the Los Angeles case suggests explanations for both the emergence of social unionism and its success. Strategic choice is obviously at the center of both explanations. Given the weakness of labor institutions, the possibilities ranged far and wide; it is difficult to see how choices could be derived from institutions or from economic, political, social, or cultural circumstances. In a context characterized by weak labor standards and institutions, union leaders made real, often surprising, choices that mattered.

The shortcomings of traditional union strategies in Los Angeles opened the door for strategic innovation by union reformers. Strategic support from national unions such as SEIU and the activism of local bridge builders combined to shape the choices and the implementation of innovative strategies. The emergence of social unionism is thus consistent with an explanation based on the weakness of insider unionism and the innovative strategies of union leaders and activists. In contrast to New York City, no powerful union locals and political insiders blocked the open field for innovative union strategies in Los Angeles in the 1990s.

The accomplishments of social unionism in Los Angeles can be measured specifically in gains by janitors and subsequent groups of workers and more broadly by a sustained process of economic and political transformation. The SEIU and Justice for Janitors found corporate vulnerability in the image concerns of large building owners, their inability to relocate, and their obvious ability to pay more for janitorial service (opportunity). Subsequent campaigns by unions targeting other employers sought similarly vulnerable targets in business and government—a learning process in which university-based researchers played a supporting role (Frank and Wong 2004). Also essential were the decisions of local union activists to build on this initial breakthrough, to replace traditional leaders with innovators, and to promote strategies based on rank-and-file mobilization and community coalitions (actor choice). Lacking the dynamism of a broad social movement context, labor nonetheless found an ethnic workforce and community ripe for mobilization, based in social networks that linked established residents with recent immigrants, legal and illegal. As initial successes ballooned in spillover processes, bridge builders mobilized the Latino community, while more unions tried out the new strategies and joined the widening circles of coalition campaigns.

Conditions for the emergence and spread of social unionism found in Los Angeles are also present, or at least latent, in other cities, including Miami and Nashville (see chapters 8 and 9). Where they are not blocked by entrenched insiders, unions pursuing social-movement–type strategies such as grassroots mobilization and coalition building may generate momentum for significant social gains. So much so that in Los Angeles unions have gained new insider status, entrenched in new bargaining relationships with employers, incorporated in a central position in local politics and government, and solidly established on a range of policy boards and agencies.[8] Yet this insider status is so far quite different from the entrenched version found in New York. On the contrary, this new institutional position, which is far more substantial than labor has ever had in Los Angeles, is being defended and expanded in continuing processes of strategic innovation and coalition campaigns. And social unionism has expanded beyond social movement strategies to include participation in economic development (Frank and Wong 2004).

---

8. See, for example, an in-depth article on L.A. County Fed president Miguel Contreras by Matea Gold, "L.A. Power Broker Faces Test," *Los Angeles Times,* March 21, 2005. In a sad twist of fate, Contreras died unexpectedly at age fifty-two in May 2005, thus opening the question of the influence of this one key person in the revitalization of the labor movement in Los Angeles.

URBAN COALITIONS AND THE PROSPECTS FOR LABOR MOVEMENT REVITALIZATION

We began this chapter with a puzzle: Why have unions in New York City, long powerful players in the political economy of this global city, declined in numbers and influence over the past fifteen years while unions in Los Angeles, historically a marginal player at best, have experienced a dramatic expansion of political and economic influence? And more specifically, why has an expansive, socially activist labor movement come to prominence in Los Angeles while a similar sort of social unionism remains to some extent marginal in the political economy of New York?

Based on our examination of coalition-building efforts and labor's role in politics, the evidence persuades us that the decisive explanatory factors are union centered: the structure of existing union incorporation in the urban political economy along with the strategic choices of union leaders and activists. In New York, powerful local unions, often at odds with one another, have long played the role of political insiders. Union leaders have used these positions of influence to negotiate contracts on behalf of their own members while showing less interest in sustained coalition building with other actors. Limited political coalitions have dominated the union landscape, narrowing the space for the potentially transformative effects of a more socially activist unionism. By contrast, a generally weak union presence, including the absence of labor integration in the centers of power, in L.A. politics left the field wide open for social mobilization. A new generation of union leaders and activists stepped forward in the 1990s to fill the vacuum with ambitious campaigns focused on organizing, collective bargaining, and politics. Based in large measure on the mobilization of a growing Latino community and the building of coalitions with social actors such as immigrant rights and religious groups, the labor movement has now become a central player in the political economy of modern Los Angeles.

Although a more rigorous testing of a systematic comparative analysis is beyond the scope of this two-city study, we have emphasized existing structure and strategic choice because these factors have emerged prominently in contrasting labor movement trajectories in contemporary New York City and Los Angeles. These findings are consistent with the evidence from other cities presented in this book.

The easiest alternative explanations to rule out are those for which similar circumstances are joined by contrasting outcomes. Political institutions and orientations are in many ways similar in both cities. Strong mayors share power with city councils elected by district, often in adversarial relationships with each other. Both cities are located in liberal "blue states" where large majorities vote Democratic (except when celebrity "Terminators" enter the field). While New York was for many decades a more politically liberal city than Los Angeles, it is hard to see how this difference could explain contemporary differences in labor movement revitalization.

Economic differences, both institutional and structural, also offer little help in explaining variation. New York and Los Angeles are both global cities of great wealth, financial centers for the global economy with world-class ports and expanding construction industries. Although light manufacturing is important in both cities, employment has shifted in recent decades to service industries at the high end (business and financial services) as well as health care, building services, transportation, public education, hotels and restaurants, domestic services, and other areas. In both cities, unions today are based primarily in services, in both the public and private sectors.

Social conditions are also similar in many ways. Both cities are major ports of entry for immigrants and have unusually large foreign-born populations. Hispanics make up the largest part of both of these groups in each city. As for other global cities (and most U.S. cities for that matter), social structure is characterized by vast inequality, with extremes of great wealth and poverty. Apart from wealthy owners and investors, large cohorts of well-paid professionals provide the services necessary to administer capital flows in an increasingly global economy. At the same time, growing numbers of lower-paid service workers, many of them immigrants, work in the buildings, hotels, hospitals, homes, schools, buses, and gardens of an expanding global city.

There are of course differences not included in our union-centered explanation. New York is an established union town while Los Angeles entered the 1990s as a "frontier," wide open for new developments such as labor movement revitalization. Although conceptually useful, especially in understanding the political insider concept, this difference in itself provides only limited explanatory value— and here we must look beyond the two-city comparison. In other chapters of this book we see clearly that frontier cities such as Miami and Nashville have as yet no L.A.-type labor resurgence, while in union towns such as Seattle and Buffalo unions have built on existing strengths to revitalize the labor movement and develop new influence in politics and society.

Perhaps the most compelling alternative explanation is social and demographic. Labor movement revitalization in Los Angeles has been built to a large extent on the mobilization of the Latino community. Although New York also has a large Hispanic population, it is more diverse, spanning a wide range of countries from the Caribbean through Mexico, Central America, and South America, and thus it is harder to mobilize in a cohesive way than the more homogenous Latino population of Los Angeles, which is largely of Mexican and Central American origin. This difference in immigrant and ethnic composition is important for understanding contrasting outcomes for labor in the past fifteen years. Still, there are large concentrations of particular ethnic groups in New York such as Haitians, eastern Europeans, Koreans, and Pakistanis that are quite capable of mobilization, especially in alliance with similar groups and supportive social actors. By contrast to salient labor strategies in Los Angeles, however, most unions in New York have limited their efforts to serving the interests of existing memberships. Finally, other large metropolitan areas such as Houston also have large and relatively homogeneous Hispanic populations without having experienced anything like the labor movement resurgence of Los Angeles.

Thus we are left with a union-centered explanation based largely on structure and strategy.[9] The bad news for unions is that they are to a significant degree responsible for the declining influence they have faced in cities such as New York. It won't do to blame employers, government, globalization, economic restructuring, or opportunity-seeking immigrants and individualist young workers. The good news is that unions, as they have done in Los Angeles, have real opportunities for expanded influence, if and when they step back from insider stagnation or outsider irrelevance to pursue innovative strategies based on union unity, coalition building, and social activism.

---

9. There is, of course, always the cultural explanation advanced by unreconstructed L.A. chauvinists: uptight, belligerently set-in-their ways New Yorkers versus loose Angelenos used to innovation, wide open for whatever the world brings along.

Part III
FRONTIER CITIES

8

STRATEGIES FOR LABOR REVITALIZATION

The Case of Miami

Bruce Nissen and Monica Russo

Miami is a "frontier city," a large urban global city with important financial and service sectors. Known as the "gateway to Latin America," its banking, investment, and trade ties with Latin American and the Caribbean are the strongest of any U.S. city. Its large immigrant population works in the service economy, which is growing from tourism and economic ties with Latin America. "Greater Miami" is Miami-Dade County, about six times as large as the city itself (2.2 million inhabitants in 2000, compared to the city's 362,000)—it contains over twenty cities. City and county economies are not easily separated; in this chapter we examine the county's labor movement.

The following section provides demographic, economic, and political information on Miami-Dade County. We then profile the local labor movement, and recent attempts to revive it, with particular attention to community coalition and network efforts. We then analyze the reasons for organized labor's traditional weakness and recent revitalization attempts. Finally, we outline the most recent strategies to push revitalization forward.

Our investigation indicates that revitalization requires that the labor movement be grounded in the community. It must fight for "community" issues such as smaller school class sizes, fair immigration policies for the foreign born, and living wages for all employed with public funds. Qualitative advance also requires a major offensive to organize key labor markets. Despite obstacles, labor progressives have built a social justice infrastructure in Greater Miami that was absent a decade ago. A county living wage ordinance and a limitation on public school class sizes were won. But labor remains stuck in tactical, not strategic, for-

This chapter is a considerably altered version of a paper first presented at the conference on "Strategies for Urban Labor Revitalization: Union Campaigns in Large, Midsize, and Global Cities," held at Cornell University, October 1–2, 2004. An earlier version appeared in an article in the March 2006 issue of *Working USA*. We thank Lowell Turner and Dan Cornfield for feedback on earlier versions of this chapter, as well as anonymous reviewers for Cornell University Press. Finally, our special thanks and admiration go to all those working to build the "social justice infrastructure" in the Miami area to the point where we can hope for real power for working people and unions in the area.

■ **Table 8.1**   Percentage of Black and Hispanic residents: United States, Miami-Dade County, and city of Miami[a]

RACE	UNITED STATES (%)	MIAMI-DADE COUNTY (%)	CITY OF MIAMI (%)
White	75.1	69.7	66.6
Black or African American	12.3	20.3	22.3
Hispanic (of any race)	12.5	57.3	65.8

[a]The numbers in each of the columns in this table do not add up to 100% for a number of reasons: Hispanics are not considered a "race"; they can self-identify as either "black" or "white," so many Hispanics may be counted twice; and there are of course other categories such as Asians and Native Americans.

mations. A long-term strategic coalition able to win union organizing breakthroughs in key industries is needed.

DEMOGRAPHIC, ECONOMIC, AND POLITICAL CONTEXT

The county and the city are very diverse, comprising immigrants from the Caribbean (Haiti, Cuba, the Dominican Republic, Puerto Rico, Jamaica, the Bahamas), Latin America (Colombia, Brazil, Argentina, Venezuela, Mexico, and Central American countries), and a sizeable native-born population of African Americans, Anglos (non-Hispanic whites), and Jews. Cubans are a majority in many areas; Haitians predominate in the city of North Miami and the Little Haiti neighborhood in Miami city; African Americans make up large majorities of cities like Opa Locka and Miami Gardens, many unincorporated county neighborhoods, and Miami city neighborhoods such as Liberty City and Overtown.

Miami-Dade County and Miami city have a higher percentage of black and Hispanic residents than does the U.S. population, according to the 2000 Census (see table 8.1).[1] The disproportionately high Hispanic population is especially apparent. Among Hispanics, the population diverges from the national pattern by being distinctively more Cuban and less Mexican, and also more Central American and South American (see table 8.2).

The county and city populations are more heavily immigrant than is the nation's (over 50% compared to less than 12% in 2000). Over 90 percent of the county and city's immigrant populations came from Latin America, compared to just over 50 percent for the nation as a whole. Almost 68 percent of the county's

1. Figures in the following text and tables are taken from the Census Bureau website, 2000 Census.

■ **Table 8.2**   Percentage of Hispanic residents by type: United States, Miami-Dade County, and city of Miami

ORIGIN	UNITED STATES (%)	MIAMI-DADE COUNTY (%)	CITY OF MIAMI (%)
Mexican	58.5	2.9	1.5
Puerto Rican	9.6	6.2	4.3
Cuban	3.5	50.4	51.9
Central American	4.8	10.0	16.8
South American	3.8	11.9	6.3
Dominican Republic	2.2	2.8	2.7

population and three quarters of the city's population speak a language other than English at home, and of these, between a third (county) and a half (city) do not rate themselves as speaking English "very well." In contrast, less than 18 percent of the U.S. population speaks a foreign language at home, and 92 percent of these rate themselves as speaking English very well. After Spanish, Haitian Kreyol is the second most spoken foreign language.

The county has a higher proportion and the city a much higher proportion of service occupations; the county has a lower proportion and the city a much lower proportion of management and professional occupations than does the United States (see table 8.3).

This mix of occupations means that wages are lower in the county, and considerably lower in the city, than in the United States as a whole.

Industrially, the county and city are less manufacturing intensive than is the country (a bit above 7% compared to 14% nationally). The public sector is smaller (4.1% and 3.3% of the county and city economies, compared to 4.8%). Wholesale trade is larger than normal (6.0% and 5.5%, compared to 3.6%). The large service sectors are mostly low-paying industries such as recreation, accommodation, food services, entertainment, and "other services," although high-level legal and financial jobs also are abundant. Women hold many low-paying service

■ **Table 8.3**   Service and professional occupations as percentage of workforce: United States, Miami-Dade County, and the city of Miami, 2000

OCCUPATION	UNITED STATES (%)	MIAMI-DADE COUNTY (%)	CITY OF MIAMI (%)	COUNTY VARIANCE FROM NATIONAL PERCENTAGE	CITY VARIANCE FROM NATIONAL PERCENTAGE
Service	14.9	16.9	22.1	+2.0	+7.2
Management or Professional	33.6	30.2	23.8	−3.4	−9.8

■ **Table 8.4**   Percentage of individuals and families in poverty in 1999:
United States, Miami-Dade County, and the city of Miami

IN POVERTY	UNITED STATES (%)	MIAMI-DADE COUNTY (%)	CITY OF MIAMI (%)
Individuals	12.4	18.0	28.5
Families	9.2	14.5	23.5

jobs. Most businesses are small: in 2001 over 98 percent of the county's businesses employed fewer than one hundred persons, and almost 90 percent employed fewer than twenty (U.S. Census Bureau, County Business Patterns 2001).

This combination of less manufacturing, a smaller public sector, more mostly low-paying service industries, and small businesses means low incomes. Median household income in the county in 1999 was over 14 percent lower than in the nation ($35,966 vs. $41,994), and the city median household income was 44 percent lower ($23,483 vs. $41,994). In 1999 the county had an official poverty level almost 50 percent above that of the nation, and the city's poverty rate was well over double that of the nation (see table 8.4).

By 2003 the county's individual poverty rate had climbed to 18.4 percent, eighteenth highest of the covered counties in the nation. The city's individual poverty rate had dropped slightly to 27.9 percent, placing it fifth highest in the nation (U.S. Census Bureau 2003, American Community Survey).

Politically, Miami-Dade County usually votes by a small margin for the Democratic candidates for president and U.S. Senate and statewide offices. To win the nonpartisan countywide mayor's race, candidates court voters in each ethnic constituency. The huge Cuban vote goes Republican by fairly large margins, offsetting the Democratic advantage with almost every other demographic group. The county's mayor is a Cuban American Republican, and the thirteen-member county commission is composed of four African American Democrats, two non-Hispanic white Democrats, and seven Cuban American Republicans.

Redistricting by the state's Republican-dominated legislature made the Miami-Dade state legislative delegation 60 percent Republican. Thirteen of the fifteen Republicans are Cuban American, with one Colombian American and a non-Hispanic white. The ten Democrats are five African Americans, two Haitian Americans, and three non-Hispanic whites. The first Hispanic to be speaker of the Florida House of Representatives is a Cuban Republican from Miami-Dade County. The four members of the U.S. Congress are three Cuban American Republicans and one African American Democrat.

The Republican edge in many local political structures does not necessarily translate into hostility to unions. More than a few Cuban American Republican politicians campaign on progressive social and economic policy issues in order to mobilize their working-class bases. They may sponsor and vote for legislation defending unions as often as some Democrats, and oftentimes more effectively. For example, a Cuban American Republican on the Miami-Dade County Commission spearheaded the drive for a living wage ordinance, and a Cuban American Republican legislator and CWA member has championed pro-union/pro-worker legislation, including a bill to secure health care for health-care workers.

On issues of direct institutional importance to organized labor such as privatization of union public sector jobs, unions in Miami-Dade County usually can defend themselves better than unions in other Republican-dominated parts of the state. Union density is low, but Cuban politicians must rely on working-class votes, thus benefiting unions to some degree.

The labor movement thus operates in a complex context. Politically, the area is divided among many nationalities and races and is split along partisan political lines. While the demographic, economic, and political divisions are obstacles for the labor movement, they create major opportunities for it to serve as a bridge to ally divided communities and become a strong voice for the growing working class.

THE LOCAL LABOR MOVEMENT AND "SOCIAL JUSTICE INFRASTRUCTURE" ORGANIZATIONS

Florida is the only Southern state with collective bargaining rights for public sector workers, but it is also a right-to-work state, so many workers covered by a union contract do not pay union dues. Employers routinely engage in vicious union-busting campaigns.

In 2005 union density in the Miami–Ft. Lauderdale area was 5.5 percent, compared to a 5.4 percent state rate (in a three-way tie for 40th–42nd of the fifty states). Local area private sector union density was 2.3 percent, compared to 2.5 percent statewide (48th in the nation). In the public sector, local area union density was 24.2 percent, slightly above the state rate of 22.3 percent.[2]

Public sector unions numerically dominate the local labor movement in Miami-Dade County.[3] A few private sector unions have high union density in a par-

---

2. See http://www.unionstats.com.

3. Largest is the teachers union (AFT), followed by AFSCME. Other public sector unions include a Transport Workers Union local representing county transit, the American Postal Workers Union (APWU) and National Association of Letter Carriers (NALC), the International Association of Fire Fighters (IAFF), an Office and Professional Employees International Union (OPEIU) local of government supervisors, a policemen's union, and an SEIU local representing county public hospital nurses. Private sector (or primarily private sector) unions include a couple of Teamsters locals, two Longshore (ILA) locals, two CWA locals, a HERE local, a number of building trades locals, transport workers and Machinists (IAM) at the airport, and an SEIU local representing nursing home and hospital workers led by one of the authors of this chapter (Monica Russo).

ticular market niche, such as the Communications Workers of America (CWA) in "traditional" telephone or the International Longshoremen's Association (ILA) at the ports. But low private sector union density limits material gains, which are sought primarily through national or regional bargaining (CWA, some International Brotherhood of Teamsters contracts) or local political influence over employers (such as airport unions and construction unions with publicly financed construction). The latter strategy has limited utility given organized labor's small size and the makeup of local elected officialdom.

In the public sector, unions usually stave off the worst assaults, such as wholesale privatization of union members' jobs. But even here organized labor is relatively weak due to the small size of the overall labor movement and internal weaknesses, making membership participation in political or other affairs quite minimal.

Most unions have done little organizing. The Carpenters, UNITE and HERE (now joined in UNITE HERE), Laborers, Teamsters, Communications Workers, SEIU nurses, and a few others have attempted to organize with mixed success. An Ironworkers local grew rapidly in the late 1990s through organizing and internal reorganizing by an exceptional organizer. But for most unions memberships are stagnating and often declining.

In the past the most dynamic union, both in organizing and in building community coalitions, was SEIU 1199 Florida, then a nursing home workers' union led by Monica Russo (coauthor of this chapter). This local had an 82 percent win rate in National Labor Relations Board (NLRB) elections between January 1996 and 2005. It organized 50 percent of the nursing home market in Miami-Dade County but less than 15 percent in its statewide jurisdiction. SEIU 1199 Florida recently merged with nurses and hospital employees to form a new local—SEIU Florida Healthcare Union—which launched a major drive to organize South Florida's acute-care hospital market and succeeded in organizing and winning contracts for over thirty-five hundred workers in four Miami-Dade hospitals in less than two years.

The central labor council had until recently been a virtual political extension of the large teachers union local, the United Teachers of Dade. The UTD, born of a mass struggle in the 1960s, had hardened into an oligarchic union led by a corrupt leader who engaged in backroom deals. In 2003 and 2004, this individual was indicted and convicted of fraud for looting the union's treasury. In 2005 the UTD elected a new progressive leadership that was willing to let the central labor council operate as an autonomous body.

The labor council is currently led by a progressive and enthusiastic labor leader, Fred Frost (from the Transport Workers Union), who rallied the labor movement to support a pro-labor (but losing) candidate for mayor of the county in the 2004 election. He has also reestablished relationships with progressive union activists as well as Change to Win unions. However, scarce resources and a far-less-than-activist leadership base among the council's member unions limit the council's effectiveness.

In short, this has been a very traditional labor movement that also includes a couple of dynamic and activist unions that have not dominated the local central labor council. However, initial steps toward revitalization in the 1997–2005 period began with what we call the growth of a local "social justice infrastructure" capable of supporting efforts to organize and empower workers locally. The past lack of a progressive infrastructure meant that organizing unions such as the SEIU Florida Healthcare Union had to create or support organizations and networks to boost union organizing drives and other working-class campaigns for social justice.

The living wage issue began the recent growth of social justice organizing (Nissen 2004). In 1997 leaders from the central labor council, a coalition of human service providers, the NAACP, Florida Legal Services, the Gray Panthers, a tenant's council, and others formed the Community Coalition for a Living Wage (CCLW) to fight for a county living wage ordinance, which was won with five hundred people, mostly union members, applauding its final passage.

But this was not a genuine social movement, as has been detailed elsewhere (Nissen 2000). The living wage ordinance passed mainly because there was no organized business opposition. As of early 2006 the CCLW had just won a living wage ordinance in the city of Miami and was working for ordinances in the cities of Hialeah and Coral Gables. But it has no sizable base to mobilize, and it relies exclusively on lobbying. One central labor council representative sits on the CCLW's steering committee, but unions play a minor role in its efforts, which are led by church-based or community activists.

Nevertheless, the passage of the Miami-Dade living wage ordinance had an important symbolic importance. It showed that victories can be won for working families in Miami. Living wage victories spread to Miami Beach, neighboring Broward County, and other urban areas of the state. The national Association of Community Organizations for Reform Now (ACORN) created chapters in South Florida and throughout the state because of these living wage victories, and it is now an established pro-labor presence in South Florida and statewide, broadening the social justice infrastructure.

In 1998 a local South Florida Interfaith Committee for Worker Justice chapter was established. This committee went through growing pains and some contentious skirmishes with an earlier generation of central labor council leaders (Nissen 2004, 75–76). But eventually it became an established organization with genuine church and synagogue buy-in to its leadership and program, though it still has a limited grassroots base.

The interfaith committee was not a major player influencing employer behavior during union organizing drives prior to 2006, although it did write letters of spiritual concern when employers resisted unions, and it has played a role in public events and rallies of support for union organizing. However, in 2006 it played a major role in supporting an SEIU Justice for Janitors struggle at the University of Miami, and it has also run a workers' rights counseling and advocacy program to help homeless day laborers and low-wage workers enforce their rights.

Another faith-based organization is a more traditional grassroots organizing project of the type pioneered by Saul Alinsky. People Acting for Community Together, which started in 1988, is a coalition of twenty-nine congregations and allied organizations in Miami-Dade County affiliated with the national Direct Action and Research Training network. It has worked on education, health-care, immigration, and transportation issues. It has a grassroots base with demonstrated mobilizing capacity. Direct relationships with the labor movement have been minimal, and it is not clear whether it will orient itself toward labor issues.

The Miami Workers Center, a political education and organizing center for low-income African American communities and low-wage workers in Miami-Dade County, was created in 1999. The center has founded an organization of and for current and former welfare recipients, low-wage workers, and public housing residents named Low Income Families Fighting Together. A somewhat similar organization, Power U Center for Social Change, exists in the African American neighborhood of Overtown. The Miami Workers Center and to some degree Power U represent a phenomenon that has appeared in many U.S. locations in the past decade: self-described worker centers that are primarily community organizing projects independent of ties to unions. Past collaboration with organized labor has been limited, but an emerging coalition to win community benefits from development projects that contains both union-related groups and these two organizations is progressing.

In 2001 SEIU 1199 Florida created Unite for Dignity for Immigrant Workers Rights in order to build stronger immigrant community ties and immigrant worker leadership. Unite for Dignity's signature program is the Leadership Academy, which has graduated over 125 emerging immigrant leaders (80% of them women) from a cross-section of the community. Unite for Dignity strengthens labor's relations with grassroots immigrant organizations and builds mobilizing capacity for immigrant community issues such as driver's licenses for undocumented workers, ending the indefinite detention of Haitian refugees, and immigrant access to health care and higher education. It also hosts a popular weekly Haitian radio program on issues of interest to workers and is establishing a Spanish radio show.

In the 2004 election campaign Unite for Dignity partnered with the newly formed Mi Familia Vota 100% (My Family Votes 100%, formerly a program of the Center for Immigrant Democracy) to train community volunteers for the largest Hispanic civic participation program in the history of Florida, registering more than forty thousand new voters. Mi Familia Vota reports that 30 percent of new Cuban/Hispanic voters in Miami-Dade County registered as Democrats, 40 percent as independents, and 30 percent as Republicans. Postelection, Mi Familia Vota is positioned to move progressive, pro-labor issues in key newly enfranchised communities, with the potential to influence Hispanic political dynamics.

In late 1999 the SEIU Florida Healthcare Union (then operating as a joint SEIU-UNITE venture under a different name) joined the local NAACP chapter and others to create a South Florida chapter of Jobs with Justice (SF JwJ). South Florida JwJ has more than twenty member organizations, including a broad cross section of South Florida unions as well as important community groups such as the Human Services Coalition and Unite for Dignity.

South Florida JwJ became an important center of the progressive working-class movement in Miami. Founded to support workers' rights to organize, it quickly found that community mobilization for labor issues required working on issues important to the community also, which required a multicultural approach. During a UNITE campaign to organize Cuban workers at Goya Foods, SF JwJ hosted events celebrating the lives of Martin Luther King Jr. and José Martí, and Cuban workers spoke on black AM radio about exploitation.

The SF JwJ chapter also was at the center of the historic March on Tallahassee to preserve affirmative action in 2000. This event put SF JwJ on the community map. SF JwJ has since been involved to various degrees in many working-class campaigns—the living wage, a statewide ballot initiative to reduce class size, a state minimum wage ballot initiative (spearheaded by ACORN statewide), voting rights, health care for all in Miami-Dade County, immigrant rights issues including equal treatment for Haitians and Dominicans and the Immigrant Workers Freedom Ride, antiprivatization campaigns, mobilizing for the Miami Free Trade Association of the Americas meeting, and development of a community benefits agreement (CBA) coalition to force developers to deliver concrete benefits to low-income communities and workers.

SF JwJ's most successful support for the right to organize was the Mount Sinai–St Francis Nursing Home campaign, where the employer claimed union "voodoo" tactics scared the workers into voting union. SF JwJ and Unite for Dignity rallied local Haitian pastors, elected officials, and radio personalities to condemn the racist and anti-immigrant tactics. It also held a workers' rights board hearing chaired by actor Danny Glover that induced the employer to abandon its tactics and negotiate a contract. This campaign built support for a worker's voice on the job and for the need to support the right to organize.

Through the various worker struggles for justice in the African American and Haitian communities, SF JwJ and its key affiliates have developed close relationships with progressive local black elected officials who have taken up pro-labor agendas at the city, county, state, and federal level. In the absence of strong black organizations in the community outside of the church, the black elected officials have become key allies in the progressive movement. This is also reflected in the composition of the workers' rights board set up by SF JwJ.

SF JwJ operates through standing committees. The Healthcare Committee addresses the lack of health-care insurance for half a million residents of Miami-Dade County. Key participants include the Human Services Coalition and the SEIU union of nurses, SEIU Local 1991. A major difficulty for SF JwJ in this area is developing local solutions for a national crisis.

A previously active committee was the Immigrant Rights Committee, co-chaired by a Unite for Dignity staffer. It organized and coordinated the segment of the national Immigrant Workers Freedom Ride originating in Miami and worked on Haitian immigrant rights and efforts to obtain Florida driver's licenses and access to education for all immigrant state residents irrespective of legal status. This committee brought SF JwJ into contact with many immigrant organizations.[4] More recently, SF JwJ outreach to immigrants has centered on a residents' committee in Little Havana to fight for community benefits from the renovation of the Orange Bowl, which is in their neighborhood.

In 2006, SF JwJ developed a network of student activists from the county's various college and university campuses, to help fill a void in local progressive organizing. It also undertook a campaign in solidarity with an independent Colombian flower workers' union, since Miami is the number one import destination in the nation for flowers.

Two new elements have been added to the area's social justice infrastructure. SEIU's new building services local (SEIU Local 11), formed in the spring of 2004, is attempting to unionize residential building service workers in the county, starting with condominiums in Miami Beach and janitorial workers at the University of Miami and other local institutions of higher education.[5] In the summer of 2006 it won a stunning victory at the University of Miami following a highly publicized

---

4. Organizations include Veye Yo, Florida Immigrant Advocacy Center and Florida Immigrant Coalition, Rezistans Lakay, Bajo el Arbol, Latinos Unidos, Famn Ayisyen nan Miami, De Inmigrantes para Inmigrantes, Comité Pro Legalización, Abriendo Puertas, and the Haitian American Grassroots Coalition. The Florida Immigrant Coalition has stepped forward to spearhead many of the efforts for immigrant rights.

5. Janitors in downtown offices are not being targeted in this drive, which is aimed at the condominium sector, a rapidly growing segment of the local housing structure, and local universities, which represent easier organizing targets.

creative militant struggle. This local is using a well-resourced Justice for Janitors–approach to organizing, with a decidedly social movement orientation. It is a valuable addition to the efforts to revitalize the local labor movement. The merger of unions to form UNITE HERE may create a synergy in organizing workers in Miami Beach buildings that are partly hotels and partly condos.

The research capacity needed to investigate, analyze, and validate issues raised by movements has been a weakness in the past. The newly created Research Institute on Social and Economic Policy (RISEP), housed at Florida International University under the direction of Bruce Nissen (coauthor of this chapter), intends to build this budding movement's capacity to move a broader social policy agenda by researching issues raised by labor, labor-community, and working-class community organizing in South Florida and in the state as a whole.[6]

REASONS FOR LABOR'S PAST WEAKNESS AND RECENT REVITALIZATION ADVANCES

Analysis of the Miami labor movement requires answers to two questions: Why has the labor movement historically been rather weak? And what explains the recent progress toward labor revitalization? Answers to both questions might focus on three factors: the social and economic context, the political opportunity structure, and internal union strategy and resource mobilization.

Organized labor's weakness in Miami in the 1990s owes much to the historical legacy of the defeat of the Eastern Airlines unions in 1989–90. When Eastern Airlines CEO Frank Lorenzo bankrupted and destroyed the airline in his drive to defeat the Machinists union (IAM) and the Transport Workers Union local representing the company's flight attendants, he destroyed Miami's most powerful private sector unions (Bernstein 1990; Baicich 1987). Demoralization gripped the local labor movement for years afterward. A second source of weakness is that a teacher's union local, whose leadership was at best lukewarm to virtually all social movement activities, dominated the labor movement and the central labor council for much of the 1990s, exerting a bureaucratic heavy hand to constrain movement activism.

The local social and economic context also made mass organizing and movement activism difficult. The county's workforce was over 50 percent foreign born and highly fragmented and divided. African Americans were economically marginalized, with high unemployment partly because few could speak Spanish. Haitian Americans could find work but faced intense discrimination on the job

---

6. See the RISEP mission statement and advisory board at http://www.risep-fiu.org.

and exceedingly low wages. The county's economy was unusually tilted toward small businesses, with a predominance of sectors such as services and wholesale trade. Highly conservative Cuban business owners controlled a great deal of the county's economic activity outside the largest companies, which were usually still led by Anglos.

Politically, Republican and conservative "yellow dog" Democrat dominance over many political formations has made the political opportunity structure less than desirable for union advance. The state's right-to-work law is also a political obstacle to organizing.

But we believe that both the contextual and political obstacles can be (and frequently are) overstated. As noted previously, Republicans in South Florida are often responsive to working-class constituencies if those constituencies are organized. The local political opportunity structure is far from closed to unions and working-class organizations, if they organize and exert power. And the stereotype of the Cuban community as one reactionary mass is wrong when it concerns domestic issues. Cuban American workers are open to union organizing, if unions work to organize them and develop leadership from within their ranks (Nissen and Grenier 2001; Nissen 2002).

By far the most important explanation for past union weakness in South Florida is the failure of unions to develop strategies and resources to organize and build working-class power. Unions that have attempted to do well-resourced aggressive organizing and to build up social justice organizations, such as SEIU Florida Healthcare Union, have been able to do so. But few unions have had a strategy to do either of these things. The internal failings of the labor movement have occurred at both the local and national level. Locally, not enough leaders are thinking and acting according to a strategic "organizing" and "progressive infrastructure-building" perspective such as that presented here. But, equally or perhaps even more important, national unions generally have not been willing to put in the resources necessary to carry out ambitious plans. Virtually all local unions need major resources (people and money) to do aggressive organizing and infrastructure building, and most national unions are not providing it. When they do and this is combined with local leadership that is strategic and determined, results are apparent. The rapid growth of SEIU Florida Healthcare Union is a clear example.

Likewise, we think that the explanation for the recent progress toward labor revitalization lies in the areas of strategy and resource mobilization. Neither the socioeconomic context nor the political opportunity structure for organized labor has improved appreciably in South Florida in the last eight years. The basic social and economic environment remains much as before, and politicians and the political terrain have not become friendlier.

What has changed is that a series of demonstrated successes both locally and nationally has fired the imaginations of decision makers and induced them to invest increasing strategic thinking and resources in labor revitalization and progressive infrastructure building. Living wage victories, successful faith-based organizations elsewhere, the prominence of worker centers around the nation, SEIU Florida Healthcare Union's successful organizing on a large scale, the national growth and prominence of Jobs with Justice, and the resurgence of labor in such California cities as Los Angeles and San Jose stimulated all the positive local developments we relate above. Local actors formed Unite for Dignity, Mi Familia Vota, South Florida Jobs with Justice, South Florida Interfaith Committee for Worker Justice, Miami Workers Center, Power U Center for Social Change, and local ACORN chapters largely because of these stimuli. National foundations and funders began putting money into some of these organizations because of the California successes and local Miami developments. And at least one national union, SEIU, decided to invest major resources in both property services and health-care organizing because previous investment in SEIU Local 1199 Florida had paid off. Just as previous revitalization successes have relied on strategic and resource questions, so must any strategy for further labor revitalization.

STRATEGIZING FOR THE FUTURE: HOW TO DRIVE REVITALIZATION FORWARD

In less than a decade, the activist elements in labor have laid the groundwork for potentially the most successful organizing yet to be done in the South—in politically charged, emotional, eclectic, and unpredictable Miami-Dade County. In 1996, the labor-progressive presence could be described as mute, invisible, disrespected, and/or utterly marginal. By 2006 there was a growing progressive social justice infrastructure to support union and political organizing.

The broader activist labor movement needs to transform itself from a progressive network into a movement capable of executing real social change. To do so, it must build and expand on key components of the area's social justice infrastructure—leadership development, research, and civic participation. Second, it needs to solicit major union investment of resources and talent that is critical to organizing markets and exponentially growing the power of the broader labor movement. And third, it needs to change the strategic direction of its coalition work.

Reinforcing the Infrastructure

Many pieces of the needed social justice infrastructure have been created, but they must be expanded, deepened, and coordinated. Organizations such as Unite for Dignity (leadership development), South Florida Jobs with Justice (labor-community coalition), Mi Familia Vota (immigrant civic participation), and the Research Institute on Social and Economic Policy (research) now exist. Some of these structures are already drawing attention from the foundation world, key unions, and political funders.

Collective leadership development programs—union based, academic, and immigrant—need to train, track, advance, and promote thousands (not dozens) of working-class leaders. More commitment and effort must be devoted to training potential labor and progressive leaders and moving them into real leadership roles throughout the movement, including directing progressive nonprofits, leading union organizing campaigns, running for elected office, hosting radio shows, and heading political campaigns and canvassing operations.

Progressive civic participation needs to be ongoing, not simply funded during federal election cycles. Organizations such as Mi Familia Vota could have a tremendous impact when they move issue campaigns in communities by deploying armies of local canvassers and organizers. This work needs to be coordinated with union organizing campaigns to amplify community support for workers under attack by their employers. These newly enfranchised communities can begin to set a new working-class agenda.

The largest working-class base in Florida is in the churches. More resources will need to be devoted to organizing in religious institutions, with faith-based organizing reaching down into the base, not simply restricted to some religious leaders.

Research capacity is also underdeveloped. Some useful research has been done on living wage movement issues, condominium workers, violations of workers' rights during organizing drives, poverty, lack of affordable housing, lack of healthcare, and Florida's poor treatment of workers in general.[7] But more, and more sharply focused, academic-labor collaborative research is needed.

Capacity building includes recruiting more talent to the movement and developing leaders, developing more sophisticated public relations, communications, websites, upgraded technology, and database systems. Unions and community-based organizations need to consider affiliations, collaborations, and sharing of staff to increase collective capacity.

---

7. For examples of this work see the studies found at http://www.risep-fiu.org.

Sustained Union Investment

There have been sporadic union election victories over the years, but only a few unions have dug in for the long haul—with resources. Drives by SEIU's property services and health-care locals and the Teamsters' solid waste and seaport truck drivers' campaigns are the only active market campaigns in Miami. The extent to which these unions recognize, commit to, and invest in strategic community-based partnerships will both determine their organizing effectiveness and the future of the progressive labor movement. Until workers win power in key markets, the progressive movement will continue to be marginal and qualitative change will be out of reach for working communities.

Strategic Focus of Coalition Work

South Florida JwJ is the broadest attempt to bring union, faith, and community activists into alliance. It has established positive relations with the new local AFL-CIO leadership in joint work beyond traditional bread-and-butter union causes, such as those against the Free Trade Association of the Americas and for voting rights. However, in the past SF JwJ focused on tactical support—"I'll be there" in solidarity at rallies, pickets, and forums. This helped to build a network and extend a progressive presence, but it has not affected policy in a major way.

For labor-progressive revitalization, SF JwJ has decided that it needs to move from tactical solidarity to a power model. Instead of saying "yes" to every organization that needs turnout at a rally it will have to learn how to say "no" to nonstrategic requests. This would allow it to focus limited resources on strategic policy and partnerships.

One approach would be policy campaigns where SF JwJ is a lead organization garnering labor and community support for important local public policy changes such as expanding access to health-care coverage, driver's licenses for immigrant workers, labor peace agreements, or community benefits agreements. In fall 2004, SF JwJ chose community benefits agreements—requiring jobs, affordable housing, and other benefits from development projects—as a strategic policy campaign, staffing a central labor council component of this work and working with many of the organizations named above in a broader CBA coalition.

The potential of a CBA policy campaign could be great. First, through its staffing of a central labor council task force, SF JwJ is bringing in unions well beyond the usual "organizing unions"—a first. Second, many community groups that have had little experience working with labor are beginning to coalesce around this issue. Broader union buy-in and potential community partners beyond the usual suspects are enormously important. Whether the union-based effort for well-paying unionized jobs in development projects will mesh well with community struggles against gentrification and for affordable housing and a healthy environment remains to be seen. But, like the living wage, CBA policy work may last for years and, if so, the ties forged should be invaluable for future union organizing.

A second strategic focus might be for SF JwJ to become the meeting place for key unions to plan joint work in industry- or area-focused organizing campaigns. To do this SF JwJ would have to ground its long-term planning in partnership with key anchor unions that have a strategic plan, along with major resources, to win a major market share. The potential is there to work with UNITE HERE in the hotel industry, Laborers International Union of North America (LIUNA) and other unions in the construction industry, SEIU in acute care and/or property services, or the Teamsters in the waste management or seaport sectors.

Both the "strategic policy campaign" focus and the "strategic partnership with unions" focus require SF JwJ to become much more disciplined, focused, and strategic. This is difficult in a coalition with such a large number of organizational members (over twenty), all with their own concerns. Many unions join SF JwJ expecting that little more will be required of them than occasional shows of token solidarity at events for others; in return, they expect the same demonstrations of solidarity for their own causes. Moving beyond this "you scratch my back, I'll scratch yours" mentality will be a major task and a measure of how successful the organization can be in becoming more strategically focused.

Real Working-Class Power

Several key grassroots organizations have recently bonded together to move the social justice agenda in Miami. Aggressive and well-resourced market organizing campaigns are ramping up and under way in building services and health care, and market campaigns are also under way in waste management and seaport trucking. The existing capacity of South Florida's social justice infrastructure is not sufficient to sustain all these major and viciously contested market campaigns, and therefore it must be consolidated and expanded. Strategic focus, base building, leadership development, research, and creative coalition building with "unusual suspects" are also needed.

This is a new moment for the working class in South Florida. It is now within the realm of possibility for one or two unions to gain a major market share in key South Florida labor markets and to win policy changes that will improve the quality of life for working-class Miamians. If that occurs, we would say that Miami-area labor has indeed been revitalized.

9

IMMIGRANTS AND LABOR IN A GLOBALIZING CITY

Prospects for Coalition Building in Nashville

Daniel B. Cornfield and William Canak

Mounting employment-related problems have accompanied the recent and rapid settlement of new immigrants and refugees in the vast, globalizing interior of the United States. Sweatshop working conditions, underemployment, unemployment, occupational injuries, and poverty are some of the problems facing the millions of new immigrants and refugees from Latin America, Africa, Asia, and the Middle East who are settling for the first time in that large swath of land between Minnesota and Texas. In this rapidly globalizing, formerly secluded interior region of the nation, local labor movements and advocates for the new immigrants are beginning to form coalitions in order to address their employment problems (AFL-CIO 2003; Fine 2006; Singer 2004; U.S. Bureau of the Census 2003b; Zúñiga and Hernández-León 2005).

Building coalitions between local labor movements and immigrant advocacy groups is an important labor revitalization strategy in the globalizing interior. Like traditionally unionized coastal regions, the globalizing interior has experienced substantial union decline over the last four decades. For example, the percentage of the labor force who are union members, that is, union density, in the states of the former Confederacy declined from 14.8 percent to 6.3 percent between 1964 and 2002 (Eckes 2005, 43). In Tennessee, where our Nashville study is situated, union density declined from 22.1 percent to 5.4 percent between 1964 and 2005 (Eckes 2005, 43; U.S. Bureau of Labor Statistics 2006). Eckes (2005) attributes Southern union decline to globalization and plant shutdowns in Southern manufacturing. The globalizing interior's vibrant service economies, however, contain a growing nonunion, culturally and economically marginalized

We are grateful to Lowell Turner, the participants in the "Urban Labor Revitalization: Large, Midsize, and Global Cities" conference at the ILR School, Cornell University, the participants in the "Power, Politics, and Social Movements" seminar in the Department of Sociology, Vanderbilt University, and two anonymous reviewers for their helpful comments on previous drafts of this chapter, and to our interviewees, who must remain anonymous, for sharing their insights about the situation of immigrant workers in Nashville. We are also grateful to the ILR School, Cornell University, for financial support.

immigrant labor force. These workers and their larger immigrant communities constitute a field where labor's established economic, organizational, and political resources find fertile opportunities for coalition building, union organizing, and possible revitalization.

The newness of immigration and immigrant organizing in the globalizing U.S. interior challenges local labor leaders and immigrant rights advocates to form coalitions. Immigrants and refugees, many of whom are not citizens, lack access to the polity and ethnic communal organizations and are often socioeconomically and culturally marginal in their new destination communities. At the same time, local labor union memberships have declined in all U.S. regions, lowering labor's bargaining power and diminishing its resources. The chief challenges for coalition building are surmounting organizational and cultural barriers and sharing organizational and cultural resources between groups that have had little or no previous contact with one another and whose mutual suspicions must be replaced by mutual trust and commonality of purpose. Immigrant-labor coalition building in the U.S. interior also is challenged by the disproportionate prevalence of antilabor state right-to-work laws in interior states. The right-to-work states include Florida and Texas, which are major ports of entry and include established, urban immigrant ethnic enclaves. Our purpose in this chapter is to examine the prospects for immigrant-labor coalition formation in Nashville, Tennessee, a globalizing city of the U.S. interior. Immigrant-labor coalition building in Nashville is recent and, as such, Nashville serves as a case of emergent coalition formation among these groups (Farris 2005).

NASHVILLE AS CONTEXT FOR IMMIGRANT-LABOR COALITION BUILDING

According to the final report of the 2002–03 Immigrant Community Assessment of Nashville, the number of foreign born, especially from Latin America, but also from Africa, Asia, eastern Europe, and the Middle East, in Nashville tripled to almost 10 percent of Nashville-Davidson County's six hundred thousand residents during the 1990s. Nashville's robust, full-employment service economy and moderate cost of living have made it an attractive destination community for immigrants and refugees over the last two decades; Nashville's percentage of foreign born is now at the U.S. average for all cities. Three-fourths of the foreign born in Nashville are not U.S. citizens and, with a 24 percent poverty rate, are twice as likely as natives to be poor. The poverty rate of Nashville's foreign born is similar to that of African Americans and Hispanics, who constitute 25 percent and 5 percent of Nashville's population, respectively (Cornfield et al. 2003; Cornfield 2004; Farris 2005; Swarns 2003).

The newness of immigration to Nashville is reflected in Nashville's relatively small foreign-born population and ethnic homogeneity. According to the U.S. Census Bureau, Nashville ranked 49th in percentage foreign-born in 2003, 179th in percentage Hispanic in 2000, and 141st in percentage Asian in 2000 among the largest U.S. cities (U.S. Bureau of the Census 2002, 2003a).

Nashville's traditionally Democratic electorate and service economy and the Tennessee anti-union "right-to-work" law contextualize collective bargaining and labor organizing. The economy is grounded in Nashville's role as the state capital and in higher education and in the health-care, finance and insurance, religious publishing, entertainment and music-recording, tourism, and retail industries. The enduring but small local labor movement of independent and AFL-CIO-affiliated unions—we estimate that no more than 10 percent of the metropolitan labor force is unionized—is based largely in the building trades, all three levels of government, public education, telecommunications,.transportation, retail, entertainment, and a few automotive and other manufacturing facilities. Nashville also is home to the headquarters of the Tennessee AFL-CIO State Labor Council. At the time this study was conducted, Nashville also was home to the headquarters of the Paper, Allied-Industrial, Chemical and Energy Workers International Union. The Nashville labor movement has operated on a traditional model of "business unionism" with few new strategies and sustained initiatives in labor organizing and coalition building.

The challenges of immigrant integration in Nashville have stimulated the development of a range of immigrant advocacy networks and organizations. These immigrant-centered networks and organizations exist in a set of loosely coupled relationships that constitute an emerging, but as yet still crystallizing, social movement to address immigrant rights and improve the livelihoods of immigrants. These include umbrella organizations for social justice, advocacy, and information sharing; ethnic community organizations, religious institutions, and cultural centers; neighborhood organizations in the southeast quadrant of Nashville (along Nolensville and Murfreesboro roads), where the majority of the foreign born of many ethnic backgrounds live; and progressive, culturally sensitive, professional social service and resettlement service providers (Cornfield et al. 2003; Cornfield 2004; Farris 2005).

According to the 2002–03 Immigrant Community Assessment of Nashville, a distinct, ethnically patterned set of employment issues has arisen for Nashville's immigrant workers. The focus group discussions of the assessment that were conducted in seven languages with African, Asian, Middle Eastern, and Latin American immigrants indicated three employment issues: (1) economic marginalization—low wages and unsafe working conditions, especially in the informal construction industry among undocumented Mexican and Central American workers; (2) underemployment and cultural exclusion—the downward social mobility of former professionals and business people who, lacking formal credentials, are employed in the secondary labor market and who may experience on-the-job religious ostracism, especially among Muslim refugees from the Middle East and Africa; and (3) insufficient refugee resettlement assistance and age discrimination—the quick placement of refugees in low-wage secondary labor market jobs, as well as discrimination against older workers, especially among refugees from East Asia (Cornfield et al. 2003; Cornfield 2004).

The 2002–03 Immigrant Community Assessment of Nashville confirms that immigrants are not addressing their employment issues by unionizing. Instead, immigrants have developed their own ethnic enclave economies (especially among Latino and Asian immigrant groups), informal networks for job referrals and making child-care arrangements, paid homework, and English-language acquisition (Cornfield 2004).

Nonetheless, immigrant rights advocates and local labor leaders have begun to develop a shared sense of purpose. In September 2003, for example, Nashville was on the national inter-coastal itinerary of rallies in the AFL-CIO's Immigrant Worker Freedom Ride. A local immigrant-labor coalition produced the Nashville rally (personal observation and AFL-CIO, 2003).

FRAMEWORK AND METHODOLOGY

To assess the prospects for immigrant-labor coalition formation in Nashville, we applied sociological "frame-alignment" and "resource mobilization" theories to develop a framework for discerning the available configuration of requisite cultural and organizational resources, and deficits in these resources, for deployment, exchange, and coalition building among Nashville's immigrant advocates and labor unions (Cornfield and Fletcher 1998, 2001). Cultural resources are elements of individual and collective cognitive frames—missions, values, attitudes, and criticisms—that are shared by and generate mutual attraction between individuals and social movements. Organizational resources are factors that facilitate purposeful worker mobilization, including leadership, multilingual communication skills, organization, finances, organizers, and technical knowledge. We gauged the available configuration of cultural and organizational resources by interviewing a purposive snowball sample of twenty-five Nashville immigrant rights advocates and labor leaders in the summer and fall of 2004. Based on a semistructured, open-ended interview schedule, each interview lasted an average of two hours and covered the interviewee's attitudes about and awareness of immigrants and labor unions; the mission and activities of the interviewee's organization; the interviewee's experience with, evaluation of, and assessment of the future prospects for immigrant-labor coalition building in Nashville; and the interviewee's personal inspiration for becoming an advocate or labor leader.

In developing our Nashville sample, we inductively mapped immigrant rights advocates in three subgroups: (1) public interest groups that pursued social justice missions; (2) immigrant ethnic communities and organizations that pursued mutual-aid, cultural preservation, and social integration missions; and (3) social service providers who specialized in immigrant and refugee integration. The fifteen at-large and organizationally affiliated immigrant rights advocates whom we interviewed included five representatives of public interest groups, including public interest lawyers and activists affiliated with immigrant social justice and general social justice organizations; four representatives of organized immigrant ethnic communities, including Hispanic-Latino, East Asian, and East African leaders; and six social service providers, including immigrant and refugee resettlement professionals and activists.

Of these fifteen, five are immigrants or refugees, eleven are men, none were born in Nashville; their ages range from twenty-seven to sixty-eight, and all eleven of the public interest group representatives and social service providers are white.

Our sample of ten Middle Tennessee labor union leaders included business agents, local union presidents, and regional or district officials who are active in their unions, but whose responsibilities involve interunion collaboration and communication at the Central Labor Council, Tennessee State Labor Council Executive Board or Building Trades Council, organizing, and social mobilization. Two of the ten represent public sector service and professional municipal employees, three represent manufacturing, and five represent a mix of craft labor and manufacturing workers. Half originally are from Tennessee, the others are from other U.S. regions; nine are white and one is black; nine are men and one is a woman; and their ages range from thirty-eight to sixty-eight. The sample included four local union presidents, four district-level representatives, and two international office representatives.

PROSPECTS FOR IMMIGRANT-LABOR COALITION BUILDING IN NASHVILLE

Our interviews suggest that the available configuration of cultural and organizational resources can inspire and facilitate mutually beneficial resource exchange and immigrant-labor coalition building in Nashville. The newness of immigration in Nashville and the short history of contact between these two local social movements, however, present cultural and organizational barriers that need to be surmounted for immigrant-labor coalitions to form. Our interviews with labor union officials indicate the presence of two types of union functional organization. First, "union-centered" unions emphasize organizational entrepreneurship, recruiting and training both members and employers with whom the union has contracts, and defining public policy and shaping broad coalitions as part of long-term union strategy. These local unions also tend to be embedded in the tightly coupled hierarchal organizational structures of their international unions, which are marked by intense and constant flows of resources and information and by the strict accountability of local leaders to meet well-defined objectives. Second, "employer-centered" unions rely on employers to recruit workers and view markets, technology, and workplace organization as beyond their interest or responsibility. These local unions also tend to be embedded in the loosely coupled organizational structures of their international unions that compel local leaders, relying on limited resources, to emphasize a reactive model of union activity that gives priority to union members' immediate employment concerns. Given their greater predisposition and capacity to undertake proactive strategic initiatives, union-centered unions are more likely than employer-centered unions to build coalitions with immigrant communities. Furthermore, employer-centered unions tend to cede coalition building to established community organizations, such as religious organizations and the United Way. In Middle Tennessee, union coalition building with immigrant organizations remains limited, intermittent, and capricious for both union- and employer-centered local unions. Even Middle Tennessee local unions whose international unions have well-established and effective strategic models for coalition building with immigrants in other regions of the United States have lagged in immigrant organizing.

NASHVILLE'S IMMIGRANT RIGHTS MOVEMENT: A BALANCE SHEET OF CULTURAL AND ORGANIZATIONAL RESOURCES

Each of the three subgroups of the Nashville immigrant rights movement possesses relevant cultural and organizational resources for coalescing with local labor unions. For each subgroup, we highlight those resources that can build trust and commonality of purpose within and between the two local social movements.

Public Interest Groups

Nashville's public interest groups possess multiple relevant cultural resources. They adhere to universalistic, pro-worker, and proimmigrant missions and ideologies and attribute social inequality and social problems generally to asymmetric power relations between social classes and between ethnic-racial groups in society. Furthermore, they are very aware of the societal role and history of U.S. labor unions and harbor a generally positive view of and willingness to work with labor unions. However, most of our interviewees had had little experience in collaborating with labor unions. Some were skeptical about the openness of the local labor movement to immigrant organizing, perceiving local labor unions as nativist and ethnocentric. They expressed a high awareness and sensitivity toward the cultural traditions of Nashville's immigrants.

Public interest groups also possess several relevant organizational resources. They have leadership skills, are experienced in working in organizations, and often possess legal and technical skills for instituting and sustaining organizations. They operate with small budgets, however, and the narrow formal jurisdictions of some of the legal-service public interest organizations limit their ability to engage in immigrant labor organizing. Most of our public interest group interviewees were bilingual in English and Spanish but lacked fluency in the many African, Asian, and Middle Eastern languages spoken by some 40 percent of Nashville's foreign-born residents. Nonetheless, Nashville's public interest groups have developed substantial social capital—trusting, reciprocal networks—with several immigrant ethnic communities, Spanish speaking and non–Spanish speaking alike.

Immigrant Ethnic Communities

In terms of cultural resources, Nashville's organized immigrant ethnic communities maintain ethnically centered missions and are inspired by a general humanism to advocate on behalf of their ethnic communities. Several of our interviewees were philosophically committed to individualistic status-attainment strategies for achieving the American Dream, such as entrepreneurialism, microenterprise, and home ownership, as distinguished from collective means such as unionization. These advocates tended to attribute social inequality and social problems to ethnocentric discrimination by U.S. natives against ethnic minorities and immigrants. They generally were unfamiliar with the societal role and history of labor unions in the United States and had little or no experience in working with labor unions. Some have engaged in local immigrant rights and peace demonstrations with public interest groups and labor unions. They tended to be skeptical about the openness of the local labor movement, which they perceived as nativist and ethnocentric, to immigrant labor organizing and about the effectiveness of unions in helping immigrants to gain access to employment training opportunities and to jobs.

Nashville's organized ethnic communities are financially poor and lack the political advantages associated with citizenship, but they are rich in leadership and social capital. The leaders are immigrants and refugees who hail from the ethnic communities they represent and are trusted and revered by their communities, about whom they are very knowledgeable. Furthermore, they are bilingual in English and the native language of their ethnic community. A few have developed important job referral networks with local employers. Some of the organized immigrant ethnic communities have developed community and cultural centers that provide English-language instruction and religious services, produce cultural events, and communicate in their native languages with their communities by newsletter, newspaper, radio, and community access television.

Social Service Providers

Nashville's professional social service providers who serve and resettle immigrants and refugees are predominantly U.S.-born and possess cultural resources that pertain to forming immigrant-labor coalitions. They are inspired by universalistic and faith-based proimmigrant missions and ideologies and attribute social inequality and social problems generally to discrimination by U.S. natives against ethnic minorities and immigrants. These social service providers are knowledgeable about and respectful of immigrant cultural traditions. Regarding labor unions, our interviewees varied in their awareness of the societal role and history of labor unions and in their personal sympathy toward U.S. labor unions. Some perceived a nativism and ethnocentrism in local labor unions that lowered labor's capacity for immigrant organizing. Social service providers, who are mainly affiliated with small-budget private nonprofit professional agencies, possess substantial organizational resources. These providers have leadership skills, organizational experience, a comprehensive knowledge base about the availability, accessibility, and eligibility criteria of a wide range of social and health services, and informal social service referral networks. Although their language proficiency is typically limited to English, they have developed trusting relations with several immigrant ethnic communities. Social service providers have had little or no involvement with local labor unions.

In sum, public interest and social service groups in Nashville are emerging as a "bridge" between Nashville's immigrant ethnic communities and the local labor movement. The public interest and social service groups possess pertinent cultural and organizational resources—including political, legal, organizational, technical, and communication skills, and knowledge about, experience in, and extensive social networks in the provider and immigrant communities, as well as having trusting relationships with several local immigrant ethnic communities for whom they can help broker relations with local labor unions. The immigrant ethnic communities possess the requisite cultural and organizational resources for unionizing immigrant workers that includes indigenous, bilingual, trusted leadership; a dense set of formal and informal social networks that extend throughout immigrant and refugee communities; and multiple means of bilingual communication.

MIDDLE TENNESSEE'S LABOR ORGANIZATIONS: PROSPECTS FOR IMMIGRANT ORGANIZING

In Middle Tennessee, union- and employer-centered labor leaders emphasize different employment and organizational issues (on union leadership, see Canak 2004). Employer-centered leaders with manufacturing memberships view union survival and worker job security as their highest priorities and address immediate employment issues, such as fair pay, job security, and health care.

Union-centered leaders, in contrast, frame worker concerns in terms of political and economic structures and processes. For example, one local leader identified the "complete abdication by state and federal officials of the costs of government." Others focused on increasing "market share" (union density); productivity (through union-based training); and union strategic mobilization for economic, social, and political objectives.

Grounded in a business model of trade unionism, Nashville union- and employer-centered leaders focus union resources on member services such as training, collective bargaining, and grievance handling. They report that they are underresourced, reactive, and harried. They attribute the demise of union mutual-aid activities, such as sports leagues, cultural events, and regular interaction in union halls, to increasingly diverse lifestyles, mass media entertainment, the geographic dispersion of union members, and the eclipse of union social activities by religious organizations.

Employer- and union-centered leaders differ in their orientations toward coalition building. Employer-centered leaders consider coalition building with immigrants as beyond their interest, understanding, or capacity. Several of these unions represent workers at sites with substantial immigrant populations, comprising as many as twenty-six nationalities. Communication with immigrant workers, many of whom exercise their right-to-work right not to join the union, tends to be initiated by the local union leaders, who often are unable to speak immigrant languages and are unfamiliar with immigrant cultures. In contrast, union-centered leaders consider coalition building and social mobilization to be a core strategy for unions. With the active support of their regional and international union offices, some of these local leaders dedicate personnel and resources for organizing to other unions. Nonetheless, employer- and union-centered unions in Nashville report negligible activity aimed at organizing.

UNION KNOWLEDGE AND PERCEPTIONS OF NASHVILLE'S IMMIGRANTS

Regardless of the number of immigrants in the economic sectors in which they operate, all of our interviewees were aware of the growing presence of immigrant workers in Nashville. They also reported that rank-and-file members of their unions viewed immigrant workers as a threat to their interests, especially their job security and wages. Typical union members were described as perceiving that immigrants are not assimilating and acculturating, as indicated by low English-speaking proficiency. They described a negative reaction by African American workers toward immigrant workers and noted, with irony, that perceptions of immigrants had unified African American and white workers. These reactions were perceived to be especially intense in unionized workplaces where immigrants chose not to join the union.

Union leaders, in contrast to their description of rank-and-file attitudes, described immigrant workers as potential union members. Leaders of bargaining units with immigrants, however, felt that their efforts to recruit immigrant workers were stymied by linguistic barriers and cultural differences centered in beliefs about gender roles and religion. Recruiting immigrant workers also was frustrated by immigrant unfamiliarity with U.S. labor organizations, which many immigrants viewed skeptically through the lens of their homeland experiences as corrupt or as agents of a repressive political regime. Furthermore, leaders perceive that most immigrant workers consider their Nashville wages and working conditions to be an improvement over that in their home countries; their immediate objectives are to work, save, and send money home; and given their intentions to return home, immigrant workers in a unionized workplace are content not to join. Those union leaders not representing bargaining units with substantial immigrant worker populations described Nashville's immigrants as "Hispanic" or "Islamic."

Union-centered leaders of bargaining units with immigrants were more aware of immigrant communities than their employer-centered counterparts. Employer-centered leaders of bargaining units with immigrants described the immigrant community as being diverse, complex, and heterogeneous, mentioning Mexicans, Laotians, Chinese, Vietnamese, and Muslims as specific groups. "I had requests for [steward manuals] in French, Farsi, Arabic, Spanish, and various

African dialects," noted one interviewee. As leaders of employer-centered local unions, however, they were the least likely to know about immigrant community associations and programs and past events or coalitions that linked local unions and immigrants in Nashville.

Union-centered leaders described the demographic complexity of immigrant communities with the same precision as that of employer-centered leaders, but they were more aware of immigrant organizations. They described the Nashville immigrant population by comparing it with immigrant communities in other areas of the United States and characterized some immigrant groups in Nashville and elsewhere, such as Cubans in South Florida and Kurds in Nashville, as "petit bourgeois," educated and professional populations with little relevance to organized labor. They know that elsewhere in the United States established immigrant communities have a dense network of associations that promote immigrants' civil rights and economic interests. Nevertheless, they were unfamiliar with such organizations in Nashville. Instead, these union leaders focus on a small set of local religious organizations for approaching immigrants. For example, one of these leaders remarked, "We have talked to some of the parishes—the Catholic Church—Father Breen and others," or "We are reaching out to immigrant organizations and we do that through religious groups."

UNION RESOURCES AND PROGRAMS LINKED TO IMMIGRANT COMMUNITIES

Despite their business unionism, Nashville's unions promote and sustain a range of organizational resources that are dedicated to strategic social justice, cultural, and political goals and immigrant workers. These include a union-financed Immigration and Naturalization Service advising office that assists immigrants, providing translations of union documents into immigrant languages, and giving financial support to labor-friendly groups such as the Tennessee Economic Renewal Network, which is spearheading a Nashville living wage campaign.

Labor tends to collaborate with established nonprofit organizations, such as United Way and Goodwill, in its community action initiatives for immigrants. For example, local unions reach immigrants indirectly by supporting Goodwill's GED educational, housing, and job search programs. In Nashville, these union resources are filtered through United Way, to which the labor movement donates substantial human and financial resources. Labor market support programs at Goodwill, however, partner mainly with nonunion employers that provide jobs for immigrants while they take English-language classes. Most of the labor leaders we interviewed were surprised to learn during the interview that union donations to Goodwill were effectively subsidizing the training expenses of non-union employers. A few unions donate resources sporadically to immigrant rights organizations. Several building-trades leaders considered immigrant workers' interests to be "critical" to the future of their unions. They were well informed about labor-immigrant coalitions elsewhere in the nation, especially in Florida, Texas, and California, and hoped to model Nashville coalitions after them. Their preliminary coalition-building activities include identifying immigrant leaders, especially in the Hispanic community, sponsoring public education forums, such as a Hispanic leadership forum, and recruiting Spanish-speaking leaders and organizers. Nevertheless, limited resources in this region have reduced their capacity to fully replicate coalition building activities in U.S. regions with larger immigrant populations.

A MODEL FOR UNION COALITION BUILDING WITH IMMIGRANT COMMUNITIES

One interviewee mentioned his international union's South Florida–based worker center as a model that can be adapted for successful immigrant organizing in Nashville. The worker center harnesses rank-and-file union member activism to target the immigrant community through a public health-and-safety awareness campaign. "Without [union rank-and-file involvement, the] membership doesn't understand what you are doing; they don't understand the program and where their dues are going and why you are doing all that, but more importantly, they are the resource that can actually bring about change."

In South Florida, this union established community-based worker centers that address a wide range of work and community issues of immigrants.[1] These worker centers inform nonunion workers about health and safety issues in construction and U.S. trade unionism and serve as recruitment sites for union political demonstrations. According to a building-trades union official,

> You get people's attention that way; you don't win everything, but you become relevant. This gets the worker contact, because you cannot go down there and create a solution some other way and expect workers to come around and understand what you are doing. So this approach is an evolution within the community.

By involving rank-and-file union members in its community operations, the worker center helps develop a cadre of union-member activists and positive

---

1. On worker centers and immigrant organizing in the United States, see Fine 2006.

union-community relations, build a database about workers and working conditions in the local area, and recruit new members, including immigrant workers. In Middle Tennessee, this union's leaders hope to adapt the Florida worker center model to help immigrant communities "put together organizational structures" and facilitate the capacity of these immigrants to "play a full part in the larger community, have a voice, an organized voice—otherwise they are out there on their own." The local union in Nashville draws on the international union for resources and opportunities through a multilevel and multistate council that is focused on delivering resources to training and mobilization in this Nashville immigrant community. At present, however, in Middle Tennessee "we do not have our membership activated" and "there isn't any particular campaign." Nevertheless, the tightly coupled and union-centered organizational structure of the international union diffuses innovations to its Nashville leaders and provides a model for union coalition building that combines rank-and-file members, union organization, and union resources to generate initiatives among immigrant workers. In sum, metropolitan Nashville labor leaders view the immigrant population as an important demographic force and potential ally for union political objectives and labor organizing. Nevertheless, they lack cultural and organizational resources, as well as rank-and-file commitment, for forging meaningful ties with immigrant workers. Union-centered local unions are those that are most poised for building coalitions with immigrants. Rather, most Nashville unions are embedded in established charitable and religious organizations that often serve nonunion employers. Union leaders are aware of labor-immigrant collaborations elsewhere in the United States, but they view such initiatives as secondary priorities for Middle Tennessee. The union leaders have little or no familiarity with local immigrant communities. International unions provide few resources or mandates for Tennessee unions to initiate partnerships with the local immigrant community, even those same unions that have successfully engaged in immigrant organizing elsewhere in the United States.

PATHWAYS TO LABOR–IMMIGRANT COALITIONS

As a globalizing city of the U.S. interior, Nashville exemplifies opportunities and constraints facing union revitalization and potential avenues for collaboration and coalition building between immigrant communities and local labor unions. These opportunities for collaboration and support remain dormant. Nevertheless, Nashville's immigrant communities and labor unions have built and sustain organizational and cultural resources that may support future coalitions.

Although Nashville's labor movement has not built a strong relationship with local immigrant communities or with workers at workplaces with a significant immigrant presence, several existing cultural and organizational resources may facilitate future positive developments. These resources include union leaders' positive attitudes toward immigrant workers, even toward nonunion immigrant workers who work in the bargaining unit of a unionized workplace, and financial and educational resources relating to national experiences in immigrant organizing that are provided to union-centered local unions by their internationals. Several deficits in cultural and organizational resources, however, limit the capacity for metropolitan Nashville's labor movement to build and sustain its revitalization through coalition building in the immigrant community. These deficits include rank-and-file union member antipathy toward immigrants; union leader commitment to a time-consuming business model of trade unionism, especially in the many employer-centered local unions; labor's unfamiliarity with immigrant languages and culture; and a state "right-to-work" law that effectively enables culturally marginalized immigrant workers not to unionize.

The immigrant rights movement can address some of these deficits in the cultural and organizational resources of Nashville's labor movement. The immigrant rights movement is rich in leadership and social capital. Yet many in this movement are unfamiliar with the societal role and history of labor unions in the United States and have had little or no experience in working with labor unions. Moreover, many are philosophically committed to individualistic status-attainment strategies that downplay trade unionism as a vehicle for accomplishing the American Dream. Immigrant ethnic community and cultural centers constitute a viable communication network and infrastructure in multiple immigrant communities: they provide English-language instruction and religious services, produce cultural events, and communicate in their native languages with their communities by newsletter, newspaper, radio, and community access television. This infrastructure presents an opportunity for local unions to communicate with immigrants, informing them about U.S. labor unions' historic role in the development of workplace rights and the current resources available only to unionized workers.

Concretely, the specific exchange of organizational and cultural resources that we have identified in a "social map" of networks within and between the local labor and immigrant rights movements favors a community-based union organizational model for immigrant organizing in the globalizing U.S. interior: that is, worker centers that effectively extend the "union-centered" local labor organization model in immigrant communities (Fine 2006).

Modeled on programs successfully established in other regions, community-based labor-immigrant coalitions operating through worker centers could open a path for a mutually beneficial exchange of cultural and organizational resources between the immigrant rights advocates and labor unions in Nashville. Such organizational exchanges and joint projects can dispel fear and prejudice, create mutual trust and awareness, and improve the prospects of further coalition building between these two movements in this globalizing interior city. Implementing union-centered worker centers in immigrant communities throughout the globalizing U.S. interior could institute a viable resource exchange and collaboration between labor and immigrant rights advocates for addressing immigrant employment needs and issues and for revitalizing the labor movement.

10

BUILDING AN INCLUSIVE CITY

Labor-Community Coalitions and the Struggle for Urban Power in San Jose

Nari Rhee and Julie Anna Sadler

Since the mid-1990s, the South Bay AFL-CIO Labor Council (SBLC), headquartered in San Jose, California, has led the regional labor movement in forging coalitions with community groups to build political power at the urban-regional scale.[1] Bolstered by local electoral victories and sophisticated policy research, coalition campaigns have achieved an escalating series of policy reforms benefiting low-wage workers and their families in Silicon Valley. This process catapulted labor as a major force in urban governance and began shifting the terms of debate surrounding local development and social equity in a region enthralled by high-tech entrepreneurship (Byrd and Rhee 2004; Brownstein 2004).

In this chapter we present San Jose as a well-developed example of the labor movement's changing role in urban governance in the context of neoliberal political economic restructuring, and of the reemergence of urban politics as a critical nexus between the historically fractured politics of workplace and residence.[2] In Silicon Valley, as in other urban regions, deregulation, social welfare cutbacks, fiscal crises, and heightened interurban competition for investment have led to degenerating working and living conditions for working-class communities, alongside enormous wealth creation.[3] As these contradictions deepened during the 1990s, the SBLC and key local unions cultivated community alliances and local political influence, not only to aid union organizing and bargaining but also

---

1. Primary data for this paper is drawn from Nari Rhee's dissertation research on working-class politics in Silicon Valley, with support from University of California Institute for Labor and Employment and National Science Foundation Grant #0327295. The views and findings expressed in this article are those of the authors and do not necessarily reflect those of these funders. Some interviews cited in this article were conducted jointly by Nari Rhee and Barbara Byrd for an article published in Byrd and Rhee 2004.

2. See Katznelson 1981 on the division of worker identity across the spheres of workplace and (ethnic) residential community, and Fine 2002 on the growing intersection between community and employment concerns.

3. See Brenner and Theodore 2002 and Merrifield and Swyngedouw 1997 on the urbanization of injustice under neoliberal political-economic restructuring.

to promote a regional working-families policy agenda. Repositioning their stakes in urban growth, key unions broadened their local political agenda from narrow concern with union jobs to building a more inclusive city. This strategy has directly benefited some unions in local sectors (public, service, and construction); however, it has not answered the challenge of organizing in the region's economic core—specifically in the volatile export-oriented high-tech industry, which remains immune to local political intervention.

THE TWO VALLEYS

The San Jose metropolitan area (coterminous with Santa Clara County) forms the geographical heart of Silicon Valley. A Sunbelt city, the area was transformed from a rich agro-industrial economy into a global center of computer and communications technology between World War II and the late 1970s. The City of San Jose, which comprises nearly 1 million of the 1.8 million county population, is the third largest city in California.[4] International immigration from Mexico and East, Southeast, and South Asia has formed a nonwhite demographic majority evenly split between Latinos and Asians.[5]

The public façade of Silicon Valley as a region dotted with sparkling industrial parks and peopled by overnight millionaires obscures marked economic inequality. The regional high-tech industry—seeded by cold war military spending and currently anchored in commercial electronics, complemented by software—has responded to growing international competition and market instability by externalizing risk through overseas production, flexible employment and contracting practices, and union avoidance. Its labor force is divided between techno-elite professionals who are disproportionately white and male—notwithstanding the growing presence of Asians—and a hyperexploited production workforce largely composed of minorities, immigrants, and women (Lüthje 2002; Benner 1997). This pattern is mirrored in the regional economy at large, with a bloated professional middle class supported by a large stratum of low-wage service workers anchored by people of color (Zlolnisky 2006; Alarcon 1997).

This inequality is deeply intertwined with the history of the local labor movement and the decline of working-class politics in the Santa Clara Valley. During the early twentieth century, Wobblies and Communists organized in factories,

---

4. California Department of Finance.

5. U.S. Census Bureau, Decennial Census, various years. California Department of Finance, Report E-7, available electronically at http://www.dof.ca.gov/HTML/DEMOGRAP/ReportsPapers/Reports Papers.asp.

fields, and neighborhoods, and across racial divides. However, in 1936 a major turning point occurred when the State Federation of Labor wrested control of the local cannery workers union from leftist organizers (Matthews 2003, 89–93). Although unions subsequently organized large segments of the local food processing, manufacturing, and commercial sectors, the valley's working-class politics splintered into workplace-based trade union politics and community organizing in Mexican and other minority communities marginalized by the New Deal.

Whatever its limitations, the valley's unions provided significant economic mobility for the white working class. However, the movement began its long decline during the 1960s as the commercial electronics industry—which remained nonunion due to cold war labor politics (Eisenscher 1993)—overtook agro-industry. Union membership among workers employed in Santa Clara County peaked at slightly above one hundred thousand in the 1970s, where it has hovered since, but union density plummeted from 52 percent in 1954[6] to 15 percent in 1985.[7] Subsequently, union members as a percentage of employed workers *living* in Santa Clara County (the only data available) increased slightly from 12.5 percent in 1986 to 15 percent in 1993, and then bottomed out at 11.5 percent in 2001 when the regional economic bubble burst and high-tech employment sharply contracted.[8]

Globalization, neoliberalism, and economic restructuring contributed to declining union strength in multiple ways beginning in the late 1960s. Unionized plants in mature manufacturing sectors, such as cement, woodworking, metal, and food processing, relocated or shut down in response to competition from lower-cost locations. An early pioneer of overseas sourcing, the commercial electronics industry stubbornly resisted unionization through spatial restructuring and a combination of paternalistic and repressive labor practices that one long-time valley labor activist has termed "the silicon fist in a velvet glove" (Lüthje 2002; Eisenscher 1993). More recently, union power has been eroded by deregulation and restructuring within such traditional strongholds as telecommunications, warehousing, and grocery chains. Finally, the explosion of business services and low-wage, in-person services has expanded the unorganized workforce.

6. California Department of Industrial Relations, Division of Labor Statistics. *Union Labor in California.* Various issues.

7. Evelyn Richards, "Local Unionizing Efforts on Upswing: Recent Filing Signals Latest, Largest Action," *San Jose Mercury News,* August 16, 1987, 1E.

8. Union-density figures are from Hirsch and Macpherson 2003, from updated data downloaded from http://www.unionstats.com.

NEOLIBERAL URBANISM IN A VELVET GLOVE

Despite its Sunbelt development pattern, San Jose has a significant tradition of progressivism due to its location in the greater San Francisco Bay Area. During the 1960s and 1970s, the women's, environmental, and Chicano movements combined with the growth of a predominantly Democratic electorate to produce a moderate-liberal governing coalition in San Jose and Santa Clara County (Trounstine and Christensen 1982). This legacy enhanced the political opportunity structure for labor-community coalition building in the coming decades.

However, the onset of neoliberalism in urban governance severely dampened possibilities for progressive redistribution. Specifically, the 1978 tax revolt in California and Reagan-era federal cutbacks permanently constrained city and county resources for social programs. Simultaneously, the San Jose Redevelopment Agency (SJRA) began to pump a river of tax money generated by high-tech industrial development in north San Jose into an ambitious downtown redevelopment campaign. This set in motion a massive regressive transfer of resources: currently, the state, county services, school districts, and San Jose's general fund collectively lose over $100 million a year to the SJRA and wealthy developers.[9]

Meanwhile, a growing share of the valley's residents struggled to secure adequate wages, health care, housing, and other necessities in the context of a growing but increasingly polarized regional social economy (Santa Clara County 1990; Benner 1998). Responding to pressure from a growing array of advocacy, social service, and grassroots community organizations, San Jose and Santa Clara County incrementally increased funding for health care, affordable housing, and other programs serving low-income residents from the late 1980s onward, albeit with frequent rollbacks during fiscal crises. Under the logic of neoliberalism, these policy choices were framed as a trade-off between growth and equity based on the assumption that cities must minimize taxes, reduce social expenditures, and increase subsidies to capital in order to induce growth.[10] It took the emergence of a broad labor-community coalition to begin to challenge this logic.

9. Editorial, "A Redevelopment Primer: How the Money Flows," *San Jose Mercury News*, March 28, 1999, P6. See also Muller et al. 2003.

10. For a discussion of this trend in cities in the global North, see Jonas and Wilson 1999 and Harvey 1989.

PROGRESSIVE TRADITIONS IN THE SOUTH BAY LABOR MOVEMENT

Despite declining union density, key developments within the South Bay labor movement during the 1970s and early 1980s strengthened progressive traditions within the local labor council, laying the foundation for the renewal of labor-community linkages during the 1990s.[11] The period witnessed the growth of service and public sector unions representing diverse, politically liberal constituencies including civil servants, teachers, social workers, and telecommunications workers. In addition, a new cadre of young men and women—many of them politicized through the United Farm Workers (UFW) and other contemporary social justice movements—permeated the leadership of a wide range of local unions.

These unionists formed a progressive majority within the Santa Clara County Central Labor Council (CLC), though marked conservative dissent was anchored in the powerful Building and Construction Trades Council (BCTC). The CLC passed a series of resolutions opposing the Vietnam War and U.S. intervention in Central America, and mobilized union members for political action in solidarity with the UFW, the Chicano movement, and the peace movement.

Looking beyond solidarity with social movements, a few labor leaders—including CLC business manager Peter Cervantes-Gautschi, elected in 1981—strove for deeper ties between unions and community members to address the declining power of the regional labor movement. Their efforts included a successful coalition campaign to regulate toxics disposal at the state and local level and an attempt to build a neighborhood-level political organization. However, internal funding was scarce and local unions remained skeptical about the potential payoffs of a broad-based strategy. Meanwhile, internal tensions mounted as competing affiliates—divided by ideological differences and personality conflicts—fought over control of the CLC. To begin mending these divisions, the CLC charter was amended in 1985 to change the top executive post from an internally elected position to a more neutral appointed position.

---

11. Data are drawn from archival research and interviews with the following former South Bay unionists: Fernando Gapasin, former secretary-treasurer of the South Bay Labor Council, phone interview, February 10, 2005; Peter Cervantes-Gautschi, former business manager of the Santa Clara County Central Labor Council, interview, November 23, 2004; Nancy Biaggini, former president, CWA Local 9423, interview, February 26, 2005; Ellen Starbird, former staff, Santa Clara County Central Labor Council, interview, February 3, 2005.

MOUNTING UNION CRISIS AND RESPONSE

From the late 1980s to the mid-1990s, as union strength continued to fail in the face of economic restructuring and a hostile political climate, some South Bay labor organizations began to enact new strategies to cope with the crisis. While many were ad hoc and defensive—such as rearguard actions against individual plant closures—several cases demonstrated the growing salience of political power and community support to unions' bargaining and organizing efforts.

AFSCME Council 101 and SEIU Local 715 provide examples from the public sector involving divergent responses to privatization. In 1994, AFSCME Council 101 faced a major privatization initiative in San Jose dubbed "New Realities," which was spurred by the coupling of neoliberal market ideology with fiscal crisis. Council 101 used a defensive political strategy, successfully incorporating language into contracting policies allowing city unions to bid for jobs on favorable terms. In contrast, when the county began outsourcing its mental health services in the mid-1990s, SEIU Local 715 followed its international union's mandate by shifting resources into organizing and invigorating its rank and file. The union organized thousands of workers in private and nonprofit mental health and health services, taking advantage of political leverage provided by public funding for these services and the union's electoral influence.[12]

In the private service sector, successful union campaigns relied increasingly on the support of communities and local politicians. In 1987, CLC business manager Rick Sawyer—armed with the council's increased electoral clout—persuaded Mayor Tom McEnery to broker a card check/neutrality deal with the owner of San Jose's flagship luxury hotel. Subsequently, HERE Local 19 unionized every major hotel in downtown San Jose.[13] In building services, SEIU Local 1877 successfully transformed immigrant worker struggles into a social justice issue through the Justice for Janitors campaign, drawing on the support of white liberals, the Latino community, emergent immigrant rights groups, and the religious community. In 1992, the Cleaning Up Silicon Valley coalition embarrassed computer giant Apple, Inc., into pressuring its janitorial service contractor to bargain with the union (Matthews 2003, 251).

Although local unions increasingly turned to local political influence and community support for organizing and bargaining, such efforts were uneven and fragmented. So was union support for community interests related to housing,

---

12. Raahi Reddy, former organizing director of SEIU Local 715, interview, October 2003.

13. Rick Sawyer, former business manager of the Santa Clara County Central Labor Council, phone interview, April 6, 2005; Gapasin interview; Pat Lamborn, HERE International Union organizer, interview, February 17, 2005.

health care, and urban quality of life. Conversely, many community organizations remained wary of unions, given their histories of racial exclusion and their consistent alliance with urban growth interests. This began to change in the mid-1990s, with a new wave of labor council progressivism.

LABOR-COMMUNITY COALITION BUILDING FOR URBAN POWER

In 1994, shortly after her advancement from political director to chief executive officer of the SBLC, Amy Dean proposed to revitalize the labor council and the valley's labor movement by undertaking a broad regional power-building program to create a friendlier local bargaining and organizing climate.[14] Crucially, the plan was backed by the executive board, thanks to its strong progressive anchor and Dean's demonstrated political acumen. The basic strategy, refined over the next several years, consisted of aggressive electoral power building, policy research and advocacy, and community coalition building behind a broad working families agenda. To bring legitimacy and critical foundation funding to bear on the work, Dean founded the nonprofit organization Working Partnerships USA (WPUSA) in 1995 to undertake research, act as a bridge between labor and community organizations, and ideally serve as a vehicle for organizing the high-tech industry (Dean 1996; Brownstein 2004; Byrd and Rhee 2004). Phaedra Ellis-Lamkins succeeded Dean in 2003, becoming not just the youngest person to lead the labor council at the age of twenty-seven but, as a self-identified biracial woman of African American and (white) Jewish descent, the first person of color to do so.

Since the original plan was set in motion, the SBLC has led a series of labor-community coalitions to win increasingly ambitious policy reforms at the city and county level. Key victories include the Santa Clara County tax abatement subsidy accountability measure (1995); the San Jose Living Wage Policy, one of the strongest at the time (1998); the Children's Health Initiative, a countywide health insurance program for low-income children (2000); the inclusion of five thousand units of affordable housing in a major land use plan in south San Jose (2001); and a community benefits agreement for a major downtown redevelopment project in San Jose as part of an ongoing campaign for accountable development policy (2003).

The scope of reform efforts has grown in tandem with community and affili-

---

14. Amy Dean, former executive director of the South Bay Labor Council and Working Partnerships USA, telephone interview, April 5, 2004.

ate union support and labor's political influence. The list of allies has expanded to include the Interfaith Council, a network of liberal clergy and activist laity; the San Jose chapter of the Association of Community Organizations for Reform Now (ACORN); People Acting in Community Together, a countywide, Alinskyite faith-based community organization; the local housing movement; homeless groups; and immigrant rights groups. On the electoral front, the SBLC has aggressively mobilized union members and Latinos, dramatically increasing voter participation in historically low-turnout districts. The strategy transformed the San Jose City Council into a solidly pro-labor majority; seated a labor-friendly majority in Sunnyvale, the largest industrial city in the county; and shifted several state and national legislative seats from moderate-liberal to left-liberal Democrats. Labor failed to capture the San Jose mayor's seat in 2006, however, due to concerted business opposition.

The SBLC's labor-community coalition work between 1994 and 2001 focused on integrating a broad social-welfare agenda into the labor movement agenda and on reframing the rights of workers, especially low-wage workers, as a social justice issue. Strategic policy goals were formulated with the input of community stakeholders. But more than that, coalition campaigns reflected the convergence of union and community interests in key policy arenas related to social welfare.

An example is the regional housing crisis. Community organizations and local housing advocates have fought for low-income housing in the valley since the late 1980s. But rapid economic growth and income polarization during the late 1990s magnified the housing crisis. In 2001, fair market (40th percentile) rent for a two-bedroom apartment skyrocketed to $1,481, and the median home sale price was $455,000, well beyond the reach of average-earning families.[15] Unions became increasingly concerned with members' hardships in finding affordable housing, and rapidly escalating housing costs ate away negotiated wage increases. Hence the SBLC and several affiliate unions, including SEIU Local 715 and SEIU Local 1877, partnered with longtime housing advocates and community organizations to support a number of local affordable housing initiatives. These included a just-cause eviction ordinance, an inclusionary housing policy in San Jose and a campaign to increase several local redevelopment agencies' housing expenditures.

As the SBLC's political power and community ties deepened, the organization forged an even broader coalition behind an urban development agenda focused on social inclusion and quality of life. In the process, key segments of the regional labor movement began to depart from their traditionally narrow focus on union job creation to embrace a broader set of social needs.

---

15. California Association of Realtors.

REFORMING URBAN ECONOMIC DEVELOPMENT: THE COMMUNITY BENEFITS INITIATIVE

The Community Benefits Initiative (CBI), a campaign for economic development subsidy accountability in San Jose, illustrates broadening perceptions of union self-interest in tandem with an effort to redefine economic development in terms of worker welfare and social goods. CBI's major target is the San Jose Redevelopment Agency, the largest local source of development subsidies in Silicon Valley with an annual budget of over $300 million.[16] Historically, the labor movement's steadfast support for downtown renewal as a source of union construction jobs earned the distrust of community groups opposed to redevelopment. But during the 1990s, SBLC and WPUSA joined other organizations nationwide in identifying the link between economic development, land use policies, and low-wage jobs—both in city-center revival and exurban big-box retail. CBI was a key product of their search for an alternative development policy.

The first campaign under CBI was launched in late 2002, when a labor-community coalition spearheaded by SBLC decided to intervene in the approval of a $200 million downtown development agreement between the city, the SJRA, and the CIM Group, a large developer. Activists demanded that the CIM Group and the redevelopment agency negotiate community benefits with the coalition. Probusiness Mayor Ron Gonzales, conservative city council members, and the Chamber of Commerce charged that this would drive investment out of the city, but the labor-backed progressive majority prevailed. The resulting community benefits agreement, negotiated in early 2003, included affordable housing additions, small business outreach, subsidized leases for child care, living wage standards for parking lot operators, and a good-faith commitment by the developer to negotiate living wage and union-neutrality provisions with hotels and grocery stores.[17]

Building on this success, the SBLC and Working Partnerships—in coalition with neighborhood associations, housing advocates, the religious community, ACORN, unions, and small businesses—launched a follow-up campaign for a citywide policy requiring the completion of a community impact report for major development projects that involve public subsidies. Such a policy would anticipate a project's social and economic effects, including those on housing, wages, and demand for services, and institutionalize greater democratic partici-

---

16. City of San Jose Redevelopment Agency, *Annual Budget,* various years.

17. Kate Folmar, "Accord Expected on S.J. Project: Labor, Housing Changes Sought Downtown," *San Jose Mercury News,* March 27, 2003, 1B.

pation in the development process (Muller et al. 2003). However, elite opposition and generalized anxiety over the valley's slow recovery from recession hindered negotiations between CBI advocates and City Hall. In the aftermath of the 2006 elections in San Jose, advocates were waiting for an opportunity to reintroduce economic development reform.

While its ultimate outcome is still uncertain, the CBI campaign illustrates deepening union stakes in local economic development policy. A number of service sector unions have been involved in CBI, including SEIU Local 1877 (building services), UNITE HERE Local 19 (hotel and restaurant), and UFCW 428 (grocery and retail). These unions hope to leverage CBI and the living wage policy to raise wage-and-benefit standards in the low-wage labor market and gain new members. Furthermore, CBI integrates working class concerns between workplace and residence, demanding that local economic development policies make sure that the workers who provide services in newly developed communities can also afford to live in them.

Importantly, several building-trades labor organizations have broken from their past stance in growth politics to support CBI. Representatives of the BCTC, Plumbers Union Local 393, Roofers and Waterproofers Local 95, and the Carpenters apprenticeship program have testified alongside community organizations and service sector unions at the city council in favor of community benefits. Significantly, the new BCTC leader, Neil Struthers, has played a critical role in easing local building-trades unions' fears that CBI will negatively affect the demand for construction labor. He stresses the long-term benefits of cooperating with other groups: "CBI gives [building-trades unions] an opportunity to work with broader coalitions to build a bigger base."[18]

Although there has been real progress, according to Struthers and staff members of the Greenbelt Alliance (a key Bay Area environmental organization), the relationship between the building-trades unions and environmental groups is still complicated, and they "don't agree on everything."[19] In the end, unions depend on the jobs generated by urban growth, and environmentalists are concerned about growth and its negative impacts. But union leaders' agreement with the principle of environmental protection and key environmental organizations' adoption of the "smart growth" solution for minimizing urban sprawl through dense, mixed-use, transit-oriented development have opened up dialogue and opportunities for strategic collaboration.

---

18. Neil Struthers, executive director of the Building and Construction Trades Council of Santa Clara and San Benito Counties, interview, December 16, 2003.

19. Jessica Fitchen, Greenbelt Alliance, phone interview, April 11, 2005; Struthers interview.

PLANNING A LIVABLE COMMUNITY: COYOTE VALLEY

Another example of the emergent labor-community agenda for equitable urban development in Silicon Valley extends beyond economic development policy to land-use planning, the heart of local state authority. In 2001, San Jose began deliberations on a new land-use plan for Coyote Valley, a 6,800-acre expanse of open space at its southern tip, part of which has been earmarked for development since 1984. Taking the initiative, the SBLC, with the support of the Greenbelt Alliance and housing advocates, successfully pressed Mayor Gonzales to commit to five thousand below-market-rate housing units in Coyote Valley as part of his housing-policy platform.

In 2002, the SBLC and the BCTC each secured a seat on the Coyote Valley Specific Plan Task Force, alongside the mayor, city council members and other local elected officials, city commission members, planners, and large developers. Since then, SBLC and WPUSA have been working closely with unions, environmental groups, and social justice organizations to influence the shape of the future community, which will include twenty-five thousand homes and fifty thousand jobs for seventy-five thousand people. They collaborated with the Greenbelt Alliance to produce a detailed "visioning plan" for development based on smart growth and "new urbanist" planning principles combined with a social equity agenda. The vision includes dense, mixed-use development built at a walkable scale; adequate public transit; affordable housing; living wage jobs; and funding mechanisms to support local health care, child care, and other community facilities.[20] These fit into an overall vision of a "new town" in which all workers—not only affluent professionals—can enjoy a high quality of life.

A long, hard fight still lies ahead for the labor-community coalition. Fraught with high-stakes contention among the various stakeholders—including agricultural, industrial, real estate, historic preservation, and NIMBY (Not In My Back Yard) neighborhood interest groups—the Coyote Valley planning process entails lengthy negotiations on a range of issues. In addition, the coalition's smart growth vision conflicts with the interests of powerful suburban developers, who stand to gain phenomenal profits from upscale, automobile-oriented residential development. If successful, the coalition's strategy regarding Coyote Valley could serve as a model for livable and socially inclusive city building, one in which environmental, labor, and low-income community organizations can find common ground.

---

20. Greenbelt Alliance, "Getting It Right: Preventing Sprawl in Coyote Valley" (San Francisco: Greenbelt Alliance, 2003).

SOCIAL JUSTICE UNIONISM AND THE LIMITS OF LOCAL POLITICAL LEVERAGE

When the South Bay Labor Council and its affiliated unions first began to build deeper coalitions with community interests and intensified their engagement with urban politics, they were "looking for a way not to be stuck in the mud" as their power in the labor market declined.[21] Maneuvering in a relatively open regional political arena, they forged an emergent urban coalition to challenge the region's commercial and development interests, deepening labor's role in urban governance and the complex project of city making. On the ideological front, they won credibility as advocates for working families in the region, and they increased public sympathy for the struggles of low-wage workers.

The process has instilled palpable pride in many unions regarding their support for campaigns that advance the welfare of working people at large, not just their own membership. For instance, the local Plumbers union (UA Local 393) broke out of the mold of building-trades conservatism early on under the leadership of the late Loyd Williams. Williams explained that its membership does not benefit directly from policies such as the living wage and the Children's Health Initiative but that the union "understands that what helps workers is good for us."[22] At the same time, the labor movement has been forced to address fundamental tensions with environmental and community interest groups, whose support it needs to steer local development policies towards better jobs. Significantly, a partial reconciliation has occurred through the articulation of a common vision for a livable and socially inclusive city.

But how has the strategy affected the strength of unions in the workplace? Labor-friendly politicians, progressive policies, and research capacity have directly improved wages and working conditions for some unions and workers. For instance, SEIU, Teamsters, HERE, and other locals have organized over six thousand service workers covered by San Jose's Living Wage Policy by leveraging its labor peace requirement. They have also helped to cushion the impact of fiscal crises on public sector workers. Indirectly, union organizing drives have been bolstered by labor-friendly local politicians in cases in which firms receive local government funds, such as nonprofit social services; fall under local land use authority, such as the expansion of a hotel; or where businesses are place-bound and vulnerable to political pressure and moral suasion, such as the health-care sector.

Unfortunately, the leverage afforded by local political power does not reach

21. Bob Brownstein, policy director, Working Partnerships USA, interview, December 2, 2004.

22. Loyd Williams, former business manager of the United Association of Plumbers and Steamfitters Local 393, phone interview, December 18, 2003.

most private sector jobs. Union density in Santa Clara County dropped faster between 1994 and 2004 than during the previous ten years, down to 11.6 percent, though it seems to have stabilized since 2001. Contributing factors are economic restructuring, a deteriorating bargaining climate in much of the private sector in line with national trends, and the fact that most unions in the valley do not devote adequate resources to organizing.

The high-tech sector still remains nonunion, with local labor leaders convinced that the high-tech workforce, particularly production workers, cannot be organized in the short or medium term because of continual offshoring and restructuring. The SBLC and WPUSA relinquished their original ambitions to organize the sector early on, though the latter does provide a health plan for temporary workers in the industry. Indeed, the SBLC has maintained a modus vivendi with the powerful Silicon Valley Manufacturing Group because the former's initiatives do not challenge the prerogatives of the latter. As former SEIU 715 political director and long-time labor activist Harry Adams observes:

> Labor has nibbled around the edges in terms of challenging the real power in the valley. . . . Yes, we should be very proud of our policy wins. Still, the real test is whether you've challenged the economic and political engines here: technology, communications, finance, core sectors with almost no union presence or organizing effort.[23]

What all of this means for the future of the valley's labor movement is that the current trajectory—assuming stable union density—will continue to yield incremental gains in electoral politics and policy reform, with benefits concentrated among public sector and select service sector workers. To tilt the balance of class power in the region, union organizing will be required on a much larger scale, no easy task in the current political climate. The current upheaval in the national labor movement may yield such an effort—the unions that recently broke off from the AFL-CIO in 2005 to form the Change to Win coalition account for a large share of the valley's union base—but this is speculative at best.

Meanwhile, in the face of continued business antipathy and growing public perception of labor as part of the political establishment, SBLC and Working Partnerships struggle with the difficult work of advancing policies that will institutionalize popular participation and economic justice in land use and economic development decision making. In Silicon Valley, where high-tech elites hardly consider low-wage workers and their families as an integral part of the region, labor and its community allies provide an important countervoice for a socially inclusive city.

---

23. Harry Adams, former political director of SEIU Local 715, e-mail to Nari Rhee, July 22, 2005.

Part IV
INTERNATIONAL COMPARISONS

11

SPECIAL INTERESTS AND PUBLIC GOODS

Organized Labor's Coalition Politics in Hamburg and Seattle

Ian Greer

Why do some unions engage in special interest politics while others pursue broader social goods? In this chapter I examine the effect of global markets for capital and local political mobilization. I argue that protecting jobs requires unions to engage in coalition politics, sometimes in pursuit of social goods that have benefits beyond the interests of union members. In cases, however, of high-stakes economic development projects involving large employers, the affected unions join business-driven coalitions with narrowly economistic pro-jobs agendas. I demonstrate this argument by comparing union involvement in the politics of economic development in Seattle and Hamburg. Because the argument holds in both Germany and the United States, labor's constraints and opportunities may increasingly have to do less with national differences than with the particulars of local politics and labor-business dependence.

LOCAL PARTICIPATION AND THE GLOBAL ECONOMY

As capital has become more global, unions have found that they have to participate in local policies to attract and retain "good jobs." This race for capital creates an unfortunate paradox. The globalization of capital and corporate organization leads to a localization or decentralization of collective labor participation. Al-

Many thanks to participants in seminars at Cornell, the European Trade Union Institute in Brussels, the Forschungsinstitut Arbeit Bildung und Partizipation in Recklinghausen, and the Max-Planck-Institut für Gesellschaftsforschung (MPIfG) in Cologne for comments on earlier presentations of this material. Thanks to Barbara Byrd, Virginia Doellgast, Lou Jean Fleron, Marco Hauptmeier, Otto Jacobi, Nathan Lillie, Nari Rhee, and Lowell Turner for comments on earlier versions of the chapter. Finally, thanks to Cornell University's New York State School of Industrial and Labor Relations, the Ford Foundation, the German Academic Exchange Service, and the MPIfG for financial support of the field research.

though trade unionists are caught up in this daily grind to attract, retain, or organize jobs in a specific place, their employers and other adversaries are organized on a much broader scale.

"Decentralization" and "localization," however, are vague concepts. Although studies of comparative politics and industrial relations tend to stress the in-plant character of participation (Kochan, Katz, and McKersie 1986; Turner 1991), worker participation can also extend beyond the workplace into the broader community and local politics (Locke 1992). Sometimes unions act as social partners and sometimes as contentious worker representatives. Their goals can be self-interested and economistic or broad and social.

Case studies can bring some clarity to the matter. In an international comparison of union political participation in two urban regions, Hamburg and Seattle, I find striking parallels. In the construction and health-care sectors, trade unionists followed a strategy to retain jobs, attract members, and innovate in the provision of broader social goods. For these unions, participation creates opportunities with broader implications for the local labor and progressive scenes. Participation, however, also has a dark side. In the aerospace sector, unions were caught up in a high-stakes race for capital investment from a major employer. Meeting corporate demands involved deep social costs beyond the camp of organized labor.

One way to understand patterns of coalition formation is to examine national patterns of labor-management relations. The nationally specific rules governing labor-management relations lead to some differences in how unions participate in the political economy. In the 1980s, researchers on the German labor movement found that, by giving workers strong participation rights, strong institutions of in-plant worker participation allowed unions to participate in industry restructuring from a position of strength (Turner 1991). "Varieties of capitalism" theory argued further that labor-management relations in Germany differ from those in the United States because of nationally specific features of capitalism that give some German employers a "comparative institutional advantage" (Hall and Soskice 2001). Baccaro, Hamann, and Turner (2003) turned institutional explanation on its head with an argument that U.S. unions are dynamic because of the relative absence of institutionalized "insider" channels of influence.

A second option is to examine urban development politics and ask how unions work with other locally organized interests to deal with policy issues that affect workers. Businesses and politicians, for example, can be close allies with labor, since they, too, favor economic development. In cities that are hemorrhaging manufacturing jobs, however, this usually involves painful compromises (Savitch and Kantor 2002), and in many younger cities "growth machines" consistently place business promotion above all other policy goals (Logan, Whaley, and Crowder 1997). If this economism is one kind of urban policymaking, postmaterialism is also a possibility. Postmaterialistic policymakers take up issues of social services, income equality, and environmental sustainability (Portnoy 2003), sometimes with the active support of unions (Rose 2000) and business interests (Sellers 2002). This approach does not rule out the national context as important but places it among the many factors shaping the "menu" of options for urban-level policy (Savitch and Kantor 2002).

The mobilizations of other business and civil society actors and their relations of dependence on their employers shape the strategies of unions in Seattle and Hamburg. Despite different sets of worker rights and bargaining practices institutionalized at the national level, unions in both cities rely on coalitions as they respond to restructuring. High-stakes races for investment combined with one-sided relations of dependence by workers on their employer require an economistic approach to coalition politics. In other areas of local policy, however, such as workforce development policy and public sector restructuring, it is possible for unions to fight for jobs while pursuing other social goods.

In this chapter I make this case by examining union approaches to growth politics in two union strongholds, Hamburg and Seattle. Both cities have seen a recent revival of labor-community coalitions, pushed in part by the unions' central coordinating bodies—the local affiliates of the Deutscher Gewerkschaftsbund (DGB, German Confederation of Trade Unions) and the AFL-CIO—and facilitated by a civil society willing to cooperate. Although Hamburg has not seen anything on the scale of the 1999 WTO protests, labor's coalition work there has produced spillovers with broad local significance. Hamburg and Seattle have both experienced declines in waterfront and defense-oriented manufacturing industries, successful efforts by local elites to develop a new economy, a growth in service employment, strong left-liberal political traditions, and intense competition in the market for capital investment. Local union officials in both cities assist in-plant worker representatives in negotiations with management, in strikes, and in local political issues such as privatization and economic development policy. Despite periodic conflicts of interest, a strong culture of solidarity in both cities prevents local unions from pulling out of central bodies or engaging in intense rivalries. Although collective bargaining is formally more centralized in Germany than in the United States, this does not affect the variables that shape union coalition-building strategies. Comparing cities with similar political cultures, levels of union strength, industry structure, and economic vitality allows a test of the relative importance of sectoral and national differences.

HAMBURG

Hamburg, Germany's second largest city, with 1.7 million residents, has a long history as an independent Hanseatic port city (*freie Hansestadt*) on the Elbe River. The Hansestadt is a city-state within the German federal system, governed by a directly elected city council that elects an executive cabinet (the Senate) and mayor. The city's territory corresponds roughly to its economic space, thanks to a Nazi-era reform annexing the nearby industrial towns of Harburg, Wilhelms-burg, and Altona. The region has been a union stronghold from the nineteenth century through World War I, through two failed Communist revolutions (including Hamburg's own Thaelmann Putsch of 1923), and the turbulent Weimar Republic. After a twelve-year period of illegality under Hitler, unions enjoyed a forty-four-year period of integration in a Social Democratic Party–led local governing coalition, ending with SPD defeat in 2001.

The 2001 defeat was a long time coming and reflected a deeper crisis in the social democratic milieu. Since 1970, white-collar employment had doubled and blue-collar employment had declined by half, blue collar unemployment had grown, and union membership had declined. At the same time, the national SPD government had pushed a painful program of welfare state retrenchment that hurt the most vulnerable working people. Poor neighborhoods shifted their votes toward right-wing populist parties and the conservative Christian Democratic Union (CDU).

Until 2001, unions were part of a local governing coalition that developed a strong postindustrial economy. Through military conversion campaigns, struggles against plant closings and the race for investment capital, their involvement in economic development policy stretches back to the 1970s. Attracting investment became a focus of the SPD in the 1980s and 1990s, especially in media, the harbor, and aerospace (Läpple 2000). The local DGB and the public sector union, Öffentliche Dienst, Transport, und Verkehr (ÖTV), similarly worked to expand the harbor. The unions and the local government also negotiated over the rationalization and privatization of public services, which most local elites viewed as bringing Hamburg into the postindustrial era. In the late 1990s, the local of the metalworkers union, IG Metall, having declined from fifty-six thousand to forty thousand members since the early 1970s, became deeply involved in a push for a new Airbus plant. These initiatives, however, had social and environmental costs and strong local opposition, often within the union camp.

This pattern of local participation and coalition politics changed with the defeat of the SPD. Unions, dealing with the same trends, found that they needed a more vocal, public approach. Their most dramatic public display of discontent came when the Senate announced its intention to privatize the public hospitals, the Landesbetrieb Krankenhaeuser (LBK). The unions organized a ballot initiative to fight privatization, which led to a series of spillover campaigns focused on local democracy (making ballot initiatives more binding) and the preservation of other public services. Contrasting union approaches at Airbus and LBK is instructive, because it shows how Hamburg's unions shifted from an insider strategy for jobs to a strategy of contesting the new government's vision of how development should proceed.

Germany's distinctive industrial relations institutions shape how worker representation happens. Unions and works councils in Germany are products of the so-called dual system of industrial relations. Unions negotiate wages and lead strikes, usually at the regional-sectoral level. IG Metall is a conglomerate union representing workers in steel, automotive, aerospace, electronics, shipbuilding, and a wide range of other manufacturing industries. Ver.di (Vereinigte Dienstleistungsgewerkschaft or United Services Union), similarly, represents workers at all levels of government and in most private service industries as well. Works councils, which may not call strikes, are elected by workers and represent the daily concerns of workers in the workplace and translate sectoral agreements into in-plant regulations.

In practice, these roles are usually blurred, and union members dominate the works councils of both Airbus and LBK (although Hamburg's Airbus works council has a substantial antiunion caucus). IG Metall in Hamburg pursues a strategy of "workplace-near" collective bargaining, in which the regional sectoral agreements, covering Germany's northern coastal regions, are customized in close consultation with the works council to deal with issues specific to the firm. One agreement at Airbus, for example, is called "Siduflex." It buffers the company's core German workforce, including thirteen thousand workers in Hamburg, from the industry's vicissitudes through a series of agreements that cover working time accounts (schemes to pay for time off during business downturns in exchange for unpaid overtime during boom periods), temporary workers, and outsourcing. Siduflex, however, has been hampered by the low degree of union organization in the white-collar areas of the plant. While union density among blue-collar workers keeps overall union density above a quarter, membership among white-collar workers (who outnumber blue-collar workers 2–1 in the plant) has slid from 15 percent to below 10 percent.

Outside the firm, therefore, union participation has proven crucial. In December 1997, Airbus's works council and IG Metall began to experience the dark side of economic development politics. Airbus managers announced a program to build a new giant airplane, the A380. Managers projected two thousand new jobs in the plant and two thousand jobs at local suppliers for the winner. A competition between local governments ensued to determine where the firm would place the investments and jobs.

Hamburg's local IG Metall leadership participated in a coalition, which included local business associations, government agencies, politicians, and the DGB, to win public expenditures to fill in a waterway for plant construction and pass a series of laws to expedite construction. Farmers, environmental groups, affluent neighbors (whose views would be spoiled by the construction site and the new production complex), and others (mainly artists and media professionals who considered the "jobs above all else" agenda an infringement on the Hansestadt's tradition of local democracy and autonomy) opposed the subsidies and land redevelopment plans. Stiff competition came from Toulouse, which had the same sorts of advantages as Hamburg. Other regions, such as Rostock and Dresden in eastern Germany, developed public policy arguments for national government officials (who still exert some influence at the company) that they had the necessary infrastructure and skills but needed the jobs more than the wealthy Hansestadt. Furthermore, Hamburg's progrowth coalition was under time pressure, since the company needed to fill in part of a local waterway before it could build new production buildings and ramp up A380 production. In the end, the company decided to accept incentive packages from both Toulouse and Hamburg and built two final assembly lines for the A380, each one carrying out various stages of assembly.

The works council and IG Metall had the support of the local DGB, business organizations led by the Chamber of Commerce, and politicians across the spectrum, including the Greens and the SPD. This coalition not only won public money for infrastructure, it helped the company steer through the land use decisions necessary to construct the plant, including the filling of the waterway and the seizure of private land through eminent domain. In February 2001 Hamburg's supreme administrative court decided the final appeal on whether or not to halt construction due to its implications for the environment and property owners. On the day of the decision, IG Metall mobilized seven thousand workers downtown to show support for the project. The court ruled in favor of the government and Airbus.

Workers, in principle, had some tools to counter this whipsawing. The unions had political channels, in that Airbus, a creation of governmental industrial policy, remains a policy instrument of governments to shape economic development. German workers, furthermore, have codetermination rules giving them extensive access to corporate decision making in areas of personnel and investment. The company could not credibly claim that it was in a time of hardship, since it had enjoyed recent successes in the global market for planes. Furthermore,

Airbus workers have an organ for international solidarity. The European Works Council brings worker representatives from throughout Europe together for meetings and even includes a special economics committee modeled on German codetermination, far beyond the legal minimum stipulated by European Union legislation. Nevertheless, the interregional competition for jobs faced no organized resistance from European or nationwide worker representation bodies.

Why did unions not resist this whipsawing between workplaces and cities? Union officials faced a dilemma, since they did not want to sacrifice environmental quality or public funds, but believed, along with local elites, in the importance of the Airbus investment for the region's economic future. Worker representatives had an extra incentive to protect jobs, since Airbus workers lacked mobility in the local labor market; there are not many employers of aerospace engineers or machinists outside of Airbus. The largest one, Lufthansa's maintenance operation, does not pay according to IG Metall's metal industry contract, and the smaller firms depend on Airbus for orders. The costs included damage to historically and environmentally important places, a heavy burden of subsidies for taxpayers, and criticism from within union ranks (Remarque 2001).

Although IG Metall continued working to help the company deal with the local politics associated with expansion, it changed its approach somewhat. By late 2004, the land-use issues were still in play, as the company fought nearby villagers to buy land for a new transport center. The union and the SPD, however, were not feeling the intense pressures of 1997–2001. With the A380 in production and the SPD out of the Senate, the unions and SPD called for a compromise to protect the local landscape.

The dilemmas facing unions in Hamburg shifted dramatically with the 2001 local election. The new right-wing coalition government continued public sector rationalization and economic development projects but eliminated the unions' previous channels of influence. Although Erhard Pumm, the head of the local DGB, retained his seat as an SPD city councilor, he lost his influence in the executive branch. The new coalition government of liberals, conservatives, and right-wing populists announced that it would privatize a majority stake in LBK. The hospital privatization fight led to a major test for the newly merged ver.di (which included the old ÖTV) and its leader, Wolfgang Rose. Pumm and Rose responded to hospital privatization by organizing mobilizations of hospital workers and community allies and by shifting the union's role from labor-management-government partnership to community mobilization.

The Senate had created LBK in 1996 as part of an effort to make public agencies independent and entrepreneurial. Because LBK accounted for about half of Hamburg's local hospital beds and fifteen thousand employees, rationalizing it had huge implications for economic development and social well-being. That year, the works council and ÖTV negotiated a series of concessions in order to make LBK more efficient, including massive outsourcing of services (cleaning, cooking, transport, maintenance, and information technology), the closure of a hospital, and the elimination of three thousand jobs. In exchange, the union and works council won policies to cushion the impact of downsizing on the workforce. This exchange was possible because of the close ties between unionists, managers, and top policymakers in the government, including an affiliation with the SPD shared by all three.

The post-2001 battle over privatization proceeded differently. In principle, Pumm, Rose, and the works council did not want to be "blockers"; they agreed with the government that updating the company's physical infrastructure would require some private financing. Unions and the SPD proposed 49 percent privatization, to retain local public control of health care, while obtaining the capital needed for upgrades. CDU health-care and public-financing experts, however, argued that private suppliers of capital would not accept a minority stake. Since hospital chains would be assuming the risks, they argued, the purchaser—in this case, for-profit hospital chain Asklepios—would require control and 74 percent ownership.

In response to the Senate's new policy, Rose rallied LBK workers, his own organization, and a range of allies to organize one of the city-state's first ballot initiatives with the slogan "Gesundheit ist keine Ware" (Health Is Not a Commodity). The coalition included other unions (especially the local DGB), political parties, globalization critics "attac," the doctors' association (Marburger Bund), individual patients, and ver.di's national office. Antiprivatization campaigners collected one hundred thousand signatures in the city's public squares and shopping areas and organized numerous rallies and demonstrations. Attendance at workplace meetings dramatically increased, and, over the opposition of management, the works council announced an unprecedented citywide meeting of LBK workers. Conservative politicians fought back with anticommunist language, equating state-owned hospitals with the combines of preunification East Germany.[1]

In late 2003, the Senate signed the privatization agreement with Asklepios and was hoping to finalize the deal before the issue went to the voters. The transfer stalled, however, when one of the governing parties imploded. A judge ruled that local elections would take place at the same time as the LBK ballot initiative. The SPD—itself a privatizer before 2001—took opposition to LBK privatization into its early 2004 election program.

---

1. Anonymous, "LBK: Koalition schießt scharf," *Hamburger Abendblatt,* May 8, 2003: http://www.abendblatt.de/daten/2003/05/08/159035.html?prx=1.

The ballot initiative was, by all accounts, a powerful tool. Conservative party officials said in interviews that the unions had been so successful in "instrumentalizing" popular feelings of insecurity that they had to focus on their mayoral candidate, the photogenic Ole von Beust, rather than controversial policy issues. For similar reasons, LBK administrators and Asklepios managers kept a low profile. Although the initiative won over three-quarters approval from the voters, the conservatives won an absolute majority on the city council.

The fate of LBK's workers thus remains far from resolved; the workplace conflict and related spillover campaigns remain active and visible. After the 2004 election, the CDU ignored the vote over the ballot initiative and continued efforts to transfer LBK to Asklepios; eventually, in December 2004, it won a court decision allowing it to privatize LBK. As a result, the NGO Mehr Demokratie, e.V. (More Democracy) jumped into the fray, working with the unions and opposition political parties on a second project, "Rettet den Volksentscheid" (Save the Ballot Initiative), to make ballot initiatives legally binding in Hamburg. Rose has initiated a national effort to encourage other Ver.di locals to use the ballot initiative process. The tactic was indeed effective in delaying privatization, improving community relations, mobilizing workers in the hospitals, winning more members, and learning how to mobilize public opinion around emotional issues. It remains unclear, however, whether this fight will help unions cope with issues inside the workplace, such as the terms of the handover. In upcoming effects bargaining, management will push to extend working hours. It is unclear what the coalitions mean for these negotiations or for the Senate's upcoming program to revise public sector labor law, privatize more services, and cut other social programs.

LBK and Airbus illustrate changes in the opportunity structure faced by Hamburg's labor movement since the 1990s. At first, labor had allied itself with a social democratic government bent on a vigorous economic development program. Under conservative governments, however, rather than a process of joint problem solving, hospital rationalization sparked a battle over privatization and a series of mobilizations and coalitions that will probably continue for years to come. This struggle helped to build a nascent local ver.di organization and revive the local DGB. The meaning of participation shifted from mobilizing as the government's junior partner to developing alternative strategies and building a new social coalition. After the 2001 election, unions had a broader menu of options because of their independence from the government and ver.di's broad scope beyond LBK and the health-care industry.

SEATTLE

Since the mid-1990s Seattle has gained a reputation as a hot spot of union revi-talization.[2] With relatively high union density, its booming service, transporta-tion, and high-tech economy has made it the economic engine of the Pacific Northwest. Like Hamburg, Seattle is an economic development success story, where progrowth politics have succeeded, albeit unevenly and with social costs. Seattle's trade unionists share many challenges with their colleagues in Hamburg. A large aircraft manufacturer's strategy of pitting regions against each other forced organized labor into a business-led coalition, sacrificing social goods for economic development. Meanwhile, in other sectors, labor has managed to com-bine its interest in job retention with other goals. Efforts by unions to retain union jobs in construction involve new policies to spread the gains from economic de-velopment to disadvantaged groups and has facilitated the revitalization of Seat-tle's AFL-CIO affiliate, the King County Labor Council (KCLC). Like Hamburg, this renewal has taken place as union membership density has declined (although economic growth and organizing have increased the absolute union membership in the region).

The economic development politics of Seattle has both probusiness and pro-gressive elements. The region is highly dependent on Boeing and focused on building up its physical infrastructure. Progressive forces, however, are also firmly entrenched, with powerful environmental and other community organizations. Compared to Hamburg's SPD, Seattle's Democrats, some of whom are among the state's most progressive politicians, have a solid base of support. Organized labor has joined this constellation of forces, after a long period of conservatism. Seat-tle Union Now, Jobs with Justice, the Worker Center AFL-CIO, the Boeing strikes, the massive WTO protests, and dozens of smaller, lesser-known campaigns and projects all attest to the ferment of Seattle labor during the 1990s. Since then, the KCLC (along with its state-level equivalent) has revived its member-mobilization program around election campaigns, introduced a new endorsement process, brought pressure to bear on labor-supported candidates, and built broad coali-tions that include environmentalists, community groups, and portions of the re-gion's business community. Although unions have had success in fusing broader social goods to the politics of construction, winning the high-stakes race for aero-space jobs has split the labor movement (though only in the short run) over the costs of development.

The training initiatives of the Seattle King County Building Trades Council are an important part of local labor movement revival in Seattle. After decades of

---

2. This section draws heavily on Byrd and Greer 2005.

fighting the minority community over job access, the building trades began around 1990 to find ways to bring women and minorities into the trades. Ron Judd, who later became head of the KCLC, was one of the initial bridge builders . who built an alliance with community groups, politicians, quasi-public agencies, private contractors, and developers to shape the way that large projects and training are governed (Rosenblum 2001). The new rules that the building-trades council and the Worker Center have constructed have secured the market share of unionized contractors, bolstered labor-governed training problems, and addressed some of the problems faced by minority and female apprentices and firms on job sites. Although community activists argue that some of the industry's racist recruitment policies continue, the programs' inadequacies have not prevented deep coalition building.

Since the late 1960s, Seattle's building-trades unions have faced two major challenges. First, like most cities, they have faced low-cost competition and non-union contractors taking over predominately unionized markets such as commercial and industrial building projects. Second, public works projects have been a flashpoint of racial tension. Federal urban renewal projects became a battleground, as organized minority contractors and workers, led by Tyree Scott, shut down job sites. Building trades council and KCLC leaders mobilized thousands of white members in rallies to sway the Republican governor and county executive to resist the insurgents' demands. Labor leaders railed against an "unholy alliance" of civil rights groups, Republicans, and contractors (Griffey 2004).

In the early 1990s, however, the building-trades council switched from this defensive approach to a more proactive coalition-based approach. Reforms in apprenticeship rules and improved community relations were central to this strategy. Judd worked with local community leaders to develop a set of rules governing building projects. The purpose was to protect the market share of union contractors and bring women and minorities into the trades. Adding social goals generated broad political support for project labor agreements (PLAs) and brought a stream of funding from the Port of Seattle.

The main policy initiative consisted of rules requiring minimum levels of apprenticeship utilization and enforceable racial and gender diversity targets. Initially, PLAs were instituted at airport expansion projects, and over the following ten years they spread to county and municipal office buildings, mass transit, schools, and new private development. Alongside the PLAs, the building trades supported several programs (mentorship, housing, transportation, preapprenticeship, and so on) to help apprentices both on and off the job, using contributions from the port, which also had an interest in spreading the proceeds of development. Despite some disagreements with the building trades over the administration of the programs, the port reported that significant improvements had been made in gender and racial diversity. The building trades and KCLC also managed to include other social goods, such as organizing rights and affordable housing, into some of the more controversial projects. By the late 1990s, Scott's group, the Northwest Labor and Employment Law Office (LELO), was helping to frame project labor agreements and taking an active role in monitoring their implementation.

The spread of PLAs—or more precisely, the apprenticeship rules in them—was a victory for the unions. Other local actors began taking unions seriously as advocates for socially responsible growth. The stabilizing effect came partly from rules stipulating that apprentices had to enroll in state-licensed apprenticeship programs. Unionized programs cover 95 percent of King County's apprentices. Furthermore, according to union leaders, they overcame some employer resistance to unionization when contractors saw that unions were flexible with their rules and could supply a high-quality workforce. The new rules eased the transition of nonunion workers into the unionized workforce, in that nonunion workers under the PLA now worked alongside union members and changed hiring rules made it easier for skilled nonunion workers to enter the union with their journeyman skills recognized. Working with business did not force a consistent progrowth position: the building trades helped environmentalists in the late 1990s to defeat a ballot initiative to overturn the state's growth management law (Rose 2000).

As the unions were healing the wounds of the past, they were creating a basis for restoring the market share of their employers and removing barriers to organizing. These local innovations laid the groundwork for national policy development. These rules inserted in PLAs have been widely disseminated, partly because the Seattle case has been publicized as a best practice by the national AFL-CIO (Working for America Institute 2002) and partly because of a shift within national construction unions toward an aggressive organizing program. Furthermore, there have been local spillovers. Seattle's building-trades unions are now trying to win apprenticeship rules without the concessions associated with PLAs. In 2005, legislation passed in the state legislature extending a 15 percent apprentice utilization requirement to public works projects statewide.

Economic development politics, however, have also had a downside for Seattle's unions. The region's largest employer, Boeing, has forced unions into some extremely difficult political positions. Boeing employs over fifty thousand workers in design and production facilities, mainly in southern King County and Everett. The company has long dominated local labor markets for skilled blue and white-collar aerospace workers and has found ways to win union support for subsidies and infrastructure investment from state and local governments. Since

Boeing became the dominant local employer during World War II, its patterns of hiring and firing have created periods of boom and bust (Markusen, Golob, and Grey 1996). In recent years, Boeing has become increasingly footloose. It has shifted its headquarters from Seattle to Chicago (where it has no production facilities) and outsourced and offshored considerable production (including some complex work such as wing production). The company's labor-relations strategy has come to emphasize union busting and downsizing—"reduce union leverage; reduce union workers"[3]—and it has met several organizing drives with union-busting tactics. Most important for Seattle's unions, however, was the company's threat to shift assembly work of a new plane, the 7E7, to a greenfield location.

Boeing's workers belong to two unions that have few members outside the company: the blue-collar International Association of Machinists District Lodge 751 and the white-collar Seattle Professional Engineering Employees' Association (SPEEA). Both organizations have considerable autonomy from their national organizations; SPEEA affiliated to a small national union in 1998 in which it is the largest affiliate. The national and transnational links between Boeing unions are extremely loose, occurring via the Coalition of Labor Unions at Boeing or the International Metalworkers Federation (which also brings together representatives from Airbus and elsewhere). The near absence of union organization in local manufacturing outside Boeing results in large wage discrepancies between unionized Boeing workers and the rest of the industry. These unions and their members are thus highly dependent on demand for aircraft and the company's decisions about how to meet that demand.

During the 1990s, the IAM and SPEEA fit Seattle labor's revitalization image. During Boeing's boom period, the unions organized successful strikes and made gains in participation rights. The 1995 IAM strike and the 2000 SPEEA strike both involved intensive cooperation with KCLC, Jobs with Justice, and with other unions and community groups. In the case of SPEEA's "No Nerds, No Birds" strike, the union won massive increases in membership in a workplace without mandatory membership. This and a major organizing drive in Boeing's Wichita plant (contested by management even after the initial certification election) allowed SPEEA to double its membership in the four years leading up to Boeing's crisis. These struggles provided an opportunity for unions and other community groups to mobilize and show solidarity.

When the market for commercial jets collapsed after the September 11 attacks and the Asian SARS outbreaks, the fight for jobs took center stage. The unions' approach has been twofold: outside the workplace they have entered coalitions

3. Dominic Gates, "A Critical Juncture for Boeing and Machinists," *Seattle Times,* June 14, 2004, A1.

with managers, Boeing lobbyists, and other partners to improve Boeing's business climate (winning subsidies, government orders, infrastructure, and other advantages); inside the workplace, they have used a partnership approach to win participation rights in work reorganization and outsourcing decisions, in hopes of preventing mismanagement and saving jobs. Union leaders have been largely dissatisfied with the results of in-firm partnership, due to management's tendency to ignore the advice of joint committees and distance joint activities from the core of strategic decision making. The IAM's training fund, for example, has been used more as a way to help unemployed workers get skills for other jobs than for its stated purpose, to improve quality at Boeing.

In late 2002, however, a flurry of job retention activities began outside the workplace. Boeing announced that it was building a new plane, the 7E7 Dreamliner. In order to choose a site for the new assembly plant, the firm solicited bids from state governments throughout the United States, in a competition that was to last a year. The governor, county executives, and mayors gathered in public displays of support for Boeing and commitment to meet the company's demands. IAM and SPEEA mobilized to win support for subsidies, infrastructure investments, and other reforms to benefit the company. IAM was especially active, organizing a volunteer effort of eight hundred shop stewards to put up yard signs, lobby, and carry out discussions with local residents and business people about the importance of supporting Boeing.

For its part, Boeing made common cause with a coalition of business groups with whom it had disagreed over past unemployment insurance reforms. The head of Boeing's commercial aircraft unit, Alan Mullaly, gave business leaders their rallying cry at a Rotary Club meeting in late 2003. When asked his opinion about local business conditions, he said, "I think we suck." Business groups in the state capital successfully used the ensuing support for Boeing-friendly legislation as an opportunity to win reforms of the unemployment insurance system, not only to help Boeing's bottom line but also to help building contractors and farmers. The proposal that passed eliminated benefits for thousands of seasonal workers, including construction workers, who use the unemployment system to survive periodic unavoidable periods of unemployment. More important for the IAM and SPEEA, Boeing won $3.2 billion in tax breaks.

Once the legislature passed the incentive package, Boeing agreed to build the new assembly plant in Everett. The building-trades unions sent angry letters to IAM leaders for accepting the unemployment insurance cuts, and the tax created difficulties for anyone advocating state government investment elsewhere. However, IAM and SPEEA's message of jobs above all else was understandable, since it came at the end of a wave of downsizing that had cost the region thirty thousand jobs. The gains were relatively small: the company projected two thousand new local Boeing jobs, plus an unknown number in local suppliers. The business press urged the public to view the subsidy package not in terms of the two thousand jobs but in terms of retaining the remaining fifty thousand jobs.[4]

At Boeing and the building trades, local unions responded to challenges from the global economy in different ways. At Boeing, a high-stakes race for investment forced the unions into a position where they had to participate in a coalition to win subsidies and other advantages to retain jobs. The legislative battle temporarily divided the state's labor movement and gutted the state's protections for seasonal workers. This decision had little positive effect on union membership, since the company's new assembly plant had few employees compared to the number recently lost. Furthermore, the unions did not represent employees at the company's major local or offshore suppliers, which would employ most of the workers on the 7E7 project. At the building trades, by contrast, the unions had to innovate in the policy arena to hold their own against nonunion contractors vying for contracts in a building boom. With the assistance of the KCLC and several quasi-public agencies, the building trades strategically built bridges to longtime adversaries in the community, diversified union membership to reflect the new construction workforce, and laid the foundations for new kinds of social regulation of private development. While Boeing's unions were coerced by crisis into working to help the company obtain public funds, the building trades responded to their crisis through innovative policies inserted in PLAs and successfully held the line on low-wage competition.

Both of these stories are rooted in the growth politics of Seattle and have implications for the local labor movement as a whole. Although union victories at Boeing before the downturn were part of the story of the revival of the local labor movement, mobilizations to win Boeing investment have threatened not only unions but also public finances and public programs. Likewise, the building-trades' initiatives have affected not only construction workers but also have been an integral part of the careers of bridge builders like Judd and Scott. The impact of coalition building in Seattle has arguably been global, in that the KCLC and LELO both played crucial roles in the 1999 WTO protests. Patterns of union-employer dependence and different opportunities in (and pressures from) the local business community, government, and civil society have thus shaped what is possible for unions in Seattle.

4. Glenn Pascall, "Take the State's 7E7 Deal, but Forget the Study," *Puget Sound Business Journal,* July 7, 2004: http://www.bizjournals.com/seattle/stories/2004/07/05/editorial3.html?page=2.

URBAN POLITICAL ECONOMY AND LABOR'S SEARCH FOR ALTERNATIVES

Unions are searching for alternatives, and, despite their dark side, the politics of local economic development holds some promise for this search. While some unions revive themselves through coalition politics to pursue broad social goods, others end up on an economistic low road. Why do unions pursue these different goods? The observed differences reflect not only differences in union strategy but also in what is possible for policymakers, what Savitch and Kantor (2002) call differences in the menu of policy choices.

I take seriously the argument made by unionists at Boeing and Airbus in interviews that they understood the trade-offs, but had no choice. While the possibility of capital flight created a threat, the interests and mobilization of local business and local government provided an opportunity. Building trades and health-care unionists, by contrast, said in interviews that they had developed something new and built bridges that had helped them both save jobs and win credibility in local policymaking that provides broad social goods.

Do inadequate industrial relations institutions in the United States spur innovative union strategies by forcing a search for alternative sources of power? Do the German institutions of workplace participation and sectoral wage bargaining continue to support participation and union strength? Neither institutional hypothesis seems helpful in this comparison. Progressive union-inclusive coalition building was visible in both cities, as was a more coercive pattern of participation. Despite national differences, union leaders such as Judd and Rose were able to innovate. Moreover, unions in both countries, regardless of formal information and consultation rights, faced uncertainty and dependence. The announcement of a race for a new production line gave unions in Seattle and Hamburg a threat and opportunity that forced them into a development coalition with narrowly economistic aims.

A second factor, the economic structure and power relations of the sector, provides more analytical leverage. Airbus and Boeing are multinational firms, competing with each other in the global airplane market, while LBK and the unionized construction sector in Seattle compete in less export-oriented industries. Furthermore, Airbus and Boeing can invest in a much wider range of locations than LBK or Seattle's building contractors (although the vast sunk costs and reserves of skilled labor make aircraft makers more locally dependent than most manufacturers).

A sectoral explanation stressing the differences between multinational manufacturing and local services leaves a few features of this comparison unexplained. It remains to be explained, for example, why unionists did not utilize the large firm structure as an opportunity, especially the Germany-wide and European works councils. Furthermore, all three sectors are *both* localized *and* globalized. While LBK and Seattle's real estate development industries also depend on su-perregional markets for capital, Boeing and Airbus face some local regulation via the influence of local politicians in national policymaking. Industrial, trade, and land-use policies still constrain these aerospace giants, despite their political power and control over the location of jobs. In addition, a focus on sectoral dif-ferences neglects changes over time in cities and firms. With a change in local pol-itics, Hamburg's unions took a different approach at both Airbus and LBK, and a change in Boeing's fortunes led to a change at IAM and SPEEA.

What are the salient differences between sectors in these places? First, the pattern of union-employer dependence shapes the menu of possible policies. Workers and unions at Boeing and Airbus are highly dependent on a single transnational firm, because finding a job as an aerospace mechanic or engineer in the adjacent region at the same pay level is difficult, and because the unions have limited presence outside of these employers. Their counterparts in heath care and construction, by contrast, organize broadly across industries, and there-fore have much less of an existential fear of job losses. These unions lack the in-tense pressure seen at Airbus and Boeing to sacrifice the environment, public funds, and welfare benefits in exchange for jobs.

Second, mobilizations of actors outside of the labor-management relationship have set up opportunities for unions (although in the high-stakes races for in-vestment seen at Airbus and Boeing, the opportunities have come with clear disadvantages). When jobs are threatened by an interregional competition for in-vestment, local politicians and business representatives gave worker representa-tives an additional set of resources to fight for jobs. Health-care and construction organizers, similarly, deal with competition with the help of community allies. The difference is the quality of the partners and their interests. Oppositional po-litical parties, community organizations, and other partners, with their wider range of interests, can help unions reach beyond the goal of job retention.

These patterns of union-firm dependence and broader mobilizations of busi-ness, government, and civil society explain the menu of options that are available for local political participation in economic development policy, in Seattle, Ham-burg, and possibly beyond. Whether a union seizes opportunities, however, is a matter of strategic choice and cannot be read from the political-economic factors highlighted here. Political economy cannot tell us whether other leaders in the same circumstances would have made the same decisions as Rose or Judd.

Union-inclusive coalition building can emerge in cities that vary by size, eco-nomic well-being, labor history, culture, and country. These coalitions, however progressive, do not usually reverse trends of declining union density, certainly not in Hamburg and Seattle. Union membership decline thus may be robbing cities of one of the most important supports of high-road economic development. On the other hand, threats to jobs and opportunities to participate might be turning unions into better local citizens.

Current economic development trends are simultaneously transforming and decimating unions. Will they be able to do more with less through smarter participation? Only time will tell.

12

ORGANIZING LABOR IN LONDON
Lessons from the Campaign for a Living Wage

Jane Holgate and Jane Wills

In this chapter we explore the extent to which union organizing strategies and practices in London have been developed to reflect the particularities of place. And, in so doing, we consider the extent to which unions are creating a new social justice infrastructure on an urban scale. It is widely acknowledged that London is a global city at the heart of the networks of capital, labor, and ideas that are producing globalization. In this chapter we consider what being a global city, and being London in particular, might mean for union organizing. We ask what it means for unions to take their location seriously, to develop a geographically sophisticated analysis about their prospects, and how this might affect union strategy and practice in London. We argue that coalition building offers a very useful way to extend the reach and influence of labor in a city of remarkable diversity, complexity and political-economic significance for Great Britain and the rest of the world. We explore the tentative steps that are being taken to establish a new movement of workers and community activists, focusing on the London living wage campaign that has been led by the East London Communities Organisation (TELCO).[1] In our conclusion, we urge unions in London to take their geography more seriously and take advantage of the positive opportunities that come from being at the heart of the city and its global networks.

DEVELOPING A GEOGRAPHICALLY SENSITIVE ORGANIZING STRATEGY FOR LONDON

Saskia Sassen (2000, 177) defines global cities as places "that are strategic sites in the global economy because of their concentration of command functions and high-level producer-service firms oriented to world markets; more generally,

We would like to thank the editors, Lowell Turner and Dan Cornfield, for their constructive comments on this chapter.

1. The material in this chapter has been gathered by the authors over the last few years while working with union organizers and living wage activists across London.

cities with high levels of internationalization in their economy and in their broader social structure." London is the quintessential global city. The "square mile," or the financial heart of the city, houses a number of important financial markets and the headquarters of many transnational corporations and banks. As these words from the London Plan indicate, London is a global city that fundamentally depends on its role in global finance and business: "[London] is one of the three world financial centres, Europe's financial capital, and the world's most economically internationalised city; it is the most culturally diverse city in the world; it is the largest city in the European Union and the UK's centre of government, culture, tourism and business" (Greater London Authority 2002, 6).

London is clearly a critical node in global politics, economy, and culture. It is a place of great strategic importance, a place where the powerful are located and a location from which globalization is made. Yet not everyone in the city is a winner from the processes of globalization. The very intensity of its global connections tends to fuel greater inequalities in the city: those who are involved in global-level transactions tend to have great power and wealth while many others are left far behind. Over the past thirty years London has been transformed. The city has lost most of its manufacturing base and become a postindustrial city "whose economy is no longer dominated by manufacturing industry but is, instead, based on finance, business services and the creative and cultural industries" (Hamnett 2003, 5). In the process, the social character of London has changed dramatically. The number of manufacturing workers in the city has declined, and there has been an explosion in jobs for white-collar qualified service workers. There are fewer opportunities for those without qualifications and, as a result, sections of London's working-class communities have been left a long way behind. Despite the great wealth generated in London, there is greater poverty here than anywhere else in the country. The Greater London Authority (GLA) have calculated that one in seven workers in London earn less than what they call a "poverty threshold wage" of £5.80 an hour, and as many as one in five earn less than a "living wage" of £6.70 an hour (Greater London Authority 2005).[2] Four hundred thousand full-time and three hundred thousand part-time workers in London are estimated to earn less than this amount.

For those in poor jobs at the bottom end of the labor market, working conditions have deteriorated over the past thirty years. Deregulation of the labor market is known to have had a disproportionate impact on those in low-paid employment, and what were once "living wage" jobs with some benefits and

---

2. The GLA's living wage unit makes an annual adjustment of the living wage rate to reflect changes in the cost of living.

prospects for advancement are now often only a means to survive through very long hours of work. The employment conditions of those performing such essential work as cleaning, catering, caring, and hospitality have tended to decline over time, particularly with privatization. As a result, London now relies on an army of low-paid workers, many of them new migrants, to perform the essential jobs on which the city depends.

In her early conceptualization of the global city, Sassen (1988) argued that immigration and ethnicity were fundamental to the ways in which the city was changing. Just as the transnationalization of capital (North to South) allowed multinational corporations and governments to find new ways of increasing profits and raising revenue in the South, the transnationalization of labor (South to North) allowed capital to find new sources of profits in the North. In parallel with global trends, rates of migration to Great Britain have increased recently, with almost one-third of the total migrant population arriving during the last decade. On arrival in the country, migrants locate in the major conurbations, with more than 40 percent of all migrants now living in London, constituting just over a quarter of the city's population. Data indicate that migrants tend to be divided between those employed in highly skilled, high-wage jobs (approximately 60 percent of all migrants) and those in clerical and routine manual jobs (Hamnett 2003, 107). Low-paid manufacturing and service work is increasingly done by black and minority ethnic (BME) migrants in London. And while many Londoners celebrate the city's ethnic diversity, little has been done to tackle the problems low-paid migrant workers face in trying to survive in a global city like London.[3]

London is a global city that embraces extremes of power and wealth. The rich and poor share the same space but live in very different worlds. The critical question for us in this chapter, however, is the extent to which this context should and does affect trade union organizing campaigns. A new stream of geographically focused research into union organizing would suggest that unions can gain a great deal from taking their geography seriously. As Herod, Peck, and Wills (2003, 176) have recently put it:

> Axiomatic for labour geographers is the claim that spatial factors—such as the inescapably uneven geographical development of capitalist economies, the geographical scale and scope of legislation, the role of distinctive regional "cultures" of industrial relations practices, the structure and dynamics of local labour markets, the spatial hierarchies

---

3. For more on the role of migrant labor in jobs at the bottom end of London's economy, see Evans et al. 2005 and May et al. 2006.

of trade union organisation, the locally-differentiated processes of social reproduction, gender and race relations, the shifting landscape of
political activism and labour-organisational capacities—really *matter*
in the practice of industrial relations and in the trajectories of workplace politics.

Geography, they would argue, matters to trade union organization, and here we
focus on three key ways in which it matters for London.

First, places and their labor markets have very particular characteristics. Due
to its idiosyncratic history and its contemporary position as a key node in networks of global political economy, London, for example, has a labor market that
is segmented among a growing business and finance sector; public services (many
of which are contracted out to the private sector); private services with a particularly strong demand for hospitality, leisure, and retail workers; and a declining
manufacturing sector. Each is very different, each is gendered and racialized in
very different ways, and, from a trade union point of view, each presents a range
of different opportunities and challenges. These opportunities and challenges
need to be assessed to direct union resources to those areas of greatest need and
potential for recruitment, bearing in mind the wider impact that trade unions can
have on the political economy of the city itself.

Second, the relative geographical fixity of capital and labor in each segment of
the labor market needs to be evaluated. Geographers have highlighted how spatial mobility can shape power relations, demonstrated most clearly in the way in
which manufacturers are able to increase their power by threatening to move production abroad to cheaper locations to avoid unionization attempts (Cravey
2004; Hale and Wills 2005). Yet in the same way, those employers seeking to serve
local markets, such as tourism, retail, and hospitality, are much less able to move.
From a geographical perspective, workers in these sectors have greater potential
for organizing than those employed in some more traditional manufacturing industries, even if service sector workers and their trade unions often remain weak.

Third, trade unions themselves have their own geographical structure: unions
are organized so that activities take place at particular spatial scales such as the
branch (local), region, national (or international in North America), and global.
These structures make a great difference to who is included, the focus of activity,
and what is possible. Increasingly, workers are spread across very small workplaces, and they may be working alongside agency colleagues; they may be very
ethnically diverse, relocate fairly often (as is common in hospitality, retail, and
contract services), and they may work part-time.[4] Such workers may have weak

---

4. For the challenges these kinds of issues pose to organizing, see Cobble 1991 and Wills 2005.

affiliations to their workplace but may feel more strongly about their occupational identity or their geographical, religious, or ethnic communities, and it can make sense to develop alternative geographical structures to reach them and organize them in new ways. Thus, in a city like London, with a large number of low-paid workers, many of them from BME groups, in sectors such as hospitality, retail, and leisure, there is a critical need to rethink the geography of existing union structures and strategies.

In the following sections we explore what unions are doing in London and focus in particular on the coalition being built around TELCO's living wage campaign, which has allowed two unions to organize low-paid contract cleaning, catering, and portering workers.

NEW LABOUR AND NEW EFFORTS AT BUILDING UNION ORGANIZATION IN LONDON

After eighteen years of Conservative rule, during which time trade unions faced an onslaught of legislation restricting their right to organize in the context of neoliberal deregulation and privatization, the trade unions enthusiastically welcomed the New Labour government in 1997. In New Labour's first term, the government enacted the Employment Relations Act of 1999, which introduced a new right to union recognition, the right to be accompanied in disciplinary and grievance hearings, as well as limited protection from unfair dismissal when undertaking strike action. In addition, the government instituted the national minimum wage, which increased hourly rates of pay for over one million low-paid workers.

Things improved a great deal for the unions, but there was no longer any *special* relationship between New Labour and the Trades Union Congress (TUC). Indeed, from 2001, the second term of New Labour's government was characterized by increasing antagonism with organized labor. At a national level it became clear that there was to be no break from the neoliberal policies introduced by the previous Tory regime. In London, however, new opportunities have arisen with the election of a union-friendly political leader in 1999. Mayor Ken Livingstone is a leading left politician, with a long history of political leadership in the city; he has popular support from Londoners and union leaders in the capital. As explained by a representative from the regional union body, there is a strong mutual relationship between London's mayor and the trade union movement:

> We are fantastically lucky that Ken Livingstone is Mayor of London. He is happy to go on record to say that workers should be members of a

trade union. He is committed to driving up health and safety across the capital, saying that there should be health and safety reps in every workplace—pretty progressive stuff.[5]

Having access to, and support from, the mayor allows the unions to have a voice and some influence in the policy environment of the city. Unions have been provided with seats on London-wide bodies such as Transport for London and the London Tourist Board, giving them input into the development of policy that has direct affect on their members (see Heselden 2001).

In addition, unions have used their influence with the mayor to create space for positive organizing campaigns. As this representative from the General and Municipal Union (GMB), a large general services union in the private and public sectors, explains in the case of their work in casinos, Livingstone's election has "had a massive influence. For example, . . . when it came to drawing up the detail for the . . . [legislation] to allow casino companies to deregulate, there is now a clause that says that local politicians can object to certain casinos because they are antiunion."[6] As part of its campaign to recruit minicab drivers across the capital, the GMB has also taken advantage of new regulations requiring all drivers to be registered. Mayor Livingstone has allowed the GMB to mail recruitment literature to all drivers and, following requests from the union, has tightened up loopholes in the regulations that make it difficult for them to recruit in the sector.

In different ways and to different extents, both nationally and locally, the climate for trade unions has improved since the late 1990s. In addition, the TUC's renewed focus on organizing is bearing some fruit. Despite initial skepticism about the TUC's Organising Academy, even those unions that have not taken part have recognized that there are benefits to employing dedicated organizers who can initiate and support unionization campaigns. Since it was established in 1998, the Organising Academy has trained more than 250 organizers and considerable numbers of full-time officers and lay activists. Most unions have now adopted the discourse of organizing, and some have recruited dedicated organizers to undertake new unionization campaigns. Many unions can point to organizing successes in sectors previously described as difficult to organize: among agency staff; migrant workers; and part-time, temporary, and contingent workers at the bottom end of the labor market (see Gall 2003; Holgate 2005a, 2005b; Kelly and Frege 2004).

Despite such efforts, however, union density has continued to decline in London (although it has stabilized at the national level). Membership in London has risen slightly from 674,000 in 1996 to 690,000 in 2005, but union density has

---

5. Interview, representative from the Southern and Eastern Region TUC, August 28, 2004.

6. Interview, GMB organizer, August 6, 2004.

fallen from 26.4 percent to 25.3 percent as a result of the increase in the number of workers in the labor market. Clearly, more needs to be done to halt this decline and to increase trade union membership, power, and influence. Although some of the small unions, facing a crisis in union membership, including Community (previously the Iron and Steel Trades Confederation), the Transport Salaried Staffs' Association, and the Graphical Paper and Media Union (now part of Amicus), have been among the unions most committed to the organizing approach, they don't tend to have the resources or reach needed to develop a successful city-wide approach. Moreover, these unions tend to be more specialist and less appropriate for the general services sector where many potential union members are working. When organizing has failed to stabilize membership, these unions are also very prone to merging as a route to survival, as has happened in the case of the Graphical Paper and Media Union, further undermining organizing attempts. In contrast, the largest private sector unions, Amicus, the GMB, and the Transport and General Workers Union (TGWU), which have the resources and reach to make a real difference to organizing in the city, have been slower to take up the challenge. That said, circumstances have changed in the TGWU following the election of a new general secretary in 2004. The union has now adopted a comprehensive national organizing strategy and has recruited a considerable number of new organizers in an attempt to transform the culture of the union. The strategy represents the largest allocation of resources by any British union to the development of new organizing campaigns. It is, however, still too early to assess what impact this is likely to have, although initial signs look promising.

Only the first steps of the organizing agenda have so far been taken in London. Although winning acceptance of the role of organizing is essential, it is not necessarily enough. So far, workplace organizing campaigns have tended to be conducted on a rather ad-hoc basis, with only a limited attempt to locate these workplaces and their workers in their wider geographical setting or to develop a strategy for the city as a whole. This causes a number of significant problems. First, it makes it harder to win campaigns. Workers are more likely to be frightened away from the union when there is no support from outside the workplace and no moral pressure being put on the employer from the community or customers to do the "right thing." Second, those workers who are brought into activity have nothing beyond their own workplace and maybe their own union structures to foster their development as leaders. Although unions provide training courses in being a representative and undertaking disciplinary and grievance work, there is only a very limited wider social and political movement into which new activists can be inducted, integrated, and developed. This makes it less likely that the unions will develop a new generation of activists who are self-confident community as well as workplace leaders for the long term.

Third, unions acting alone, workplace by workplace, are not developing an urbanwide strategy for London. There is no union-led effort to develop a geographically sensitive and systematic organizing strategy for the city. This would involve unions in identifying key workers, allies, and possible campaigns, and working together to influence the political-economic development of the city itself. The reasons for this are twofold. First, regional TUC bodies, because of their structures, have restricted influence on the activities of individual unions. They are instructed by union affiliates to carry out programs of work and are dependant on the willingness of unions to forge a common agenda; there are no signs of this developing in the near future. Second, the grassroots structures, such as local trade union councils, are very weak and do not have the resources to undertake the organizing required.[7]

The development of new structures and strategies would make a significant difference in union organizing attempts. In London, the launch of a living wage campaign in April 2001 has allowed a coalition to develop involving religious, community, and trade union organizations. This coalition has had impressive results and does highlight what can be achieved by working together in very new ways.

THE EAST LONDON COMMUNITIES ORGANISATION'S LIVING WAGE CAMPAIGN

TELCO was established in 1995 and now works in five local authority districts in East London. The organization is a coalition of about forty local organizations including churches, mosques, schools, community centers, and trade union branches representing at least fifty thousand people. In philosophy and practice, TELCO follows the model of the Industrial Areas Federation (IAF), established in the 1950s by Saul Alinsky, in developing broad-based collective organization for community empowerment and progressive change (Alinsky 1971). Before the launch of the living wage campaign in 2001, TELCO was essentially an organization based in the religious community. The coalition led local campaigns related to supermarket pricing in poor communities, the quality of local hospital services, for the sale of land to a local mosque, and the paucity of labor market opportunities for local people. It is only since the launch of the living wage campaign in 2001 that TELCO has been able to successfully recruit trade union branches into membership. There is now a strong relationship with the public sector union

---

7. Although for an exception in South London, see Wills and Simms 2004.

UNISON and a more recent relationship with the Transport and General Workers Union.[8]

East London's living wage campaign was officially launched in April 2001. Since then, the campaign has had a number of strands to its work. The first has been tackling the incidence of low pay in the public sector, highlighting the pay and conditions of hospital cleaners and other public sector workers employed by private contractors. The second has been working with unions to organize cleaning contractors at the wealthy office development at Canary Wharf. The third has been urging Mayor Livingstone to act on this issue, and this has encompassed efforts to secure an ethical Olympics for London, which will host the games in 2012. More recently, campaigns have secured agreements to pay living wages to cleaners contracted to work at a number of nonprofit organizations and at Queen Mary, University of London.

Hospital trusts and area health authorities have been a particular focus. By combining moral pressure on public officials (using the media to good effect) with the demand for improvements from UNISON members, contract staff have secured major improvements in their terms and conditions of work. Moreover, the campaign has helped rebuild union organization at the hospitals concerned. At the start of the campaign, UNISON had very low union membership among contract staff in the five major hospitals in the area (Homerton, Mile End, Royal London, Newham General, and Whipps Cross). Following privatization, low morale, the corrosive effects of low pay and poor conditions, and high labor turnover had made it difficult to retain a strong union organization. There was no union forum for sharing experiences or developing strategy across the five sites even though there are at least one thousand domestic, catering, portering, and security workers employed. Through joining TELCO, the union branches at these hospitals were put in touch with one another on a more regular basis. TELCO and UNISON organizers worked with each branch and spent time meeting and recruiting workers, organizing events, and promoting the campaign. Hundreds of contract staff joined UNISON, a considerable number attended union training courses, and there are now shop stewards from the contractor companies at each site.

Examples of community-union pressure during the campaign include the lobbying of a meeting of Homerton's National Health Service (NHS) trust board in May 2002. TELCO and UNISON mobilized at least forty contract workers along with representatives from local mosques, churches, colleges, and the media to participate in this event. After handing over a petition with six hundred signa-

---

8. For more on the background to the living wage campaign, see Wills 2004.

tures from hospital staff, the case for a living wage was presented with quiet passion by a nun from a religious community in Hackney. The trust was forced to concede the moral case for improved pay and conditions, but they restated the financial limitations they faced. Similar initiatives at the other hospitals resulted in UNISON activists deciding to submit a detailed claim for improved wages and conditions (a living wage) to the contractors at five East London hospitals in July 2002. This unique initiative sought immediate improvements in pay and conditions, leading contract workers closer to parity with NHS terms and conditions, with the ultimate goal of full parity by April 2006. Launched with a demonstration at Whipps Cross Hospital, the claim was featured on the BBC television news and in the local press, increasing interest in the campaign.

But six months later and despite promises from the contractors to move forward in negotiations, no progress had been made at any of the hospitals. Although they were now well organized, UNISON members employed by the contractors at the hospitals became increasingly frustrated and decided to pursue ballots for industrial action. In each case, the ballots were successful and UNISON moved toward strike action. At the eleventh hour, the NHS trust boards and ISS and Medirest (the two contractors) put together improved offers that were accepted at the Homerton and Mile End hospitals but rejected at Whipps Cross. In the latter case, two days of very successful strike action in June 2003 led to new talks and an improved offer. A similar deal was subsequently made at the Royal London Hospital for ISS staff and at Newham General for Medirest staff, even though they were less involved in the campaign.[9]

In contrast to the public sector, in the early days of the campaign it proved much more difficult to build strong union-community alliances in order to organize the contract cleaners employed in the private sector at Canary Wharf. Canary Wharf is home to the British/European/global headquarters of a number of major financial and business organizations, including Barclays, Morgan Stanley, HSBC, and Citigroup. The site was a controversial state-led development initiated by the Conservative government during the 1980s, and it remains an island of wealth employing white, middle-class commuters, situated in a very poor and multicultural sea.[10] Services such as cleaning, catering, and security are provided by contractors, which have historically paid minimal wages and few, if any, benefits to their largely immigrant staff. In 2001, the contract cleaning workers employed in the financial district at Canary Wharf were not unionized and no attempt had been made to organize them.

---

9. The Royal London Hospital took the domestic staff back in house during 2005 as part of a private finance initiative at the site. These workers are now paid well above the London living wage. For more information about the impact of better conditions on the workers involved, see Sokol et al. 2006.

10. For a flavor of the debates about the development, see Merrifield 1993.

The unions that would be expected to organize cleaners, catering, and security staff in the private sector, such as the TGWU and the GMB, were reluctant to get more involved. These unions have stronger traditions in manufacturing and were only slowly coming to terms with the structural changes in London's economic base that had decimated their membership and influence in their traditional heartlands. Moreover, they have tended to be led by those who are hostile to working with religious organizations (reflecting a longtime strand of leftist thinking in the United Kingdom) and to the need to share decision making with an "outside" organization such as TELCO. The situation has changed only since the TGWU, under new leadership, started to work with the SEIU to develop a more systematic effort to organize cleaners across London at Canary Wharf, the City, and the underground service.

To focus the campaign in the early days, before any union involvement, TELCO targeted the new global headquarters of HSBC that opened in mid-2002, demanding that the tower be cleaned by those earning a living, rather than a minimum, wage. By picketing a retail bank branch on Oxford Street, lobbying the company's Annual General Meeting (AGM) with the media present, and applying ongoing pressure, they forced the company to improve pay and conditions for contract cleaners in 2004. This followed a major breakthrough when Barclays agreed, following discussion with TELCO about socially responsible contracting procedures, to improve the contracting arrangements at its new headquarters. Barclays was the first private sector employer at the Wharf (and probably in the United Kingdom) to set out minimal standards for the pay and conditions of cleaning staff as part of its contracting arrangements. The contract would be awarded only to a contractor that met a costed commitment to pay £6 an hour, with fifteen days sick pay and eight extra days of annual leave. This agreement was featured on the national media and increased the pressure on HSBC.

In early 2004, two TGWU organizers started to build union organization, recruiting several hundred workers and developing a number of enthusiastic workplace activists. More recently, the union has increased this investment in organizing and allocated a number of additional minority ethnic organizers to work on the campaign. Influenced by the SEIU's Justice for Janitors campaign in the United States, the union has developed a sophisticated approach to organizing throughout the cleaning sector in London, and much greater resources have been devoted to the campaign at Canary Wharf. In addition, the union has come round to working with TELCO. Its new members in the cleaning sector have affiliated with the TELCO alliance and are committed to working together. As in the hospitals, TELCO is acting as the community arm, providing solidarity and targeting the clients while the union organizes the staff. The campaign has made a number of significant breakthroughs at Canary Wharf and is now planning to target the City.

London Citizens is the pan-London body to which TELCO belongs. In 2005, and following pressure from London Citizens[11] during the 2004 mayoral election campaign, Mayor Ken Livingstone's team at the GLA announced an official living wage rate for London, set at £6.70 an hour (Greater London Authority 2005; Jamoul 2006). Livingstone has agreed to ensure that this wage is paid to all those working for the GLA and Transport for London, including those contracted to work for them. Furthermore, the wage rate is now a benchmark for the capital and provides a target for further organizing campaigns. Following pressure from London Citizens, the need to pay living wages was also included in the recent Olympic bid, to provide living wage jobs when the games come to London. This shows the benefit for labor in working in a coalition that provides community backing and political muscle to hold politicians, business leaders, and public officials accountable, and it helps to create the space for unions to organize from below. In TELCO, community pressure and organized strength have combined to form a sum much greater than the strength of the parts. Not only have workers made significant gains but the unions have gained significant numbers of new members and additional strength. The living wage is now being taken up by progressive organizations in the third sector and by campaigners in the university and hotel sectors in London. Despite such gains, however, the lessons have yet to be widely discussed in the labor movement in London, and many unions remain less than convinced of the benefits of working in broad-based organizations, particularly with the religious community.

THE FURTHER PROMISE OF COMMUNITY– UNION COALITIONS IN LONDON AND THE UNITED KINGDOM

Our research found ongoing organizing activity in London but, with the exception of the strategic campaigning being developed by TELCO and a number of unions, it is largely responsive rather than strategic. There is much to be gained by unions taking their geography seriously and developing a more appropriate, coalition-based strategy in London. Three-quarters of all workers in London do not belong to a union, and it is critical that the labor movement make some assessment of the possibilities and challenges of working with nonunion groups in order to direct resources to where they are most needed and might have greatest

---

11. London Citizens comprises TELCO, South London Citizens, and West London Citizens. While these broad-based organizations have their own local structures and strategies, they also work on London-wide issues together.

effect. As we have seen, those employed in private sector services such as cleaning may be better reached through community-union campaigns that deploy media and corporate campaigns alongside more traditional efforts at union recruitment. Such campaigns can create the space for more effective organizing campaigns from below and provide a social movement infrastructure into which new activists can be integrated and developed as leaders.

As we have shown, London is a unique place, and it has a richness of global and national connections. Trade unions, which once relied on their industrial strength to organize for better terms and conditions, had little need for support from local communities. Yet as trade union membership has fallen and union's heartlands have been devastated by the decline in primary and secondary industry, this is no longer the case. From their position of weakness, trade unions need to recognize that in many cases they do not have the connections or experience to organize in some sections of the labor market and that only by working *with* local communities will they be able to establish a solid base from which to recruit and organize. TELCO's living wage campaign suggests that there is considerable potential to improve the presence and influence of trade unionism in London. However, as yet, the benefits of this approach have not spread as far as they might. There is considerable potential to further develop community–union coalitions in London and other cities across the United Kingdom.

13

RESTRUCTURING WITHOUT UNIONS
The Polycentric Region of Greater Frankfurt

Otto Jacobi

For many years, the polycentric Greater Frankfurt metropolitan region has been going through a process of transformation in response to the demands of globalization and structural change. Frankfurt is regarded as Germany's most Americanized city on account of its globally networked economy, international mix of inhabitants, and, not least, its gleaming skyscrapers. It is in these modern cathedrals that the financial sector has set up shop and, to paraphrase that master of sociological observation Pierre Bourdieu (1982), to gain control over space is a privileged method of exerting and demonstrating power. Cities are now dominated by service industries rather than factories, and the latter are being demolished or at best converted into centers for the entertainment industry. This is no longer the world in which the trade unions came of age. Nor is it yet a world in which they have started to feel at home. Their classic constituency of industrial workers is shrinking. High-earning employees in the service industries do not feel they represent their interests, and they have not yet turned their attention to the category of low-paid workers.

German trade unions are well established and institutionally protected organizations. They are represented in dozens of public and semipublic bodies at the federal, state, or municipal level. More important, the unions are the monopoly-like actor on the workers' side in the industrial relations system (Jacobi 2003). The main field of activity is collective bargaining. The coverage rate of the approximately fifty thousand binding collective agreements settled at the sector and/or company level, which define wage levels, working time, and working conditions, is around 80 percent. At the company level employees are represented by works councils elected by the entire workforce and empowered with information, consultation, and codetermination rights.

The umbrella organization DGB (Deutscher Gewerkschaftsbund) is weak compared with its eight industry organizations, which are in charge of collective bargaining. The affiliated individual unions are organized along sectoral rather than local or regional lines, and this has the fatal result that their specific and often contradictory industry-specific interests prevent them forming a united front within metropolitan regions. Because of the decline of the unions, nonlabor organizations, and cooperatives, they have lost the means to form modern urban society. This is a worrying fact, for, according to the French historian Jacques Le Goff (1997), it is in the city that the future is shaped.

ECONOMIC FEATURES OF THE POLYCENTRIC METRO REGION OF GREATER FRANKFURT

Since Germany's reunification in 1990 Berlin has become the political center, and other functions within the economy and society are distributed across various metropolitan regions: Düsseldorf, Frankfurt, Hamburg, Cologne, Munich, and Stuttgart. They all have roughly equal status, focusing on a specific formation of societal, economic, or cultural strength. None of the German metropolitan regions is in any way comparable in terms of centralization and sheer size with cities such as London or Paris (see table 13.1). In population, economic power, and share of national GDP, London and Paris have achieved dimensions well beyond those of Greater Frankfurt or any other German metropolitan region. In all three conurbations, per capita GDP is well above the national average. In the Greater Frankfurt region, the figure of €35,000 compares with a national average of just under €26,000.

In a comparison of economic performance made in the early 1990s of the approximately three hundred regions in the European Union, Greater Frankfurt came in third, but it has now slipped back to 12th. Measured in terms of economic potential, Greater Frankfurt remains in the lead, but in comparison with its most important European competitors it has lost some of its momentum. Other studies reach different conclusions: the 2005 European Cities Monitor ranks Frankfurt as the third best company location in Europe. In the Mercer study of quality of life in 215 cities worldwide, Frankfurt comes in fifth behind Zurich, Geneva, Vancouver, and Vienna. Domestic comparisons of quality of life, academic achievement, employment levels, and economic prospects come up with

■ **Table 13.1**   London, Paris, and Frankfurt, basic data 2002

REGION	SIZE (KM²)	POPULATION (MILLION)	GDP (BILLION €)	SHARE OF NATIONAL GDP (%)	GDP PER CAPITA (€)
Greater London	1,600	7.2	248	15	34,000
Paris—Ile de France	11,000	11.7	456	30	38,000
Greater Frankfurt	7,400	3.8	135	6	35,000

Source: Eurostat

virtually the same ranking every year: Greater Munich leads, ahead of Greater Frankfurt.

There are four sectors that have made Frankfurt a global city rivaled only by other European, rather than German, cities. First, Frankfurt is the heart of the German financial industry (Holtfrerich 1999; Spahn 2002). It may lag far behind London, but it is comparable to Paris in its role as a continental financial center. The European Central Bank, which is responsible for managing the euro, and the Deutsche Bundesbank, the German national reserve bank, both have their head-quarters in Frankfurt, making the city a center for international monetary policy.

Second, the Frankfurt-based Deutsche Börse, Germany's biggest stock exchange, is responsible for more than 90 percent of trading in stocks and shares. Measured in market shares, Deutsche Börse is second in Europe behind London, but it exceeds its rival in market capitalization. Deutsche Börse also operates on the international stage. Eurex, its futures market subsidiary, has the biggest turnover in the world.

Third, the congress and trade fair business is a further element in the international services offered by Frankfurt. The public company Messe Frankfurt has long been an international business responsible for organizing major trade fairs both at home and abroad. The biggest of these is the International Motor Show, and the best known is the International Book Fair, the world's leading event for the global publishing sector. In 2003 Messe Frankfurt was second after the British company Reed Exhibition as the world's trade fair organization with the biggest turnover.

Fourth, Frankfurt Airport is by far the biggest international airport in Germany. Within Europe, only London Heathrow processes more passengers and Paris Charles de Gaulle a similar number. According to the Boston Consulting Group, Frankfurt Airport has the potential of becoming one of the nine global mega hubs that will dominate future air traffic. The airport operator, Fraport, which is still largely in public hands despite being partly privatized, has also developed into a multinational business with holdings all over the world.

These four industries have spawned clusters of related service industries: consultancies, legal firms, advertising agencies, hotels, restaurants, catering companies, transport operators, as well as the information technology and media sectors. The business-friendly, conservative *Frankfurter Allgemeine Zeitung* is Germany's leading political broadsheet. Although the region still has important companies in the automotive (GM-Opel) and chemical industries, traditional manufacturing industry has declined dramatically following widespread closures and transfers of production elsewhere.

Greater Frankfurt is dubbed a "polycentric metropolitan region." What is meant is that only the region as a whole, consisting of the city of Frankfurt and the surrounding area, fulfils the functions of a metropolis and is able to make the necessary infrastructure available. The biggest problem faced by Greater Frankfurt is a political one: the region does not constitute a political unit. It does not have a parliament responsible for further development or an independent executive in the form of a regional government. There is considerable rivalry among the cities within the region, particularly between Frankfurt and its neighbors, over taxation revenue and sharing of costs. This "suburban free-ridership" and "chaos of competition" among cities of a metro region is also a well-known phenomenon in the United States (Phares 2004, 23, 165).

LABOR MARKET, EMPLOYMENT, AND TRADE UNIONS

Compared with the national average, the Greater Frankfurt region has low levels of unemployment (see table 13.2). Of the 3.8 million people in Greater Frankfurt, 2.2 million are gainfully employed and 170,000 are jobless. Just under 60 percent of the region's inhabitants have a job, compared with the national average of well under 50 percent. In the city of Frankfurt itself, the core city has considerably more jobs than inhabitants, making it the economic hub for the region. People work in the city and live in its immediate surroundings.

The changes in the labor market and the dramatic decline in the influence of the trade unions on the development of the region are closely linked to the deindustrialization of its central urban core. Since the early 1970s, there has been a continuous process of closures and transfers of traditional industrial companies away from the city. The city is now virtually devoid of industry, with almost 90 percent of the working population employed in the services sector; only 25 percent of employees in Greater Frankfurt work in manufacturing industries. The context in which the trade unions have traditionally operated—blue-collar workers with their housing estates and leisure facilities—has largely disappeared, and the working population has undergone a radical transformation. To a large extent the trade unions have lost their foothold in the city, because they have not

■ **Table 13.2** Labor market, 2002

	POPULATION	ENTIRE WORKFORCE	EMPLOYEES	UPPER END OF LABOR MARKET	LOWER END OF LABOR MARKET
Greater Frankfurt	3,800,000	2,200,000	1,500,000	350,000	350,000
City of Frankfurt	650,000	1,000,000	500,000	250,000	250,000

Source: Planungsverband Ballungsraum Frankfurt/Rhein-Main, Statistical Trends, October 2002; own calculations

succeeded in recruiting new members from the private services sector. The average level of union membership across all sectors is 25 percent. Union density is disproportionately high in the few remaining manufacturing industries as well as in public administration and in many former state-owned companies that have now been partly or fully privatized. GM-Opel and Frankfurt Airport are, for example, union bastions. Membership levels in the private services sector do not even reach 10 percent. The situation is mitigated somewhat by the works councils in the major private service companies.

If we look at the labor market from the point of view of employment security, income levels, and social security, then it is impossible to ignore the changes since the golden age of postwar Germany. The labor market has three main segments.

First, there are those who are registered with the social security system, which accounts for about 70 percent of the region's workforce, respectively 50 percent of the core city's workforce. These workers have permanent employment contracts and receive a collectively agreed wage that entitles—and obliges—them to participate in the social security system. They are covered by the social security system in the case of sickness, unemployment, and retirement; the contributions to this semistate insurance system are divided between employers and employees, and both are represented on the supervisory board. Most trade union members are drawn from this segment of the labor market.

Second, about 16 percent of the regional but 25 percent of the city workers have above-average incomes and a social status that enables them to opt out of the social security system and take out private insurance. They include middle and top managers, technicians, and civil servants as well as independent employers and tradesmen, self-employed individuals, freelancers, consultants, and lawyers.

Third, a growing group of the regional labor market consists of employees at the lower end of the market, approximately 16 percent in Greater Frankfurt and 25 percent in the city. The common feature of this otherwise very varied category is that it consists exclusively of low-wage workers who are excluded from participating in the system of social security because they have not met the formal requirements. Some, such as spouses and students with family connections, are protected under the umbrella of the social welfare system; most low-wage workers, however, depend on minimum state aid if they need medical care or financial support in older age. There is a huge range of people in the low-wage sector: conventionally employed individuals or their partners trying to supplement their household income, students financing their studies, single mothers with children and unemployed or impoverished individuals who have organized a modest additional income to supplement state benefits, and immigrants without work permits. Jobs for all these categories are available in the commercial sector but also increasingly take the form of personal services to private households. The low-pay sector can be largely regarded as an informal labor market that forms the core of a growing moonlight economy.

The really significant new development is the growth and expansion of this informal labor market, as a result of which the income gap has visibly widened—boosted also by the increasing number of top earners in an urban region like Frankfurt. In both absolute and relative terms there are now more rich people but also more poor people in Greater Frankfurt. There has been a distinct increase in social polarization.

Unemployment and the low pay-sector represent a challenge for the trade unions, which have yet to come up with any convincing response. Although they have made many attempts to gain recognition as the political and social voice of the unemployed, the trade unions have failed to make themselves into organizations of and for the unemployed. This is partly because trade unions in Germany are primarily organizations for the working population, and partly because the unemployed are perceived as being difficult to mobilize and organize. Thus a state of mutual frustration exists between the unions and the unemployed (Albrecht-sen 2004).

The unions are divided as to whether a minimum wage is desirable. In Germany there is no uniform minimum wage laid down by the government for all branches of industry. The increasing significance of the low-pay sector has triggered widespread discussion about the issue. The chemical workers' union rejects statutory minimum wages, which it fears would endanger its collective bargaining autonomy. Other trade unions, like the hotel and catering union, are confronted with a substantial informal sector and are in favor of nationwide statutory minimum wages. Another group under the leadership of the construction workers' union has come out in favor of the collectively agreed introduction of sectoral minimum wages. As of January 2005 the minimum wage for an unskilled construction worker is €10.36 per hour and for skilled workers €12.47. All domestic and foreign companies operating on German construction sites are obliged to adhere to them. In the summer of 2005 the multibranch union ver.di (public and private services) launched a campaign for binding minimum wages. The union hopes that minimum wages will have a ratchet effect against downward wage spirals and help forge new alliances with low-wage workers. The campaign for minimum wage was initiated by the trade union leadership after consideration of experiences in neighboring countries.

Based on U.S. models, ver.di has also started campaigns against unfair working conditions in chain stores. With mixed success, the trade union attempted to mobilize the workers, to create transparency by publicly effective media work, as well as to form a coalition with consumers and city dwellers. Here is a rare example where innovative local trade union activities received nationwide coverage.

In 2004, the construction workers' union launched a highly innovative initiative: the establishment of the European Migrant Workers Union. The idea is to encourage immigrants, particularly those from central and eastern Europe, to join a trade union whose full-time staff comes from their home countries and whose function is to help them to become integrated. The aims of the new organization are (a) to ensure that the immigrants gain access to all the statutory welfare benefits and collectively agreed rates to which they are entitled; (b) to conclude collective agreements tailored to the needs of immigrants; (c) to help immigrants procure residence and work permits; and (d) to support the immigration of family members and help them integrate into German society.

This initiative reflects the changed economic and social environment of foreign workers. Modern immigration to Germany started in the 1960s and has continued ever since. In the Greater Frankfurt region the proportion of foreign citizens is 20 percent and the corresponding figure for the city of Frankfurt is 30 percent. In terms of integration one has to differentiate between first- and second-generation immigrants. In the 1960s, immigrants came almost exclusively from southern Europe—from Turkey to Portugal—to a country with a booming labor market. They were quickly absorbed into German working life: they received the collectively agreed wage, were incorporated into the social security system, joined trade unions, and were granted the right to vote and stand for office in works council elections. The second wave of immigration started with the collapse of the Communist regimes. This generation of immigrants came from the countries of central and eastern Europe and entered a labor market that was no longer booming. They did not have work permits and were excluded from the social security system. Therefore, they had to put up with low wages in Germany—albeit ones that were relatively high by the standards of their home country. These workers often compete with the established workforce by offering both low wages and social as well as professional qualifications. The low-pay segment, which was not created but was enlarged by immigrant workers, undermines the collectively agreed wage levels. There is a risk of hostile international wage competition but also the potential for transnational workers' solidarity. The German trade unions are confronted with a double dilemma: (a) the more they defend the interests of the German workers, the more they neglect the social integration of the new generation of immigrant workers, and (b) the more they represent the interests of the high-skilled workforce, the more they disregard the needs of the unskilled and marginalized workers.

LACK OF UNITY AMONG TRADE UNIONS

Four of the member unions of the DGB are based in Frankfurt: IG Metall (metalworking, engineering, vehicles, aircraft, shipbuilding, steel, electrical engineering), with 2.5 million members, is the biggest single German trade union; IG BAU (construction, agriculture, environment) has just under half a million members; TRANSNET is the railway union, with approximately three hundred thousand members; and the teachers union, GEW (Gewerkschaft Erziehung und Wissenschaft), has a membership of around 250,000 (Jacobi 2003). One might think that the trade unions would be particularly active in Greater Frankfurt and would have left their mark on the region. That this is not the case has to do with the typical organizational structure of German trade unions. The individual industrial unions are organized along sectoral lines, and their activities therefore concentrate on developments in a particular economic segment rather than in regions or cities. At the same time, they have a centralized structure. As a result, regional and local subunits have little freedom to act autonomously; local unions in the American sense do not exist in Germany. The consequences for trade union representation at the regional level are profound—and Greater Frankfurt offers a particularly good example.

First, trade unions represent sectoral political interests and, as a result, are frequently rivals pursuing divergent goals. As one example among many, the trade union for the chemical industry defends the pharmaceutical industry and calls for greater efficiency in the running of hospitals, whereas the public services union, ver.di, is fighting for security of employment in the health sector and criticizes the pharmaceutical industry for the exorbitant prices it charges for medicines, accusing it of profiteering and exploitation of the insurance system. The sectoral orientation of trade unions also results in a number of disagreements, in particular over globalization and environmental protection. Germany is massively dependent on exports, so it is understandable that the trade unions in export-intensive industries are much less critical of globalization than those in industries with a high degree of immigration.

Conflicts of interest can result in irreconcilable clashes in the regions. The biggest bone of contention is the planned expansion of Frankfurt Airport. Almost seventy thousand people are directly employed by Frankfurt Airport, and two hundred thousand people in the surrounding region are indirectly employed. Airport expansion is set to boost employment by 50 percent and will consolidate the airport's position as a competitor for London, Paris, and Amsterdam. Some trade unions are in favor of expansion; others reject it as irresponsible in environmental terms.

Theoretically, the problem of diverging views is understood, and there is even a formal solution to it: the DGB, as an umbrella organization, is responsible for regional policy. However, the reality is fairly depressing. One almost exclusively comes across frustrated, cynical DGB representatives who complain about regional offices that are completely underresourced in staffing and financial terms. There are structural reasons for this. The individual trade unions do not want a strong umbrella organization and keep the DGB on a leash. However, as the individual trade unions frequently pursue divergent and even conflicting interests, it is a leash that is both short and tangled. It is therefore no coincidence that the regional DGBs do not produce leaders who would be in a position to reverse the relationship with the individual trade unions. The DGB cannot resolve conflicts between the trade unions and can therefore do little to create a unified front.

The absence of the unions as prime actors in the ongoing process of regional restructuring causes major concern. The activities of the works councils are an exception. Democratically elected, they are the respected representatives of the company's workforce. Works councils are present on the local, national, and European levels of the firm. In recent years they have attained a new authority: on the one hand, by the Europeanization of business in the context of the completion of the single market; on the other hand, by the decentralization of operational entities and their requirement for location-specific working conditions. The works council at GM-Opel's traditional German headquarters plays a leading role in Greater Frankfurt. It has settled supplemental labor provisions in order to safeguard the long-run competitiveness of the plant. Simultaneously, it acted as representative of the European works council on behalf of all of GM's European subsidiaries. It settled an agreement with the stipulation that the restructuring of GM-Europe must occur without the closure of any plant. Works councils, especially those of big companies, balance the vacuum created by the insufficient presence of the unions, strengthen the economic position of subnational regions, and contribute to transnational solidarity.

COALITION-BUILDING AND LOST HISTORY

Caught as they are in an organizational framework that is inappropriate for maintaining a regional presence, it is not surprising that the trade unions in Greater Frankfurt have failed to work with other forces in civil society to develop innovative forms of cooperation capable of mobilizing popular support and of becoming involved in shaping the regional development of Greater Frankfurt. Any cooperation that does take place takes the form of alliances between the offices of the associations involved, but it is far from constituting a revitalization campaign with grassroots support. A list of coalitions may clarify the highly diverse character of trade unions relations with nonlabor organizations:

- One area where there is well-established and smooth-running cooperation is with the Lutheran Church and the Catholic Church. There is a considerable degree of overlap here when it comes to combating poverty, integrating immigrants, and protecting human rights. The longstanding trustful relations of the trade unions with both the Lutheran Church and the Catholic Church must be regarded as a indispensable surety for safeguarding a social justice infrastructure.
- Combating the new right-wing radicalism in collaboration with antifascist groups is also a well-established tradition.
- The relations between the unions and the women's movement are characterized by a friendly climate. Often, these coalitions are centrally guided and lack a regional groundwork.
- More problematic—because there is disagreement among the unions on the subject—are coalitions with environmental groups. Even when much effort is exerted to balance ecological and union interests, the result is often disagreement and conflict.
- Relations with the worlds of culture, art, or science are similarly poor, even though in regions such as Greater Frankfurt they play an important role in the formation of public opinion, the establishment of the social climate, and the integration of foreign workers. There is one major exception: the regional DGB and some individual unions have been involved in a project aimed at preserving the industrial heritage of the region. In close cooperation with historians and museums, a regionwide path of industrial culture (an open-air museum of industrial sites) heavily welcomed and supported by the residents has been established.

As Frankfurt is an extremely international city and has official partnerships with cities in Europe and overseas, the DGB has attempted to build up parallel partnerships with international trade unions. Links were forged with trade unions in Barcelona, Lyon, and Milan and a few meetings organized. However, this partnership, which was supposed to be extended to include Frankfurt's partner cities overseas following a consolidation phase, was put on the backburner because the individual, sector-oriented unions showed little interest. There are similar problems with cooperation with critics of globalization. For some trade unions (ver.di), coalition with the Frankfurt-based "attac" organization is a strategic alliance, whereas others (the chemical industry union) see "no future in an alliance" with this organization. Nevertheless, official representatives of the national DGB and some affiliates actively support the World Social Forum movement.

Most of the multinationals headquartered in Greater Frankfurt have established European works councils. At this level an ever denser network of transnational European cooperation between the elected representatives of the workforces is emerging. Works councils of multinationals have settled partnership agreements with the workforces of subsidiaries in threshold or developing countries. Additionally, IG Metall in particular tries to establish agreements over codes of conduct with transnational firms. Most of these coalitions are centralized at the headquarters and are not deeply rooted at the regional level. At the municipal level, the relations between the unions and foreign-born fellow citizens are underdeveloped, fostering trends toward parallel societies. Instead of becoming integrated, large segments of immigrant citizens remain in their cultural ghettos.

The trade unions' limited ability to enter into alliances and the fact that they have lost the character of a social movement also has much to do with their fragmented history. In the past they were influential players in the major industrial cities. Urban development played an important role, because the trade unions made housing, health, education, consumer affairs, leisure activities, and many other issues part and parcel of a socially oriented regional planning policy. They set up cooperative ventures in all these areas, many of which developed into major businesses. This union-dominated cooperative sector received an unexpected boost following World War II, but then fell victim to a concerted onslaught by capitalist companies. A certain lack of professionalism, and in some cases fraudulent actions by trade union managers, contributed to their decline. As a result, the economic empire of the trade unions has now largely evaporated. In Frankfurt it is possible to visit a former trade union cathedral: the skyscraper that now houses the European Central Bank was once the seat of the fourth biggest German bank, the union-owned Bank für Gemeinwirtschaft (Co-operative Bank). The trade unions have lost the means by which they could have achieved a degree of regional orientation in addition to their sectoral alignment.

The term "sclerotic blockage"—taken from an article about the metropolitan region of Hamburg (Läpple 2001)—is used to express the fact that the German trade unions face a huge challenge in adapting to the conditions in metropolitan regions and in finding the strength to revive a regional presence. Making the increasing inequality a political issue in global cities and forging alliances will require trade union organizational structures that are more balanced or networked between sectoral and regional interests, on the one hand, and union strategies, on the other, that are aimed at bridging gaps between the established and the marginalized workforces.

CONCLUSION

Seeking Solidarity . . . Why, and with Whom?

Daniel B. Cornfield

The many cases of labor-inclusive coalition building described in *Labor in the New Urban Battlegrounds* occur during a historical moment that presents labor with opportunities and obstacles to its revitalization. This contemporary moment consists of converging forces—globalization and economic restructuring, employer resistance, immigration and identity politics, union bureaucratization, and social unionism—that challenge labor to transform itself into a movement that resonates widely and deeply with workers of diverse social backgrounds and identities. In the U.S. service economy based in urban markets, these forces converge in cities that contextualize labor revitalization initiatives and labor-inclusive coalition building.

As the cases in this book show, these urban contexts of coalition building generate labor's many prospective partners which, as shown in Sellers's cross-national comparative chapter, abound in the United States with its tradition of voluntary associations. The European cases—Frankfurt, Hamburg, London—also depict the impact of the urban context of coalition formation in ways that are not inconsistent with U.S. patterns. These urban contexts often call for coalitions that address wide issues of concern to diverse worker groups, such as urban living wage campaigns and community-based participatory initiatives tailored to specific worker groups, as shown by Luce's and Reynolds' chapters on living wage campaigns and power-building strategies, respectively. Applegate's chapter shows a convergence in interest in community economic development among unions

For their insightful commentary on the meaning of the labor movement, and on previous drafts of this chapter, I am grateful to Fran Benson, Bill Canak, Janice Fine, Ian Greer, Ed Heery, Jane Holgate, Larry Isaac, John Logan, Ruth Milkman, Enrique de la Garza Toledo, the participants of the "Urban Labor Revitalization: Large, Mid-size and Global Cities Conference" at the ILR School, Cornell University, the "Power, Politics, and Social Movements Seminar" in the Department of Sociology, Vanderbilt University, the Seminar on "Cambio en las Relaciones Laborales en el Mundo" of the Universidad Autónoma de México and the International Labor Organization, the Montague Burton Seminar at the Cardiff Business School, Cardiff University, and the Political Economy of Immigration and Migrant Labor Workshop of the *British Journal of Industrial Relations*, and two anonymous reviewers. I am also grateful to the ILR School, Cornell University for financial support. Lowell Turner is a wonderful colleague who has shared his vast knowledge of labor and insights about humanity with me over the last several years—it has been a pleasure collaborating with him on *Labor in the New Urban Battlegrounds*. I am indebted to my wife, Hedy Weinberg, and our daughter, Hannah Cornfield, for their constant enthusiasm and inspiration.

and empowerment community-based development organizations, such as the Association of Community Organizations for Reform Now, as manifested by their growing collaboration in living wage and corporate campaigns.

Urban contexts are increasingly relevant to labor organizing and labor-inclusive coalition building in the growing service economy (Cornfield 2005). Services, in contrast to global manufacturing industries, often operate in local, urban labor and product markets. Indeed, Change to Win (CTW), the new national labor federation founded in 2005, announced in March 2006 its thirty-five-city, multiunion campaign to organize fifty million workers in major service industries. According to CTW chair Anna Burger, the campaign is designed "to create strong local organizations that include unions as well as community activists" (Amber 2006).

This concluding chapter distills from the many cases in this book patterns of association between different urban contexts and the shaping of labor-inclusive coalitions. Urban contexts are both an historical and spatial context and opportunity structure for strategic, revitalizing labor action (Cornfield 2005; Katznelson 1981; Milkman 2006; Turner 2003, 2004b, 2005). Historically, urban contexts exist during labor's "third historical moment," a moment in which very large multijurisdictional unions are transforming themselves into movement organizations by practicing social unionism. They are practicing social unionism in that they conceive of workers as having multiple social identities—for example, ethnic, racial, gender, and economic identities—and they are collaborating with multiple allies among consumers and in the realm of identity politics to organize workers not only in workplaces but also in communities. Spatially, urban contexts are typically local service economies and destinations to which workers of diverse social backgrounds and identities migrate and which house local labor movements of variable strength (Smith 2001). The cases of coalition building in this book, consistent with Jones-Correa's (2001) theory of urban coalition building, show that the breadth and depth of coalition issues, partners, and actions are associated with the strength and history of local urban labor movements and the ethnic-racial complexity of a city. Although the separation of work and community, according to Katznelson (1981), has tended to undermine labor solidarity in U.S. cities, the coextensive operation of urban product and labor markets in the service economy may lessen the work-community divide, raising new possibilities for linking producers and consumers, as well as workers of diverse social identities, in urban, labor-inclusive coalitions.

LABOR'S THIRD MOMENT

The several instances of contemporary labor-inclusive coalition building reported in *Labor in the New Urban Battlegrounds* occur during a third moment in the institutional history of the labor movement. Each moment is an epoch in which labor, as a strategic actor (Cornfield 2005; Milkman 2006; Turner 2004b, 2005), institutionalizes a new strategy for organizing and representing workers that resonates in a structure of opportunity characterized by new worker identities and emerging organizational forms of economic production. The historical moments cumulate, responding to changes in worker identities and the organization of economic production, widening the repertoire of labor's strategic actions.

The eras of craft unionism and industrial unionism constitute the first two moments, respectively, of the modern U.S. labor movement. The first moment, of craft unionism, was signaled by the founding in 1886 of the American Federation of Labor (AFL). Unlike the more short-lived inclusive labor organizations of the late nineteenth and early twentieth centuries, such as the Knights of Labor and the Industrial Workers of the World (IWW, or Wobblies), each of the AFL-affiliated craft unions organized a skilled trade in construction, manufacturing, or transportation, paralleling the craft organization of economic production in these economic sectors. As institutional "providers," the local craft union controlled the entry of craft-identifying workers into the trade through union apprenticeships and controlled the labor supply through a union hiring hall, often exclusively for native white men; negotiated wages and working conditions for the trade in local (urban) labor markets; and provided a range of union-financed social welfare services, such as unemployment insurance and retirement pensions (Cornfield and Fletcher 2001; Lichtenstein 2002; Montgomery 1987).

The second historical moment, of industrial unionism, was signaled by the factionalized departure from the AFL in 1936 of a group of insurgent unions associated with the Committee for Industrial Organization, the new rival labor federation that subsequently renamed itself the Congress of Industrial Organizations (CIO). In contrast to the occupationally exclusive strategy of AFL craft unionism, the CIO strategy of universalistic industrial unionism organized occupations of all skill levels in a single industry, defined by its chief product, such as the automobile industry, and united workers of diverse ethnic, racial, and gender backgrounds. The advent of industrial unionism paralleled and was a strategic response to the rise of oligopolistic, large-corporate mass production manufacturing that produced for growing national and international markets through the 1960s, while eliminating many skilled trades with its Fordist assembly line production technology, which lowered and minimized differences in skills between production occupations. What is more, the CIO membership was more socially diverse than the AFL craft union membership, as the CIO organized the many immigrants from eastern, central, and southern Europe, Southern migrants in Northern urban factories, ethnic-racial minorities, and women workers who made up a disproportionate share of the new factory workforce (Cornfield 2006; Fine 2006; Mink 1986). Functionally, industrial unions pursued national, industrywide pattern bargaining that was developed by local unions, which tended to represent workers whose seniority-based livelihoods and careers unfolded in the "internal labor market" of a single, large corporate employer. As institutional "advocates," in contrast to craft union "providers," industrial unions advocated on behalf of their members by bargaining for employer-provided fringe benefits and training and career advancement opportunities, by filing grievances on behalf of individual workers, and by becoming a major national political lobbying force for the continuing expansion of the New Deal welfare and regulatory state. Between the first and second moments, control of labor supply, training, and the provision of social welfare had effectively passed from the union to the employer and state. By the time of the AFL-CIO merger in 1955, the newly constituted labor federation comprised 135 national craft and industrial unions (AFL-CIO 1955; Cornfield and Fletcher 2001; Dubofsky 1994; Lichtenstein 2002).

Contemporary labor-inclusive coalition building is associated with the current third moment of national realignment of the labor movement. The realignment consists of a division between, on the one hand, unions, such as the former CIO unions, that are threatened by and declining in the face of globalization, outsourcing, and plant shutdowns; and, on the other hand, unions that are organizing workers in sectors that are relatively buffered from the ravages of globalization, including economically and culturally marginalized workers in the low-wage, growing corporate service economy and construction, and professionals and other "interactive service workers" who provide urban middle-class families with a wide range of vital services in the public and private sectors (Cornfield 2005).[1]

The third moment is signaled by the fractious formation of the CTW in 2005. The CTW unions, including those that split from the AFL-CIO in August-September 2005, are mainly former AFL unions that have morphed into large multi-jurisdictional unions dedicated to extending CIO-style universalistic industrial unionism to the growing number of economically and culturally marginalized workers in the emerging, large-corporate sector of the national service economy (Milkman 2006). Change to Win's five-point "Agenda for Worker Strength" (2006b)

---

1. See also the August 2000 special issue of *Work and Occupations* on "Workers, Customers, and Clients."

calls for: (1) organizing workers and merging unions along industry lines; (2) embracing the diversity of the national labor force, including organizing immigrants, ethnic-racial minorities, and women; (3) consolidating union financial strength; (4) building global labor unity; and (5) building a broad coalition for winning affordable, quality health care and retirement security for all.

The CTW (2006a) has developed "sector coordinating committees" to diffuse universalistic industrial unionism into the service economy. These committees are designed to coordinate multiunion organizing campaigns conducted by CTW unions in these fifteen service industries: airline catering, food manufacturing, food services, gaming, health care, hotels, laundry, nonfood retail, package handling and delivery, printing, property services, retail food, transportation, warehousing/distribution, and waste.

Compared with the second-moment CIO unions in manufacturing, the third-moment CTW unions and their jurisdictions are relatively buffered from globalization and thereby constitute a stable organizational basis for extending unionization to low-wage service workers. According to the CTW (2006c):

> The central objective of the Change to Win Strategic Organizing Center is to unite the more than 50 million American workers who work in industries that cannot be outsourced or shipped overseas into strong unions that can win them a place in the American middle class—where their jobs provide good wages, good health care, good pensions and a voice on the job. . . .
>
> There was a time when blue-collar jobs in the auto, steel, electrical, rubber and other manufacturing industries were considered low wage jobs. Through union organization, these "low wage jobs" became "good paying jobs, with good benefits" that led to the creation of America's middle class and defined the elements of the American Dream. Millions of those manufacturing jobs have been eliminated or shipped overseas in recent years.
>
> Jobs in today's growing service sector are the "low wage" jobs of today. Whether it is caring for the sick, attending to hotel guests, or transporting goods across the country, these jobs cannot be outsourced to foreign lands. They are critically important to the economy and to the quality of life in this country. And nowhere is it written that these jobs must be low wage–low benefit jobs. In fact, the wages and benefits of service workers that are represented by a union today are substantially higher than those that are not.

Third-moment unionism differs from craft and industrial unionism primarily in terms of the concept of its membership jurisdiction. These multijurisdictional unions tend to organize workers of multiple occupations, industries, or both, often the lowest-wage and most marginalized workers in a broad economic sector, and they tend to be concentrated in services and peripheral manufacturing. Functionally, these unions tend to be institutional "advocates" like second-moment industrial unions. What is more, they define their membership jurisdictions broadly, frequently encompassing a range of worker identities, such as ethnic, racial, gender, consumer, community, and family themes and identities.

The following self-descriptions of the CTW-affiliated SEIU, Teamsters, UFCW, and UNITE HERE illustrate variations on the theme of third-moment union membership jurisdictions that encompass a wide range of social identities of low-wage workers in the service sector. The 1.8 million-member Service Employees International Union, founded in 1921 as the AFL's Building Service Employees International Union janitors craft union, adopted its current name in 1968 and describes its diverse membership as follows:

Health Care—hospital, nursing home, clinic, and home care workers
Public Employees—federal, state, county, municipal, and school employees
Building Service—janitors, elevator operators, and security guards
Industrial & Allied—industrial, racetrack, and ballpark workers

Members of SEIU work as nurses, doctors, social service workers, building cleaners, police and corrections officers, librarians, head start employees, maintenance workers, lab technicians, nurse assistants, and more.

SEIU represents a diverse membership. A majority of members are women. Some 20 percent are African American. SEIU represents more immigrant workers than any other union in the U.S. (SEIU 2005)

The Teamsters, originally an AFL craft union of wagon drivers founded in 1903, is now a 1.4 million-member general union that defines itself pragmatically and instrumentally:

Today, it would be hard to identify a Teamster on the streets because we are everywhere. The union represents everyone from A to Z—from airline pilots to zookeepers. One out of every ten union members is a Teamster. . . . The best-known Teamsters work in the freight industry. More than 120,000 Teamsters are covered by multiple employers under the National Master Freight Agreement. . . . Teamsters operate computers; protect families as law enforcement officers; work as technical employees in both the public and private sectors; care for patients in hospitals and nursing homes, work as public defenders; assist customers at car rental agencies; work at leading hotels; work in schools as both principals and custodians; repair highway bridges and collect tolls on thruways and turnpikes; process, store and deliver food products; and transport automobiles, trucks, SUVs and other vehicles. (Teamsters 2005)

The 1.4 million-member United Food and Commercial Workers, itself the creature of multiple mergers of old AFL craft and CIO industrial retail unions, appeals to workers as community and family members and as workers:

> We work in front of customers and behind the scenes. Look for us operating the register in a local department store, stocking produce in a supermarket aisle, taking a child's temperature in a hospital, slicing a cut of beef before it is delivered to a grocery store, or caring for your grandparents in a nursing home. We are the UFCW—North America's Neighborhood Union. . . . We are from all backgrounds and walks of life in big cities, small towns, and suburbs. We work in a wide range of industries, including health care, meatpacking, poultry and food processing, manufacturing, textile and chemical trades, and retail food. . . . Our commitment to being North America's Neighborhood Union only begins at work. We contribute to the communities in which we work in hundreds of ways, including raising millions for the Leukemia and Lymphoma Society, fighting hunger through our Women's Network annual food drive, registering hundreds of thousands of voters, and awarding scholarships to top students. Together, UFCW members work to make a better life for North America's workers and families. . . .
>
> The UFCW is about workers helping workers achieve better wages, better benefits, and safer working conditions. Despite the challenges of soaring health care premiums, costly prescription medications, retirement insecurity, and economic instability, the UFCW is a powerful voice for working men and women, leading efforts to protect and improve the livelihoods of all workers. (United Food and Commercial Workers 2005)

UNITE HERE, a 450,000-member union whose founding merger of UNITE (Union of Needletrades, Industrial, and Textile Employees) and HERE (Hotel Employees and Restaurant Employees) in 2004 culminated several decades of mergers of late nineteenth-century and early twentieth-century AFL and CIO needle trades unions and hospitality industry unions, emphasizes its commitment to organizing a wide range of economically and culturally marginalized workers:

> UNITE and HERE always organized and represented some of the most harassed workers in North America—recent immigrants, African Americans, women and workers in the South. . . . The union represents

more than 450,000 active members and more than 400,000 retirees throughout North America. UNITE HERE boasts a diverse membership, comprised largely of immigrants and including high percentages of African-American, Latino, and Asian-American workers. The majority of UNITE HERE members are women. . . . Organizing the unorganized in our industries is the top priority for UNITE HERE. Over 50% of the new Union's national budget will go toward organizing. . . . UNITE HERE represents workers in the following major sectors: apparel and textile manufacturing, apparel distribution centers, and apparel retail, industrial laundries, hotels, casinos, foodservice, airport concessions, [and] restaurants. (UNITE HERE 2005)

The third-moment realignment not only results from first- and second-moment union decline but has been emerging and is partly shaped by globalization and economic restructuring since the 1960s. As U.S. corporate manufacturers led the exodus of manufacturing out of the United States in search of cheaper labor in developing nations, U.S. manufacturing employment, the membership base of U.S. industrial unionism, and many middle-income manufacturing jobs declined. The U.S. economy was restructured from a manufacturing economy to one dominated by a service sector that now employs some three-fourths of the national labor force (Cornfield 2006).

With the hollowing out of middle-income unionized manufacturing jobs and the growth of high-wage and low-wage nonunion jobs in the services, U.S. income inequality has increased steadily since the late 1960s, creating a service economy of "haves" and "have-nots." For the most part, then, third-moment unionism organizes the growing pool of nonunion have-nots in the service sector. Similarly, the German labor movement, as Otto Jacobi shows in his chapter on Frankfurt, has begun to organize and lobby for labor legislation on behalf of low-wage service workers and immigrant workers, partly in coalition with the Catholic Church and the Lutheran Church.

Other parallel processes are shown in the European cases of London and Hamburg. Holgate and Wills's chapter on London and Greer's discussion of Hamburg in his comparative Seattle-Hamburg chapter show that viable labor-community coalitions have been formed in the health-care sectors in both cities. In both cities, community groups, including consumers and religious groups, brought consumer and moral pressure on employers to protect or raise low-wage health-care workers' wages.

At the same time, worker identities have diversified in a complex identity politics fueled by late twentieth-century movements for social justice and increasing immigration to the United States of documented and undocumented workers from all world regions, especially from Mexico and Central America (Holgate 2005b; Greenhouse 2006; Isaac, McDonald, and Lukasik 2006; Milkman 2006). The movements for civil, women's, Latino, immigrant, and gay rights have arisen to address deep social inequalities that are embedded in workplaces, labor markets, and communities, and that cut across the lines of economic inequality addressed by the labor movement during the first and second moments of labor's institutional history. Consequently, worker social identities have diversified and become more salient. Third-moment unionism, then, addresses the interests of have-not workers of the service sector not only in economic terms but also in terms of their ethnicity-race, gender, place of origin, sexual orientation, and other social characteristics (Delgado 1993; Fine 2006; Greenhouse 2006; Milkman 2000, 2006; Ness 2005).

Labor-inclusive coalition building is an important tactic for unionization during the third moment, when alliances with nonlabor groups can help strengthen a shrinking labor movement weakened by globalization, economic restructuring, neoliberalism, and tremendous employer resistance to unionism. From its all-time high of 35 percent during the early 1950s, the percentage of the U.S. labor force that belongs to unions has declined to 12.5 percent in 2005, back to the level from which its ascent began in the 1920s (Cornfield and Fletcher 2001; U.S. Bureau of Labor Statistics 2006). What is more, third-moment unions tend to organize less skilled service workers who are often replaceable and lack "positional power" to disrupt multiple economic sectors and large numbers of consumers by striking. Indeed, the frequency of striking has steadily declined during the post–World War II transition between the second and third historical moments (Fantasia and Voss 2004, 71). As the labor movement mobilizes to strengthen, revitalize itself, and grow, building coalitions with nonlabor groups is an important tactic for exchanging requisite resources—human, financial, political, and symbolic—for mobilizing workers with nonlabor groups who share labor's interest in improving the livelihoods of economically and culturally marginalized working families (see, for example, the chapters by Cornfield and Canak, Holgate and Wills, Luce, Reynolds, and Sellers).

In this third-moment era of identity politics, coalition building is also an important means for a multijurisdictional union, as a very large, complex organization, to make membership recruitment inroads among workers who harbor multiple and diverse social identities, as Holgate and Wills show in their chapter on labor-community organizing in London. Unlike the "provider" craft unions of the first moment, third-moment unions often are "advocates" that lack the union-provided and -financed labor supply and social welfare benefits that once made the union an especially meaningful institution in workers' daily lives. And in an era of identity politics, third-moment unions must articulate an advocacy mission that resonates not only with workers' economic interests but also with their social identities, identities on which a large, complex labor organization alone cannot make a legitimate moral claim (Chaison and Bigelow 2002, 24–27; Cornfield and Fletcher 2001; Fine 2006; Holgate 2005b; Ness 2005).

Therefore, building labor-inclusive coalitions with a wide range of social justice movements that are engaged in identity politics is a major prong of contemporary social unionism (Cornfield 2005; Fantasia and Voss 2004; Johnston 1994; Lopez 2004; Turner, Katz, and Hurd 2001). Social unionism is also a tactically militant, inclusive, and participatory trade unionism that effectively transforms bureaucratically inert labor organizations into meaningful labor unions in multiple worker communities. The labor movement has been developing multiple bridges for building coalitions with a wide range of social justice movements during its third moment since the 1960s (Cornfield 2005; Obach 2004). For example, the AFL-CIO (2005) has developed official "constituencies," listed in chronological order of their founding year: A. Philip Randolph Institute, 1965; Coalition of Black Trade Unionists, 1972; Labor Council for Latin American Advancement, 1973; Coalition of Labor Union Women, 1974; Asian Pacific American Labor Alliance, 1992; and Pride at Work, 1997. Similarly, SEIU (2005) maintains these "caucuses": Asian Pacific Islander Caucus, Native American Caucus, Lavender Caucus, Latino Caucus, National African American Caucus, People with Disabilities Caucus, Retiree Caucus, and Women's Caucus.

Coalition building, then, is an important tactic of labor's contemporary third moment. But with whom should labor partner? The urban contexts in which labor strategizes and acts afford labor the opportunities and configure the range of issues and prospective coalition partners labor pursues.

URBAN CONTEXTS OF LABOR-INCLUSIVE COALITION BUILDING

The city contextualizes labor-inclusive coalition building during the third moment. Unlike factory workers whose employers operate in national and international product markets, providers of the wide range of public and private retail, hospitality, distributive, personal, health-care, social-welfare, educational, and other business and professional services work in urban, coextensive labor and product markets. In an urban labor market, the bargaining power of service workers rests on the extent of the dependence of urban consumers on their services, local public sympathy with labor, labor's influence in city government and integration into civil society, and the degree of mutual affinity between labor and social justice movements associated with the identity politics of culturally and economically marginalized groups. Therefore, the city—including its exposure to globalization; its local labor and migration history; its economy, politics, social demography, and its patterns of residential and occupational segregation—constitutes labor's opportunity structure for building coalitions with other urban social actors (Jones-Correa 2001; Katznelson 1981; Smith 2001).

Labor-inclusive coalitions vary in their objectives and partnerships. In their New York–Los Angeles comparative chapter, Hauptmeier and Turner distinguish between social and political coalitions: "*Social coalitions* . . . include labor and other social actors such as community, religious, environmental, and immigrant rights groups, focused on a range of political, economic, and social campaigns. *Political coalitions* refer to cooperation between unions and parties, politicians, and other social actors, focused largely on elections and policy-making processes."[2] The distinction between social and political coalitions suggests that social coalitions are likely to form in cities in which identity politics are developed and labor has been able to link to social justice groups involved in identity politics, and that political coalitions are likely to form in cities in which labor has had a long presence in local politics and participation in government contract work. It also suggests that forming either type of labor-inclusive coalition depends on labor's political and economic strength and the demographic and mobilization patterns of ethnic-racial minorities in the city (Jones-Correa 2001; Katznelson 1981).

As an opportunity structure for labor-inclusive coalition building, the city is a relevant social arena in two ways. First, the city is an arena of strategic labor action taken by revitalizing third-moment unions and by preexisting unions of the first and second moments. As such, the city poses for labor the enduring challenge of Michels's "iron law of oligarchy," in which the self-perpetuating leaders of entrenched, complacent oligarchical unions are disinclined to shift from business unionism to social unionism, lest they upset the internal union political order with the entry of new constituencies into the union. Second, the city is an arena of ongoing identity politics, based on its ethnic-racial composition and patterns of occupational and industrial ethnic-race segregation. As an arena of identity politics, the city poses for labor the enduring challenge of "American exceptionalism," namely, the attainment of labor solidarity by a multiethnic labor force in an employer-segmenting labor market (Cornfield 1993; Katznelson 1981).

As an urban opportunity structure, then, the city poses for labor opportunities and obstacles to the attainment of labor solidarity. The status-conflict theory

---

2. For similar typologies of labor-inclusive coalitions, see Frege, Heery, and Turner 2004.

of leadership change states that, as a strategic actor, labor can achieve multi-ethnic and gender labor solidarity if an embattled and declining union harbors a universalistic ideology and its leaders perceive the importance for union revitalization of incorporating new underrepresented worker groups into the union leadership and membership (Cornfield 1993), much like the universalistic industrial unionism practiced by the CIO and CTW. The Buffalo-Seattle comparative chapter by Greer, Byrd, and Fleron and Cornfield and Canak's Nashville chapter refer to the importance of labor leaders and community coalition partners as cultural agents who act as "political entrepreneurs" and "bridge builders" outside the daily local organizational confines of unions to diffuse innovations from experienced to less experienced local labor unions, often of the same national union, and thereby widen the "cognitive frames" by which labor unions reach out to new underrepresented worker groups (see Cornfield and Fletcher 2001 and Obach 2004). Adopting this strategy often requires leadership change, an event that occurred immediately before the establishment of many of the innovative coalitions reported in this book.

To derive a link between labor-inclusive coalition building and urban context, the eleven U.S. cities in this book can be cross-classified by the strength of the local labor movement—as a "union town" or a "frontier town," as defined in the introductory chapter, and by the ethnic-racial and nativity characteristics of its residents. The union town, including cities of the Northeast and Great Lakes regions, developed during the first and second moments of institutional labor history with a strong local labor movement that participated in the rise and construction of the manufacturing economy and that suffered through post–World War II deindustrialization associated with globalization and economic restructuring. Similarly, the European cities of London and Hamburg are union towns that have undergone deindustrialization and economic restructuring. The frontier towns, including cities of the U.S. interior, South, and Sunbelt, have sustained low levels of unionization during all three historical moments, and especially in the disproportionately large number of states in these regions that around 1950 enacted state laws prohibiting union-shop union security agreements, also called state right-to-work laws by their antilabor proponents (Canak and Miller 1990; Eckes 2005). Late to (de)industrialize, frontier cities tend to be growing, urban and suburban, service economies. Regardless of city type, the eleven U.S. cities covered in this book are now mainly service economies. According to the U.S. Bureau of the Census (2005), the percentages of these eleven local urban labor forces employed in manufacturing did not exceed 21.5 percent in 2003.

The eleven cities reported in this book also vary in the ethnic-racial and nativity characteristics of their residents. Using U.S. Bureau of the Census (2005) data, we classify these cities in terms of the national rankings (above or below the median rank) among the largest U.S. cities of each of three percentages: the percentages of their residents who are (1) black or African American, (2) Hispanic or Latino, and (3) foreign born, because these groups are the largest of the mobilized groups in U.S. identity politics for which data are available. The following characterizations are intended to convey the dominant ethnic-racial patterns in these cities for the sake of constructing a typology of urban contexts and are not intended to mask the inevitably greater ethnic-racial complexity in each of these cities. The "multiethnic cities" are those with high percentages of all three groups (exceeding the median ranking of 25 percent on each of the three categories)—Boston, Houston, Miami, and New York. The "biethnic cities" are those in which one ethnic-racial minority predominates. Those in which African Americans predominate are Buffalo, Cleveland, and Nashville; and those in which Hispanics or Latinos (and foreign born) predominate are Denver, Los Angeles, and San Jose. Finally, Seattle is the only city of the eleven U.S. cities in this book with a high percentage of foreign born and low percentages of blacks or African Americans and Hispanics or Latinos. In 2000, Seattle's Asian population as a percentage of all residents (13.1%) ranked twenty-fifth highest of the largest U.S. cities, exceeding those of the other cities covered in this book except San Jose, and therefore we classify Seattle as a "biethnic" city.

Cross-classifying the eleven U.S. cities by their ethnic-racial characteristics and labor movement strength yields the following typology of urban contexts:

Ethnic-Racial Characteristics	Union Town	Frontier Town
Multi-ethnic	New York	Houston
	Boston	Miami
Bi-ethnic, African American	Buffalo	Nashville
	Cleveland	
Bi-ethnic, Latino		Los Angeles
		San Jose
		Denver
Bi-ethnic, Asian	Seattle	

The types of coalitions, characterized by their objectives, actions, and partners, vary among different urban contexts. In the union towns, preexisting local labor unions of the first and second moments tend to address a wide range of urban revitalization issues associated with economic restructuring that are especially relevant to the livelihoods and job security of existing union memberships in long-standing bargaining units and local political arrangements. The cases of London and Hamburg in this book, however, show that some strategic European unions have seized the "greenfield" opportunities for social coalition formation to address the livelihoods of health-care workers in these deindustrialized cities, where entrenched local labor movements have otherwise emphasized the interests of manufacturing workers or have pursued service-worker organizing on their own.

In contrast, it is in the frontier towns where third-moment unionism frequently leads coalition building and labor organizing. The chapters covering frontier towns show that CTW unions, such as SEIU, UFCW, and UNITE HERE, other service-sector unions, and local-area central labor bodies led by recently elected social movement activists are taking the lead in forming social coalitions and community-based initiatives.

Furthermore, the urban context of ethnic-race relations partly shapes labor-inclusive coalitions. The chapters on the multiethnic union towns—Hauptmeier and Turner's on New York and Kwon and Day's on Boston—show how public sector and building-trades unions with established ties to local government and employers form narrow, short-term, instrumental political coalitions to generate jobs and secure wages, often in conflict with other unions. In contrast, the seven-cities chapter by Reynolds and the Buffalo-Seattle comparative chapter by Greer et al. show how several unions in the biethnic union towns of Buffalo and Cleveland have jointly developed broad community-based social coalitions that attempt to improve job training opportunities for minority workers and address a wide range of civil rights and urban economic development issues. In Seattle, a relatively ethnically homogeneous city compared to the ten other U.S. cities covered in this book, many of the several innovative initiatives described by Greer et al. have been coalitions among labor unions, involving few nonlabor community actors, that have addressed a wide range of employment and urban economic development issues, including several successful political coalitions. The 1999 WTO protests were the chief exception and involved a social coalition of labor, environmental, religious, neighborhood, student, and other groups.

Coalition building in the frontier towns also is mediated by the urban context of ethnic-race relations. In these towns, coalition building is challenged by a variety of factors, not the least of which are the historical weakness of the local labor movement, especially in cities located in states with right-to-work laws, and the newness of immigration in interior regions. The chapters on the multiethnic, frontier towns—Nissen and Russo's chapter on Miami and Reynolds's chapter that includes Houston—show the ethnically variegated pattern of social coalition building within these ethnically complex cities located in right-to-work states. In these cities, grassroots social coalitions address a wide range of social justice, living wage, employment, and community economic development issues with political campaigns and participatory, community-based direct actions and initiatives, such as worker centers. Several of these coalitions are geared toward specific ethnic minority and immigrant groups.

In the Western biethnic frontier towns where established Latino communities constitute the dominant ethnic minority group, broad-based labor-inclusive social coalitions, subsequently generating pro-labor political coalitions, have formed to address a wide range of urban economic development, employment, living wage, and social justice issues. The chapters on these towns—Reynolds's portion on Denver, Los Angeles, and San Jose; Rhee and Sadler's on San Jose; and Hauptmeier and Turner's on Los Angeles—show how multiple unions have partnered with immigrant rights, Latino, small-business, religious, environmental, neighborhood, and other community stakeholders, as Rhee and Sadler put it. Deep in the right-to-work zone of the rapidly globalizing U.S. interior, Nashville's labor movement and emerging multiethnic immigrant rights community are beginning to coalesce around a range of employment issues. As Cornfield and Canak's Nashville chapter shows, local social justice public-interest groups and national unions have the potential to serve as important bridges for the exchange of organizational and cultural resources between the new immigrant ethnic communities and a declining local labor movement, building familiarity and trust between these two groups.

Summing up, the eleven U.S. urban contexts in *Labor in the New Urban Battlegrounds* present labor, as a strategic actor, with opportunities and obstacles for building coalitions and achieving labor solidarity. The chief opportunities in any one city are the historical emergence of a disenfranchised and aggrieved group of workers and a local labor movement history of organizing the unorganized. At the same time, these opportunities challenge strategic, transformative unions with social justice missions to harness and transcend the challenges of "American exceptionalism" stemming from a labor force that is segmented by race and ethnicity, and of the "iron law of oligarchy," the legacy of past labor successes that have since become bureaucratized.

Cities, therefore, contextualize and shape labor-inclusive coalition building. Political coalitions tend to form in multiethnic union towns and, subsequently, on the foundation of successful social coalitions already formed in biethnic frontier towns. Progressive unions and local-area central labor bodies are building social coalitions in the frontier towns, whose ethnic-racial complexity reflects that of the cities in which they emerge. In multiethnic frontier cities, social coalitions that address broad issues, such as living wage campaigns that effectively raise the "prevailing wage" for all workers in an urban labor market, generate labor solidarity by benefiting multiple ethnic and racial groups. Grassroots, community-based social coalition initiatives, such as worker centers, directly engage the worker with an otherwise bureaucratically remote labor union, promoting labor solidarity with isolated and segmented ethnic-racial minority groups of workers.[3] Furthermore, grassroots community-based initiatives are especially pertinent for labor organizing in states with labor-divisive right-to-work laws.

LABOR REVITALIZATION AND COALITIONS IN CITIES

Cities are the chief arenas in which contemporary initiatives to revitalize the labor movement in the service economy occur. Cities also are the arenas of converging forces—employer resistance to unionization, neoliberal globalization and economic restructuring, labor migration, past and enduring labor struggles, ethnic-racial identity politics, and social movement unionism—that pose for labor, as a strategic revitalizing actor, opportunities and obstacles for achieving a new inclusive labor solidarity.

Urban labor revitalization takes place at a historical moment that challenges large multijurisdictional unions to transform themselves into dynamic social movement organizations that can meaningfully engage a growing, increasingly diverse national low-wage service labor force. Each city, with its local labor movement legacy and social configuration of diverse worker identities, contextualizes the many innovative coalition-building initiatives that are reported in this book.

The urban context of labor revitalization is an opportunity structure for strategic actors, such as labor unions, to develop and shape urban coalitions. Together, the many cases of urban labor-inclusive coalition building reported in this book show how a range of coalitions are forming in different urban contexts. Inclusive social coalitions—addressing wide issues such as living wage campaigns and community-based initiatives such as worker centers that mutually and directly engage workers and unions—are often formed by progressive multijurisdictional unions and local-area central labor bodies in ethnic-racially diverse cities that lack an institutionalized labor movement. These labor-inclusive social coalitions partner with communitywide groups and with groups representing specific ethnic-racial minorities. Political coalitions are forming on the foundation of these social coalitions, as well as in cities whose institutionalized labor movements have an enduring place in the local political scene.

Labor in the New Urban Battlegrounds addresses the relationship between opportunity and strategic action undertaken by large complex labor unions that

---

3. On worker centers, see Fine 2006 and Greenhouse 2006.

practice social unionism in multiple urban contexts of a diverse service labor force. The many cases of innovative coalition building in this book show that no single strategy for labor revitalization fits all urban contexts. Rather, each city presents labor with a set of opportunities and obstacles for achieving labor solidarity through coalition building. Reading urban contexts and seizing local opportunities will continue to develop and strengthen labor's repertoire of strategic and tactical action for revitalizing and transforming itself into a movement that resonates widely and deeply with workers.

References

Abu-Lughod, Janet L. 1999. *New York, Chicago, Los Angeles: America's Global Cities.* Minneapolis: University of Minnesota Press.

AFL-CIO. 1955. *Report of the 1st Constitutional Convention.* December 5–8, New York.

———. 2003. "Immigrant Workers Freedom Ride." *America@Work* 8, no. 8: 8–11.

———. 2005. *AFL-CIO: America's Union Movement,* http://www.aflcio.org/, downloaded September 22, 2005.

Alarcon, Rafael. 1997. "From Servants to Engineers: Mexican Immigration and Labor Markets in the San Francisco Bay Area." Chicano Latino Policy Project Working Paper. Berkeley: Institute for the Study of Social Change.

Albrechtsen, Helge. 2004. "The Broken Link—Do Trade Unions Represent the Interests of the Unemployed?" *TRANSFER—European Review of Labour and Research* 10, no. 4: 569–87.

Alinsky, Saul. 1971. *Rules for Radicals: A Pragmatic Primer for Realistic Radicals.* New York: Vintage.

———. 1972. "Focus on Saul Alinsky: An Interview with the Outspoken Community Organizer." North Hollywood, Calif.: Center for Cassette Studies.

Amber, Michelle. 2006. "Change to Win to Launch Campaign in April: Targeting Major Industries in Over 35 Cities." Change to Win Daily Labor Report, March 21, 2006. http://www.changetowin.org/press/DLR032106.html, downloaded April 15, 2006.

Baccaro, Luccio, Kerstin Hamann, and Lowell Turner. 2003. "The Politics of Labour Movement Revitalization: The Need for a Revitalized Perspective." *European Journal of Industrial Relations* 9, no. 1: 119–33.

Baicich, Paul. 1987. "Machinists vs. Mismanagement at Eastern Airlines." *Labor Research Review* 10, no. 6: 85–101.

Benner, Chris. 1997. "Shock Absorbers in a Flexible Economy: The Rise of Contingent Labor in Silicon Valley." Working Partnerships USA Policy Brief. San Jose: Working Partnerships USA.

———. 1998. "Growing Together or Drifting Apart? Working Families and Business in the New Economy." Working Partnerships USA Policy Brief. San Jose: Working Partnerships USA.

Bernstein, Aaron. 1990. *Grounded: Frank Lorenzo and the Destruction of Eastern Airlines.* New York: Simon and Schuster.

Betten, Neil, and Michael J. Austin. 1990. *The Roots of Community Organizing, 1917–1939.* Philadelphia: Temple University Press.

Black Commentator. 2002. "The Living Wage Movement: A New Beginning. Bread, Power and Civil Rights in 19 Languages." 2 (May 8). http://www.blackcommentator.com/wage_1.html. Accessed September 15, 2004.

Bourdieu, Pierre. 1982. *Die feinen Unterschiede.* Frankfurt: Suhrkamp Verlag.

Boyle, Kevin. 1995. *The UAW and the Heyday of American Liberalism, 1945–1968.* Ithaca: Cornell University Press.

Brenner, Neil, and Nik Theodore, eds. 2002. *Spaces of Neoliberalism: Urban Restructuring in North America and Western Europe.* Oxford: Blackwell.

Bronfenbrenner, Kate. 1998. "It Takes More than House Calls: Organizing to Win with a Comprehensive Union-Building Strategy." In *Organizing to Win,* edited by Kate Bronfenbrenner et al. Ithaca: Cornell University Press.

Bronfenbrenner, Kate, Sheldon Friedman, Richard W. Hurd, Rudolph A. Oswald, and Ronald L. Seeber, eds. 1998. *Organizing to Win: New Research on Union Strategies.* Ithaca: Cornell University Press.

Brownstein, Bob. 2004. "Working Partnerships: A New Strategy for Advancing Economic Justice." In *Partnering for Change: Unions and Community Groups Build Coalitions for Economic Justice,* edited by David B. Reynolds, 190–203. Armonk, N.Y.: M. E. Sharpe.

Bruyn, Severyn, and James Meehan, eds. 1987. *Beyond the Market and the State: New Directions in Community Development.* Philadelphia: Temple University Press.

Byrd, Barbara, and Ian Greer. 2005. "The King County Labor Council: Building a Union City on the Pacific Rim." Report to the AFL-CIO's Central Labor Council Advisory Committee.

——. "Building a Union City on the Pacific Rim." Manuscript, Wayne State University. http://www.laborstudies.wayne.edu/Power/Seattle.doc.

Byrd, Barbara, and Nari Rhee. 2004. "Building Power in the New Economy: The South Bay Labor Council." *Working USA* 8, no. 2: 131–54.

Canak, William. 2004. "Labor Movement." In *Encyclopedia of Leadership,* edited by George R. Goethals, Georgia J. Sorenson, and James MacGregor Burns, 812–20. Thousand Oaks, Calif.: Sage.

Canak, William, and Berkeley Miller. 1990. "Gumbo Politics: Unions, Business, and Louisiana Right-to-Work Legislation." *Industrial and Labor Relations Review* 43, no. 2: 258–70.

Chaison, Gary, and Barbara Bigelow. 2002. *Unions and Legitimacy.* Ithaca: Cornell University Press.

Change to Win. 2006a. "Resolution on Sector Coordinating Committees." http://www. changetowin.org/pdf/SCCRes.pdf, downloaded April 15, 2006.

——. 2006b. "Restoring the American Dream: Building a 21st Century Labor Movement That Can Win." http://www.changetowin.org/pdf/AmericanDream.pdf, downloaded April 17, 2006.

——. 2006c. "Strategic Organizing Center." http://www.changetowin.org/organizing .html, downloaded April 16, 2006.

Clark, Terry Nichols. 2000. "Old and New Paradigms for Urban Research: Globalization and the Fiscal Austerity and Urban Innovation Project." *Urban Affairs Review* 36, no. 1: 3–45.

Clavel, Pierre. 1986. *The Progressive City.* New Brunswick, N.J.: Rutgers University Press.

Clavel, Pierre, and Wim Wiewel, eds. 1991. *Harold Washington and the Neighborhoods: Progressive City Government in Chicago, 1983–1987.* New Brunswick, N.J.: Rutgers University Press.

Clawson, Dan. 2003. *The Next Upsurge.* Ithaca: Cornell University Press.

Cobble, Dorothy Sue. 1991. *Dishing It Out: Waitresses and Their Unions in the Twentieth Century.* Urbana: University of Illinois Press.

Cooper, Michael. 2004. "In Tardy Albany, A Torrid Finish." *New York Times,* December 9, B5.

Cornfield, Daniel. 1993. "Integrating U.S. Labor Leadership: Union Democracy and the Ascent of Ethnic and Racial Minorities and Women into National Union Offices." In *Research in the Sociology of Organizations,* edited by Samuel Bacharach, Ronald Seeber, and David Walsh, 51–74. Greenwich, Conn.: JAI.

——. 2004. "Immigrants, Employment, and Labor Action: Strategies for Addressing Im-

migrant Employment Needs in Nashville, Tennessee." Presented at the 99th annual meeting of the American Sociological Association, San Francisco, August.

———. 2005. "Tactics and the Social Context of Social Movement Unionism in the Service
Economy." *Labor History* 46, no. 3: 347–55.

———. 2006. "Immigration, Economic Restructuring, and Labor Ruptures: From the
Amalgamated to Change to Win." Forthcoming in *Working USA: The Journal of
Labor and Society* 9 (June): 215–223.

Cornfield, Daniel, Angela Arzubiaga, Rhonda BeLue, Susan Brooks, Tony Brown, Oscar
Miller, Douglas Perkins, Peggy Thoits, and Lynn Walker. 2003. *Final Report of the
Immigrant Community Assessment,* available online at ftp://ftp.nashville.gov/web/
finance/immigrant-community-assessment-nashville.pdf

Cornfield, Daniel, and Bill Fletcher. 1998. "Institutional Constraints on Social Movement 'Frame Extension': Shifts in the Legislative Agenda of the American Federation of Labor, 1881–1955." *Social Forces* 76, no. 4: 1305–21.

———. 2001. "The U.S. Labor Movement: Toward a Sociology of Labor Revitalization." In
Sourcebook of Labor Markets, edited by Arne Kalleberg and Ivar Berg, 61–82. New
York: Plenum.

Cornfield, Daniel, and Holly McCammon, eds. 2003. *Labor Revitalization: Global Perspectives and New Initiatives.* Amsterdam: JAI Press.

Cravey, Altha J. 2004. "Students and the Anti-Sweatshop Movement." *Antipode* 36, no. 2:
203–8.

Dean, Amy. 1996. "Working Partnerships USA: The Latest Initiative for a Council on the
Cutting Edge." *Labor Research Review* 24 (summer): 43–48.

Delgado, Gary. 1986. *Organizing the Movement: The Roots and Growth of ACORN.*
Philadelphia: Temple University Press.

Delgado, Héctor. 1993. *New Immigrants, Old Unions: Organizing Undocumented Workers
in Los Angeles.* Philadelphia: Temple University Press.

Delp, Linda, and Katie Quan. 2002. "Homecare Worker Organizing in California: An
Analysis of a Successful Strategy." *Labor Studies Journal* 27, no. 1: 1–23.

Democracy Now. 2005. "Student Hunger Strike Secures Living Wage for Georgetown
Workers." Radio transcript. March 25.

DeNavas-Walt, Carmen, Bernadette D. Proctor, and Cheryl Hill Lee, U.S. Census Bureau.
2004. *Income, Poverty, and Health Insurance Coverage in the United States.* Washington, D.C.: U.S. Government Printing Office.

Dewan, Shaila K. 2002. "Some Members Balk at Union Support for Pataki." *New York
Times,* October 1, B3.

Dogliani, Patrizia. 1992. *Un Laboratorio di socialismo municipale: La Francia (1870–
1920).* Milan: Franco Angelli.

Dubofsky, Melvyn. 1994. *The State and Labor in Modern America.* Chapel Hill: University of North Carolina Press.

Eckes, Alfred. 2005. "The South and Economic Globalization, 1950 to the Future." In
Globalization and the American South, edited by James Cobb and William Stueck,
36–65. Athens: University of Georgia Press.

Eimer, Stuart. 2001. "Fighting for Justice beyond the Contract: The Milwaukee County
Labor Council and Sustainable Milwaukee." In *Central Labor Councils and the Re-
vival of American Unionism,* edited by Immanuel Ness and Stuart Eimer, 53–78.
Armonk, N.Y.: M. E. Sharpe.

Eisenscher, Michael. 1993. "Silicon Fist in a Velvet Glove." Unpublished manuscript.

Erickson, Christopher L., Catherine L. Fisk, Ruth Milkman, Daniel J. B. Mitchell, and
Kent Wong. 2002. "Justice for Janitors in Los Angeles: Lessons from Three Rounds
of Negotiations." *British Journal of Industrial Relations* 40, no. 3: 543–67.

Esping-Andersen, Gøsta. 1985. *Politics against Markets: The Social Democratic Path to Power*. Princeton: Princeton University Press.

Evans, Peter, ed. 2002. Introduction to *Livable Cities?* edited by Evans. Chicago: University of Chicago Press.

Evans, Yara, Joanna Herbert, Kavita Datta, Jon May, Cathy McIlwaine, and Jane Wills. 2005. *Making the City Work: Low Paid Employment in London*. Working Paper 1. London: Department of Geography, Queen Mary, University of London.

Fantasia, Rick, and Kim Voss. 2004. *Hard Work: Remaking the American Labor Movement*. Berkeley: University of California Press.

Farris, Anne. 2005. "New Immigrants in New Places: America's Growing 'Global Interior.'" *Carnegie Reporter* 3 (Fall). http://www.carnegie.org/reporter/11/newimmigrants/index.html.

Fine, Janice. 2002. "From City Trenches to City Tunnels: The Promise and the Limits of Community Unions in the United States Today." Presented at the Urban Affairs Association meeting, March 20, Boston, Mass.

——. 2006. *Worker Centers: Organizing Communities at the Edge of the Dream*. Ithaca: Cornell University Press.

Fisher, Robert. 1994. *Let the People Decide: Neighborhood Organizing in America*. Boston: Twayne.

Fleron, Lou Jean, and Ron Applegate. 2004. "Building a Two-Lane High Road: Unions and Economic Development in Western New York." *Perspectives on Work, The Magazine of LERA* 8, no. 1: 10–12.

Fleron, Lou Jean, Howard Stanger, and Eileen Patton. 2000. *Champions at Work: Employment, Workplace Practices, and Labor-Management Relations in Western New York*. Buffalo: ILR Great Lakes Region.

Frank, Larry, and Kent Wong. 2004. "Intense Political Mobilization: The Los Angeles County Federation of Labor." *Working USA* 8, no. 2: 155–85.

Freeman, Joshua. 2000. *Working-Class New York: Life and Labor since World War II*. New York: New Press.

Freeman, Richard B. 2005. "Fighting for Other Folks' Wages: The Logic and Illogic of Living Wage Campaigns." *Industrial Relations* 44, no. 1: 14–31.

Frege, Carola, Edmund Heery, and Lowell Turner. 2004. "The New Solidarity? Trade Union Coalition-Building in Five Countries." In *Varieties of Unionism: Strategies for Union Revitalization in a Globalizing Economy,* edited by Carola Frege and John Kelly, 137–58. Oxford: Oxford University Press.

Frege, Carola, and John Kelly, eds. 2004. *Varieties of Unionism: Strategies for Labor Movement Renewal in the Global North*. Oxford: Oxford University Press.

Fricke, Werner, and Peter Totterdill. 2004. *Action Research in Workplace Innovation and Regional Development*. Philadelphia: John Benjamins.

Frost, Jennifer. 2001. *"An Interracial Movement of the Poor": Community Organizing and the New Left in the 1960s*. New York: New York University Press.

Gall, Gregor. 2003. *Union Organizing: Campaigning for Trade Union Recognition*. London: Routledge.

Gerschenkron, Alexander. 1962. *Economic Backwardness in Historical Perspective: A Book of Essays*. Cambridge: Belknap Press of Harvard University Press.

Gittell, Ross. 1992. *Renewing Cities*. Princeton: Princeton University Press.

Goldman, Mark. 1983. *High Hopes: The Rise and Decline of Buffalo, New York*. Albany: State University of New York Press.

Gordon, Colin. 1999. "The Lost City of Solidarity: Metropolitan Unionism in Historical Perspective." *Politics and Society* 27, no. 4: 561–85.

Gottlieb, Robert, Mark Vallianatos, Regina Freer, and Peter Dreier. 2005. *The Next Los Angeles: The Struggle for a Livable City.* Berkeley: University of California Press.

Greater London Authority. 2002. *The London Plan: Spatial Development Strategy.* London: GLA.

———. 2005. *A Fairer London: The Living Wage in London.* London: GLA.

Greenhouse, Steven. 2000. "A Valone Bill Bars Purchases in Sweatshops." *New York Times,* February 8, B5.

———. 2001. "Labor a Divided House in Mayoral Race: Each Democrat Has a Union's Support." *New York Times,* September 4, B4.

———. 2006. "Groups Provide Advice and Support for Immigrant Workers Fighting for Rights." *New York Times,* April 23, A17.

Greer, Ian, and Lou Jean Fleron. 2005. "Labor and Urban Crisis in Buffalo, New York: Building a High Road Infrastructure." Presented at the United Association of Labor Educators meeting, March 30–April 1, Philadelphia.

Griffey, Trevor. 2004. "No Separate Peace: Militant Protest, Civil Disorder, and the Struggle for Affirmative Action in the Seattle Building and Construction Trades Unions." Manuscript, University of Washington.

Hale, Angela, and Jane Wills, eds. 2005. *Threads of Labour: Garment Industry Supply Chains from the Workers' Perspective.* Oxford: Blackwell.

Hall, Peter, and David Soskice, editors. 2001. *Varieties of Capitalism: The Institutional Foundations of Comparative Advantage.* New York: Oxford University Press.

Halpern, Robert. 1995. *Rebuilding the Inner City: A History of Neighborhood Initiatives to Address Poverty in the United States.* New York: Columbia University Press.

Hamnett, Chris. 2003. *Unequal Cities: London in the Global Arena.* London: Routledge.

Harvey, David. 1989. *The Condition of Postmodernity.* Oxford: Blackwell.

Hawken, Paul. 2000. "On the Streets of Seattle." *Amicus Journal* (Spring): 29–51.

Herod, Andrew. 1998. *Organizing the Landscape: Geographical Perspectives on Labor Unionism.* Minneapolis: University of Minnesota Press.

Herod, Andrew, Jamie Peck, and Jane Wills. 2003. "Geography and Industrial Relations." In *Understanding Work and Employment: Industrial Relations in Transition,* edited by Peter Ackers and Adrian Wilkinson, 176–94. Oxford: Oxford University Press.

Heselden, Laurie. 2001. "Coming in from the Cold: The Role of Trade Unions on Public Policy Bodies at the Regional Level, with a focus on London, the South East and the East of England." *Antipode* 33, no. 5: 753–62.

Hirsch, Barry T., and David A. Macpherson. 2003. "Union Membership and Coverage Database from the Current Population Survey: Note." *Industrial and Labor Relations Review* 56, no. 2: 349–54.

———. 2006. "Union Membership and Coverage Database." http://www.unionstats.com/.

Holgate, Jane. 2005a. "Trade Union Recognition in Asian Workplaces: A Springboard to Further Union Organising/Recognition Campaigns." In *Union Recognition: Organising and Bargaining Outcomes,* edited by Gregor Gall, 134–50. London: Routledge.

———. 2005b. "Organising Migrant Workers: A Case Study of Working Conditions and Unionisation at a Sandwich Factory in London." *Work, Employment and Society* 19, no. 3: 463–480.

Holtfrerich, Carl-Ludwig. 1999. *Finanzplatz Frankfurt—Von der mittelalterlichen Messestadt zum europäischen Bankenzentrum.* Munich: Verlag Beck.

Horan, Cynthia L. 1996. "Coalition, Market, and State: Postwar Development Politics in Boston." In *Reconstructing Urban Regime Theory: Regulating Urban Politics in a*

Global Economy, edited by Mickey Lauria, 149–70. Thousand Oaks, Calif.: Sage Publications.

Horwitt, Sanford D. 1989. *Let Them Call Me Rebel: Saul Alinsky—His Life and Legacy.* New York: Knopf.

Howard, Marc. 2003. *The Weakness of Civil Society in Eastern Europe.* Cambridge: Cambridge University Press.

Huber, Evelyne, and John Stephens. 2001. *Development and Crisis of the Welfare State.* Cambridge: Cambridge University Press.

Hurd, Richard W. 2004. "The Failure of Organizing, the New Unity Partnership, and the Future of the Labor Movement." *Working USA* 8, no. 1: 5–25.

Hurd, Richard W., Ruth Milkman, and Lowell Turner. 2003. "Reviving the American Labour Movement: Institutions and Mobilization." *European Journal of Industrial Relations* 9, no. 1: 99–117.

Inglehart, Ronald, Miguel Basanez, and Alejandro Moreno. 1998. *Human Values and Beliefs: A Cross-Cultural Sourcebook.* Ann Arbor: University of Michigan Press.

Isaac, Larry, Steve McDonald, and Greg Lukasik. 2006. "Takin' It from the Streets: How the Sixties Breathed Life into the Labor Movement." Forthcoming in *American Journal of Sociology,* July.

Jacobi, Otto. 2003. "Renewal of the Collective Bargaining System?" In *The Changing Contours of German Industrial Relations,* edited by Walther Müller-Jentsch and Hansjörg Weitbrecht, 15–38. Munich: Rainer Hampp Verlag.

Jamoul, Lina. 2006. "The Art of Politics: The Context, Potential and Limitations of Broad-based Organising in Britain." Forthcoming in *Urban Studies.*

Johnston, Paul. 1994. *Success While Others Fail: Social Movement Unionism and the Public Workplace.* Ithaca: Cornell University Press.

——. 2001. "Organize for What? The Resurgence of Labor as a Citizenship Movement." In *Rekindling the Movement: Labor's Quest for Relevance in the 21st Century,* edited by Lowell Turner, Harry Katz, and Richard Hurd, 27–58. Ithaca: Cornell University Press.

Jonas, Andrew E. G. 1996. "In Search of Order: Traditional Business Reformism and the Crisis of Neoliberalism in Massachusetts." *Transactions of the Institute of British Geographers* 21, no. 4: 617–34.

Jonas, Andrew E. G., and David Wilson, eds. 1999. *The Urban Growth Machine: Critical Perspectives Two Decades Later.* Albany: State University of New York Press.

Jones-Correa, Michael. 2001. "Structural Shifts and Institutional Capacity: Possibilities for Ethnic Cooperation and Conflict in Urban Settings." In *Governing American Cities: Inter-Ethnic Coalitions, Competition, and Conflict,* edited by Michael Jones-Correa, 183–209. New York: Russell Sage Foundation.

Karson, Tom. 2004. "Confronting Houston's Demographic Shift: The Harris County AFL-CIO." *Working USA* 8, no. 2: 207–28.

Katznelson, Ira. 1981. *City Trenches: Urban Politics and the Patterning of Class in the United States.* New York: Pantheon Books.

Katznelson, Ira, and Aristide Zolberg. 1986. *Working Class Formation in Western Europe and the United States.* Princeton: Princeton University Press.

Kelly, John, and Carola Frege, eds. 2004. *Varieties of Unionism: Struggles for Union Revitalization in a Globalizing Economy.* Oxford: Oxford University Press.

Klein, Naomi. 2002. *Fences and Windows: Dispatches from the Front Lines of the Globalization Debate.* New York: Picador.

Kochan, Thomas, Harry Katz, and Richard McKersie. 1986. *The Transformation of American Industrial Relations.* New York: Basic Books.

Ladd, Carl Everett. 1999. *The Ladd Report.* New York: Free Press.

Läpple, Dieter. 2001. "Globalisation and the Urban Economy—The Case of the Metropolitan Region of Hamburg." In *Globalisation and the Social Contract*, edited by David Foden and Jürgen Hoffmann, 33–54. Brussels: European Trade Union Institute.

Le Goff, Jacques. 1997. *Pour l'amour des villes*. Paris: Les éditions textuel.

Levi, Margaret, and David Olson. 2000. "The Battles in Seattle." *Politics and Society* 28, no. 3: 309–29.

Lichtenstein, Nelson. 1995. *The Most Dangerous Man in Detroit: Walter Reuther and the Fate of American Labor*. New York: Basic Books.

———. 2002. *2002 State of the Union: A Century of American Labor*. Princeton: Princeton University Press.

Linder, Marc. 2000. *Wars of Attrition: Vietnam, the Business Roundtable, and the Decline of Construction Unions*. 2nd ed. Iowa City: Fanpihua Press.

Linz, Juan J., and Albert Stepan. 1994. *Problems of Democratic Transition and Consolidation*. Baltimore: Johns Hopkins University Press.

Locke, Richard. 1992. "The Demise of the National Union in Italy: Lessons for Comparative Industrial Relations Theory." *Industrial and Labor Relations Review* 45, no. 2: 229–49.

———. 1993. *Re-Making the Italian Economy*. Ithaca: Cornell University Press.

Logan, John, Rachael Whaley, and Kyle Crowder. 1997. "The Character and Consequences of Growth Regimes." *Urban Affairs Review* 32, no. 5: 603–30.

Lopez, Steven Henry. 2004. *Reorganizing the Rust Belt: An Inside Story of the American Labor Movement*. Berkeley: University of California Press.

Luce, Stephanie. 2001. "The Fight for Living Wages." In *From ACT-UP to the WTO: Urban Protest and Community Building in the Era of Globalization*, edited by Benjamin Shepard and Ronald Hayduk. London: Verso.

———. 2002. "Life Support: Coalition Building and the Living Wage Movement." *New Labor Forum* 10 (Spring–Summer): 81–91.

———. 2004. *Fighting for a Living Wage*. Ithaca: Cornell University Press.

Luce, Stephanie, and Mark Nelson. 2004. "Starting Down the Road to Power." *Working USA* 8, no. 2: 183–206.

Lüthje, Boy. 2002. "The Detroit of the New Economy: The Changing Workplace, Manufacturing Workers, and the Labor Movement in Silicon Valley." Presented at the annual convention of the American Historical Association, January 6, San Francisco.

Mantsios, Gregory. 2001. "Labor and Community." In *Rethinking the Urban Agenda: Reinvigorating the Liberal Tradition in New York City and Urban America*, edited by John H. Moellenkopf and Ken Emerson, 75–91. New York: Century Foundation.

Markusen, Ann, Elyse Golob, and Mia Grey. 1996. "Big Firms, Long Arms, Wide Shoulders: The 'Hub-and-Spoke' Industrial District in the Seattle Region." *Regional Studies* 30, no. 6: 657–67.

Martin, Isaac. 2004. "The Living Wage Movement at Ten: A Report for the Rockridge Institute." Berkeley, Calif.: Rockridge Institute.

Matthews, Glenna. 2003. *Silicon Valley, Women, and the California Dream: Gender, Class, and Opportunity in the Twentieth Century*. Stanford: Stanford University Press.

May, Jon, Jane Wills, Kavita Datta, Yara Evans, Joanna Herbert, and Cathy McIlwaine. 2006. *Keeping London Working: Global Cities, the British State, and London's New Migrant Division of Labour*. Working Paper 2. London: Department of Geography, Queen Mary, University of London.

McAdam, Doug, Sidney Tarrow, and Charles Tilly. 2001. *Dynamics of Contention*. New York: Cambridge University Press.

McCarthy, John D., and Mayer N. Zald. 1977. "Resource Mobilization and Social Movements: A Partial Theory." *American Journal of Sociology* 82, no. 6: 1212–41.

McDonnell, James. 1970. *The Rise of the CIO in Buffalo, New York, 1936–1942.* PhD diss., University of Wisconsin.

Medoff, Peter, and Holly Sklar. 1994. *Streets of Hope: The Fall and Rise of an Urban Neighborhood.* Boston: South End Press.

Merrifield, Andy. 1993. "The Canary Wharf Debacle: From 'TINA'—There Is No Alternative—to 'THEMBA'—There Must Be an Alternative." *Environment and Planning A.* 25, no. 9: 1247–65.

——. 2000. "The Urbanization of Labor: Living-Wage Activism in the American City." *Social Text* 18, no. 1: 31–54.

Merrifield, Andy, and Erik Swyngedouw, eds. 1997. *The Urbanization of Injustice.* New York: New York University Press.

Meyerson, Harold. 2002. "Union Seeks Republicans." *American Prospect* 13, no. 19: 25.

——. 2004. "A Tale of Two Cities." *American Prospect* 15, no. 5: A8–A9.

Milkman, Ruth. 2000. Introduction to *Organizing Immigrants: The Challenge for Unions in Contemporary California,* edited by Milkman, 1–24. Ithaca: Cornell University Press.

——. 2002. "New Workers, New Labor, and the New Los Angeles." In *Unions in a Globalized Environment,* edited by Bruce Nissen, 103–29. Armonk, N.Y.: M. E. Sharpe.

——. 2006. *L.A. Story: Work and Unionism in an Immigrant City.* New York: Russell Sage Foundation.

——, ed. 2000. *Organizing Immigrants: The Challenge for Unions in Contemporary California.* Ithaca: Cornell University Press.

Milkman, Ruth, and Kent Wong. 2000. "The 1992 Southern California Drywall Strike." In *Organizing Immigrants: The Challenge for Unions in Contemporary California,* edited by Ruth Milkman, 169–98. Ithaca: Cornell University Press.

Mink, Gwendolyn. 1986. *Old Labor and New Immigrants in American Political Development.* Ithaca: Cornell University Press.

Mollenkopf, John. 1983. *The Contested City.* Princeton: Princeton University Press.

——. 1992. *A Phoenix in the Ashes: The Rise and Fall of the Koch Coalition in New York City Politics.* Princeton: Princeton University Press.

Montgomery, David. 1987. *The Fall of the House of Labor: The Workplace, the State, and American Labor Activism.* Cambridge: Cambridge University Press.

Muller, Sarah, Sarah Zimmerman, Bob Brownstein, Amy B. Dean, and Phaedra Ellis-Lamkins. 2003. "Shared Prosperity and Inclusion: The Future of Economic Development Strategies in Silicon Valley." Working Partnerships USA Policy Brief. San Jose: Working Partnerships USA.

Ness, Immanuel. 2005. *Immigrants, Unions, and the New U.S. Labor Market.* Philadelphia: Temple University Press.

Ness, Immanuel, and Stuart Eimer. 2001. *Central Labor Councils and the Revival of American Unionism: Organizing for Justice in Our Communities.* Armonk, N.Y.: M. E. Sharpe.

Nissen, Bruce. 2000. "Living Wage Campaigns from a 'Social Movement' Perspective: The Miami Experience." *Labor Studies Journal* 25, no. 3: 29–50.

——. 2002. "The Role of Labor Education in Transforming a Union toward Organizing Immigrants: A Case Study." *Labor Studies Journal* 27, no. 1: 109–27.

——. 2004. "The Effectiveness and Limits of Labor-Community Coalitions: Evidence from South Florida." *Labor Studies Journal* 29, no. 1: 67–89.

——, ed. 2002. *Unions in a Globalized Environment.* Armonk, N.Y.: M. E. Sharpe.

Nissen, Bruce, and Guillermo Grenier. 2001. "Local Union Relations with Immigrants: The Case of South Florida." *Labor Studies Journal* 26, no. 1: 76–97.

Obach, Brian. 2004. *Labor and the Environmental Movement: The Quest for Common Ground.* Cambridge: MIT Press.

O'Connor, Alice. 2001. *Poverty Knowledge: Social Science, Social Policy, and the Poor in Twentieth-Century U.S. History.* Princeton: Princeton University Press.

Offe, Claus, and Helmut Wiesenthal. 1985. "Two Logics of Collective Action." In *Disorganized Capitalism,* edited by Claus Offe, 170–220. Cambridge: Polity.

Osterman, Paul. 2002. *Gathering Power: The Future of Progressive Politics in America.* Boston: Beacon Press.

Pastor, Manuel. 2001. "Common Ground at Ground Zero? The New Economy and the New Organizing in Los Angeles." *Antipode,* 260–89.

Phares, Donald. 2004. *Metropolitan Governance without Metropolitan Government?* Aldershot, England: Ashgate.

Pierre, Jon. 1999. "Models of Urban Governance: The Institutional Dimension of Urban Politics." *Urban Affairs Review* 34, no. 3: 372–96.

Pollin, Robert, Mark Brenner, and Jeannette Wicks-Lim. 2004. "Economic Analysis of the Florida Minimum Wage Proposal." Washington, D.C.: Center for American Progress.

Portnoy, Kent. 2003. *Taking Sustainable Cities Seriously: Economic Development, the Environment, and Quality of Life in American Cities.* Cambridge: MIT Press.

Putnam, Robert D. 2000. *Bowling Alone: The Collapse and Revival of the American Community.* New York: Simon and Schuster.

Remarque, Paul. 2001. " . . . Seit Der Apollo Die größte Technologische Herausforderung." *IG Metall Küste Rundbrief.* 4, no. 1: http://www.labourcom.uni-bremen.de/ak-alternative_fertigung/rundbrf/rundbrf/rund

Research Institute on Social and Economic Policy (RISEP). http://www.risep-fiu.org, with research reports related to South Florida labor-based social movement activities.

Reynolds, David. 2002. *Taking the High Road: Communities Organize for Economic Change.* Armonk, N.Y.: M. E. Sharpe.

——, ed. 2004. *Partnering for Change: Unions and Community Groups Build Coalitions for Economic Justice.* Armonk, N.Y.: M. E. Sharpe.

Robbins, Tom. 2001. "Labor's Election Day Flop." *Village Voice* 46, no. 47: 20.

Rose, Fred. 2000. *Coalitions across the Class Divide: Lessons from the Labor, Peace, and Environmental Movements.* Ithaca: Cornell University Press.

Rosenblum, Jonathan. 2001. "Building Organizing Capacity: The King County Labor Council." In *Central Labor Councils and the Renewal of American Unionism: Organizing for Justice in Our Communities,* edited by Immanuel Ness and Stuart Eimer, 163–87. Armonk, N.Y.: M. E. Sharpe.

Safford, Sean C., and Richard M. Locke. 2001. "Union on the Rebound: Social Embeddedness and the Transformation of Building Trades Locals." *MIT Sloan School Working Paper* 4175–01. Cambridge: MIT Sloan School.

Sahu, Saura James. 2001. "Living Up to the Living Wage: A Primer on the Legal Issues Surrounding the Enactment and Enforcement of Living Wage Laws." Detroit: Guild Law Center.

Santa Clara County Department of Planning/Advanced Planning Office. 1990. "Alternative Futures: Trends and Choices—A Trends Report from the County of Santa Clara Strategic Vision Steering Committee." Executive Summary. San Jose: Santa Clara County Department of Planning.

Sassen, Saskia. 1988. *The Mobility of Labor and Capital: A Study in International Investment and Labor Flow.* Cambridge: Cambridge University Press.

——. 2000. *Cities in a World Economy.* 2nd ed. London: Pine Forge.

——. 2001. *The Global City: New York, London, Tokyo.* 2nd ed. Princeton: Princeton University Press.

Savitch, Hank, and Paul Kantor. 2002. *Cities in the International Marketplace: The Political Economy of Urban Development in North America and West Europe.* Princeton: Princeton University Press.

Saxenian, Annalee. 1989. "In Search of Power: The Organization of Business Interests in Silicon Valley and Route 128." *Economy and Society* 18, no. 1: 25–70.

Schneirov, Richard. 1998. *Labor and Urban Politics: Class Conflict and the Origins of Modern Liberalism in Chicago, 1864–1897.* Urbana: University of Illinois Press.

Sclar, Elliott D. 2001. *You Don't Always Get What You Pay For: The Economics of Privatization.* Ithaca: Cornell University Press.

Seidman, Gay W. 1994. *Manufacturing Militance: Workers' Movements in Brazil and South Africa, 1970–1985.* Berkeley: University of California Press.

SEIU. 2005. *SEIU Stronger Together.* http://www.seiu.org/, downloaded September 16, 2005.

Sellers, Jefferey. 2002. *Governing from Below: Urban Regions and the Global Economy.* Cambridge: Cambridge University Press.

——. 2005. "Re-Placing the Nation: An Agenda for Comparative Urban Politics." *Urban Affairs Review* 40, no. 4: 419–45.

Silderberg, Susan Crowl. 1998. "South Boston: Planning in a Reluctant Community." MCP diss., MIT.

Singer, Audrey. 2004. "The Rise of New Immigrant Gateways." Living Cities Census Series, Center on Urban and Metropolitan Policy. Washington, D.C.: Brookings Institution.

Sirianni, Carmen, and Lewis Friedland. 2001. *Civic Innovation in America: Community Empowerment, Public Policy, and the Movement for Community Renewal.* Berkeley: University of California Press.

Skocpol, Theda. 2003. *Diminished Democracy: From Membership to Management in American Civic Life.* Norman: University of Oklahoma Press.

Slayton, Robert A. 1986. *Back of the Yards: The Making of a Local Democracy.* Chicago: University of Chicago Press.

Smith, Michael. 2001. *Transnational Urbanism.* Malden, Mass.: Blackwell.

Sokol, Martin, Jane Wills, Jeremy Anderson, Marg Buckley, Yara Evans, Claire Frew, and Paula Hamilton. 2006. Forthcoming in *The Impact of Improved Terms and Conditions on Workers at the Royal London.* London: UNISON/Queen Mary, University of London.

Spahn, Paul Bernd. 2002. *Position und Entwicklungsperspektiven des Finanzplatzes Frankfurt.* Wiesbaden: Hessisches Ministerium für Wirtschaft.

Steger, Manfred. 2003. *Globalization: A Very Short Introduction.* Oxford: Oxford University Press.

Steinmetz, George. 2001. *Regulating the Social.* Princeton: Princeton University Press.

Stiglitz, Joseph. 2002. *Globalization and Its Discontents.* London: Penguin.

Stone, Clarence. 1989. *Regime Politics: Governing Atlanta, 1946–1988.* Lawrence: University Press of Kansas.

Stone, Clarence, and Haywood Sanders, eds. 1987. *The Politics of Urban Development.* Lawrence: University Press of Kansas.

Streeck, Wolfgang, and Kathleen Thelen. 2005a. *Beyond Continuity: Institutional Change in Advanced Political Economies.* Oxford: Oxford University Press.

———. 2005b. "Institutional Change in Advanced Political Economies." In *Beyond Continuity: Institutional Change in Advanced Political Economies,* edited by Streeck and Thelen, 1–39. Oxford: Oxford University Press.

Swarns, Rachel. 2003. "U.S. a Place of Miracles for Somali Refugees." *New York Times,* July 20, 1, 23.

Tarrow, Sidney. 1998. *Power in Movement: Social Movements and Contentious Politics.* 2nd ed. Cambridge: Cambridge University Press.

———. 2002. *Power in Movement.* Cambridge: Cambridge University Press.

Tarrow, Sidney, Doug McAdam, and Charles Tilly. 2001. *Dynamics of Contention.* Cambridge: Cambridge University Press.

Taylor, Henry Louis. 1990. *African Americans and the Rise of Buffalo's Post-industrial City, 1940 to Present.* Buffalo: Buffalo Urban League.

Teamsters. 2005. *International Brotherhood of Teamsters: The World's Most Powerful Labor Union.* http://www.teamster.org/, downloaded September 17, 2005.

Tilly, Charles. 1978. *From Mobilization to Revolution.* Reading, Mass.: Addison-Wesley.

———. 2003. "Living Wage Laws in the United States: The Dynamics of a Growing Movement." University of Massachusetts-Lowell Working Paper. Lowell: University of Massachusetts.

———. 2004. *Social Movements, 1768–2004.* Boulder, Colo.: Paradigm Publishers.

Thelen, Kathleen. 1991. *A Union of Parts.* Ithaca: Cornell University Press.

Trounstine, Philip, and Terry Christensen. 1982. *Movers and Shakers: The Study of Community Power.* New York: St. Martin's Press.

Turner, Lowell. 1991. *Democracy at Work.* Ithaca: Cornell University Press.

———. 2003. "Reviving the Labor Movement: A Comparative Perspective." In *Labor Revitalization: Global Perspectives and New Initiatives,* edited by Daniel Cornfield and Holly McCammon, 23–57. Amsterdam: JAI Press.

———. 2004a. "Globalization and the Logic of Participation: Unions and the Politics of Coalition Building." Presented at the IIRA 7th European Congress, September 7–11, Lisbon.

———. 2004b. "Why Revitalize? Labour's Urgent Mission in a Contested Global Economy." In *Varieties of Unionism: Strategies for Union Revitalization in a Globalizing Economy,* edited by Carola Frege and John Kelly, 1–10. Oxford: Oxford University Press.

———. 2005. "From Transformation to Revitalization: A New Research Agenda for a Contested Global Economy." *Work and Occupations* 32, no. 4: 383–99.

Turner, Lowell, and Richard Hurd. 2001. "Building Social Movement Unionism: The Transformation of the American Labor Movement." In *Rekindling the Movement: Labor's Quest for Relevance in the 21st Century,* edited by Lowell Turner, Harry Katz, and Richard Hurd, 9–26. Ithaca: Cornell University Press.

Turner, Lowell, Harry Katz, and Richard Hurd, eds. 2001. *Rekindling the Movement: Labor's Quest for Relevance in the 21st Century.* Ithaca: Cornell University Press.

United Food and Commercial Workers. 2005. *UFCW: A Voice for Working America.* http://www.ufcw.org/, downloaded September 17, 2005.

UNITE HERE. 2005. *UNITE HERE!* http://www.unitehere.org/, downloaded September 15, 2005.

U.S. Bureau of Labor Statistics. 2006. *Union Members in 2005,* news release USDL 06–99, table 5, downloaded March 23, 2006 from http://www.bls.gov/news.release/pdf/union2.pdf.

U.S. Bureau of the Census Website. 2000 Census data, 2003 American Community Survey data, and 2001 County Business Patterns data.

———. 2002. *County and City Data Book: 2000,* tables C-1 and C-2, downloaded August

8, 2005 from http://www.census.gov/statab/ccdb/cit1130r.txt and http://www.census.gov/statab/ccdb/cit2141r.txt.

——. 2003a. *2003 American Community Survey,* downloaded August 8, 2005 from http://www.census.gov/acs/www/Products/Ranking/2003/R15T160.htm.

——. 2003b. *Migration of Natives and the Foreign-Born: 1995 to 2000.* Census 2000 Special Reports, CENSR-11. Washington, D.C.: U.S. Government Printing Office.

——. 2005. *American Community Survey,* Data Tables: Multi-Year Profiles 2003. http://www.census.gov/acs/www/Products/Profiles/Chg/2003/ACS/index.htm, downloaded September 15, 2005.

Van Meter, Bob. 2004. "CDCs in Gentrifying Neighborhoods: Giving Low-Income Residents a Chance to Bloom in a Changing Market." *Shelterforce Online* 133 (January–February).

Verba, Sidney, Norman Nie, and Jae-On Kim. 1975. *Participation and Political Equality.* Chicago: University of Chicago Press.

Voss, Kim, and Rachel Sherman. 2000. "Breaking the Iron Law of Oligarchy: Union Revitalization in the American Labor Movement." *American Journal of Sociology* 106, no. 2: 303–49.

WAI. 2002. *Helping Low-Wage Workers Succeed through Innovative Union Partnerships.* Washington, D.C.: AFL-CIO.

Waterman, Peter. 1993. "Social Movement Unionism: A New Model for a New World Order." *Review* 16, no 3: 245–78.

Weir, Margaret. 2004. "Challenging Inequality." *Perspectives on Politics* 2, no. 4: 677–81.

Wills, Jane. 2004. "Organising the Low Paid: East London's Living Wage Campaign as a Vehicle for Change." In *The Future of Worker Representation,* edited by Geraldine Healy, Edmund Heery, Phil Taylor, and William Brown, 264–82. Oxford: Oxford University Press.

——. 2005. "The Geography of Union Organising in Low Paid Service Industries in the UK: Lessons from the T&G's Campaign to Unionise the Dorchester Hotel in London." *Antipode* 37, no. 1: 139–59.

Wills, Jane, and Melanie Simms. 2004. "Building Reciprocal Community Unionism in the UK." *Capital and Class* 82 (Spring): 59–84.

Yaro, Robert D., Tony Hiss, and Regional Plan Association. 1996. *A Region at Risk: The Third Regional Plan for the New York–New Jersey–Connecticut Metropolitan Area.* Washington, D.C.: Island Press.

Zlolnisky, Christian. 2006. *Janitors, Street Vendors, and Activists: The Lives of Mexican Immigrants in Silicon Valley.* Berkeley: University of California Press.

Zúñiga, Víctor, and Rubén Hernández-León, eds. 2005. *New Destinations: Mexican Immigration in the United States.* New York: Russell Sage Foundation.

Contributors

Ron Applegate is senior lecturer at the School of Industrial and Labor Relations at Cornell University.

Barbara Byrd is a senior instructor at the Labor Education and Research Center at the University of Oregon.

William Canak is a professor of sociology at Middle Tennessee State University.

Daniel B. Cornfield is a professor of sociology at Vanderbilt University and editor of the journal *Work and Occupations*.

Benjamin Day is executive director of Mass-Care: The Massachusetts Campaign for Single Payer Health Care.

Peter Evans is a professor of sociology at the University of California at Berkeley.

Lou Jean Fleron is director of workforce, industry, and economic development at the School of Industrial and Labor Relations at Cornell University.

Ian Greer is a postdoctoral research fellow jointly affiliated with Cornell and Leeds universities.

Marco Hauptmeier is a PhD candidate at the School of Industrial and Labor Relations at Cornell University.

Jane Holgate is research fellow at the Working Lives Research Institute at London Metropolitan University and coordinator of the London Union Research Network.

Otto Jacobi is head of the Laboratorium Europa and coeditor of *TRANSFER*, the quarterly journal of the European Trade Union Institute.

Heiwon Kwon is a PhD candidate at the School of Industrial and Labor Relations at Cornell University.

Stephanie Luce is an associate professor and the research director at the Labor Center, University of Massachusetts—Amherst.

Bruce Nissen is the director of research at the Florida International University Center for Labor Research and Studies, as well as an executive board member of the South Florida Jobs with Justice chapter.

David Reynolds is a faculty member at the Labor Studies Center, Wayne State University, in Detroit, and the coordinator for the Building Regional Power Research Project (http://www.powerbuilding.wayne.edu).

Nari Rhee is a PhD candidate in geography at the University of California at Berkeley.

Monica Russo is president of SEIU Florida Healthcare Union and international vice president of the Service Employees International Union.

Julie A. Sadler is an assistant professor of leadership in the School of Urban Affairs and Public Policy at the University of Delaware.

Jefferey M. Sellers is an associate professor of political science, geography, and public policy at the University of Southern California.

Lowell Turner is a professor of international and comparative labor at the School of Industrial and Labor Relations at Cornell University.

Jane Wills is a professor of human geography at Queen Mary, University of London.

Index

Action for Grassroots Empowerment and Neighborhood Development Alternatives (AGENDA) (Los Angeles), 75–76
actor-driven institutional change perspective, 14
Adams, Harry, 190
aerospace industry, 76, 113, 194, 196, 197–99, 202, 204–7
AFL-CIO: Change to Win split (2005), 118, 126, 190; and civil rights movement, 114; creation of, 238; and economic development, 53; and labor movement revitalization, 108; and political coalitions, 109; and project labor agreements, 204; and regional power building, 74, 76, 77; and Seattle WTO protests, 2, 116; and social coalition building, 116, 135, 136, 161, 195, 244. *See also* Change to Win
AFL-CIO Field Mobilization Department, 93
African American communities: and city types, 247; and community organizing, 60–61, 63; and living wage campaigns, 27, 33; Miami, 148, 156, 157; and social justice groups, 154. *See also* minority communities; minority-union tensions
Airbus, 196, 197–99, 208, 209
airline industry. *See* transportation industries
Alexandria, Virginia, 30, 31
Alinsky, Saul: and empowerment community organizing model, 56, 57–58, 59, 60, 61; and government co-optation, 62; and London living wage campaign, 218; and Miami organizing, 154; and union-CBDO relations, 67
American Federation of Labor (AFL), 180, 237. *See also* AFL-CIO
American Federation of State, County and Municipal Employees (AFSCME), 28, 113, 119, 133, 151 n, 183
American Federation of Teachers (AFT), 119, 151 n
American Postal Workers Union (APWU), 151 n
Amicus (United Kingdom), 217
antifascism, 233

anti-sweatshop campaigns, 125, 135
Anti-Sweatshop Procurement Law (New York), 135
antiunion employer strategies: and Boston political unionism, 102, 104; and high-road economic development, 127; and living wage campaigns, 28; Los Angeles, 129, 138; Miami, 151, 155, 157; and opportunity structure, 12–13; and regional power building, 90; San Jose, 180; Seattle, 205
Apollo Alliance (Washington), 116, 124
Apple, Inc., 183
apprenticeship. *See* training programs
Area Labor Federation (ALF) (Buffalo), 126
Arroyo, Felix, 106
Asian American communities, 9, 132, 179, 247. *See also* minority communities
Association of Community Organizations for Reform Now (ACORN): and labor movement revitalization, 159; and living wage campaigns, 25, 27, 71–72, 153; Miami, 153, 159; and regional power building, 75, 82, 91; San Jose, 82, 185; and union-CBDO relations, 69, 71–72, 75
Atlanta, 26
Australia, 42
automobile industry. *See* manufacturing industries

Baccaro, Luccio, 194
Back of the Yards Neighborhood Council (BYNC), 58–59
Bahr, Morton, 124
Baltimore, 21
Beck, Dave, 114
Believe in Buffalo Niagara campaign, 123
Bell Aircraft strike (1949), 120
Benjamin, Steve, 27
Bennett, Marty, 26–27
Benson, Roger, 134
Berkeley, 30
Bethlehem Steel, 119
Beust, Ole von, 201
biethnic cities, 247, 248, 249
Big Box Ordinance (Chicago), 34

International Union of Electronic, Electrical, Salaried, Machine and Furniture Workers—Communication Workers of America (IUE-CWA), 107
Italy, 44

Jacobs, Ken, 28, 32
janitors, 29–30, 103–4, 156–57, 183. *See also* Justice for Janitors
Japan, 41, 44
job retention coalitions: Buffalo, 120–21; and globalization, 193–94; Hamburg, 197–99, 208; Seattle, 202, 205–6, 208. *See also* capital mobility
Jobs with Justice (JwJ): Boston, 104, 107, 124; Buffalo, 121; and leadership, 79; and living wage campaigns, 25; Miami, 155–56, 159, 160, 161–62; New York, 135; and regional power building, 92–93; Seattle, 114, 115, 202, 205
Johnson, Lyndon, 61, 62, 63
Jones-Correa, Michael, 236
Jubilee 2000, 117
Judd, Ron: leadership, 114–16; and organizing, 119; and Seattle WTO protests, 2, 76, 115, 116–17; and training programs, 203, 207
Justice and Equality in the Workplace Partnership (Houston), 77
Justice Bus (Houston), 77
Justice for Janitors (JfJ): Boston, 27, 103–4, 105; Houston, 7n; and London organizing, 221; Los Angeles, 103, 104, 137–38, 139, 140; Miami, 154, 157; San Jose, 183

Kantor, Paul, 208
Katznelson, Ira, 236
Kemp, Jack, 66
Kennedy, Robert, 61
King County Labor Council (KCLC) (Seattle), 114–16; and economic development, 202, 203, 204; and electoral strategies, 117–18; and labor movement revitalization, 205, 207; and organizing, 118–19, 127; and Seattle WTO protests, 2, 76, 114, 115, 116–17, 207
Knights of Labor, 237
Korea, 44
Korean Immigrant Workers Association, 139

Labor and Employment Law Office (LELO) (Seattle), 116, 204, 207
Labor-Community Leadership Institute (San Jose), 88, 89, 90

labor councils. *See* central labor councils
Laborers International Union of North America (LIUNA), 162
Laborers union, 152
labor-management cooperation, 71, 120–24, 127. *See also* job retention coalitions
labor movement revitalization: and Boston political unionism, 108–9; and civil society revitalization, 13–14; definitions, 14–15; importance of, 1; and living wage campaigns, 31–34; Los Angeles, 129, 139–40, 141–43; Miami, 158–59; Seattle, 2, 202, 207; and social coalition building, 112–13, 243, 250–51
labor peace provisions, 28, 189
Labour party (United Kingdom), 215
Landesbetrieb Krankenhaeuser (LBK) (Hamburg), 197, 199–201, 208, 209
Latino communities. *See* Hispanic/Latino communities
Leaders Development Institute (San Jose), 84
leadership: bridge builders, 5, 89, 112, 139; and immigrant communities, 154, 170; Miami, 160; and nonworker organizations, 26; and opportunity structure, 5, 245–46; and regional power building, 79, 88–89, 90, 93; and social coalition building, 112, 245–46; status-conflict theory, 245–46; and strategic planning, 93
Leadership Academy (Miami), 154
Le Goff, Jacques, 225
Lewis, John L., 58
Lipsitz, Richard, Jr., 121
Livingstone, Ken, 12, 215–16, 222
living wage campaigns, 21–34; Buffalo, 125; coalition partners, 24–25; and economic development, 22, 28, 85–86; and labor movement revitalization, 31–34; and labor peace provisions, 28, 189; London, 211, 218–22; Miami, 30, 147, 151, 153, 159; movement overview, 21–24; and nonworker organizations, 25–26, 29; and organizing, 27–30; and regional power building, 75, 76, 85–86, 90; San Jose, 26, 30, 184, 189; and union-CBDO relations, 69, 71–72; union involvement motivations, 26–27
Living Wage Resource Center, 71
localization, 193–94
local political context, 35–52; Hamburg, 196, 198, 199, 200–201; historical background, 35–36, 137; importance of, 51–52; institutional infrastructure types, 51–52; and living wage campaigns, 25, 27, 85;